# PANDEMIC

## THE SPANISH FLU IN AUSTRALIA 1918-1920

**Ian W. Shaw** is an acclaimed writer of narrative nonfiction who has made an important contribution to Australian history and to the understanding of our nation. After a decade of school teaching and 25 years working as a security risk analyst for both government agencies and large private companies, Ian became a full-time writer in 2012. Ian has published eight works on Australian and military history, all of which are characterised by his ability to locate and access hidden tales from our past, and for his meticulous and far-reaching research.

## Books by Ian W. Shaw

*Operation Babylift*

*Murder at Dusk*

*The Rag Tag Fleet*

*Glenrowan*

*The Ghosts of Roebuck Bay*

*On Radji Beach*

*The Bloodbath*

*Other Side of the Mountain*

# PANDEMIC

## THE SPANISH FLU IN AUSTRALIA 1918-1920

# IAN W SHAW

WOODSLANE
PRESS

Woodslane Press Pty Ltd
10 Apollo Street
Warriewood, NSW 2102
Email: info@woodslane.com.au
02 8445 2300  www.woodslane.com.au

First published in Australia in 2020 by Woodslane Press
© 2020 Woodslane Press, text © 2020 Ian W. Shaw

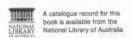 A catalogue record for this
book is available from the
National Library of Australia

Book design by Luke Harris, WorkingType Studio
Printed in Australia by McPhersons

Front cover images:
Hospital Beds in Great Hall During Influenza Pandemic, Exhibition Building, Melbourne, February 1919, State Library of Victoria
City of Sydney staff during the influenza pandemic, c.1918-19, City of Sydney Archives
Back cover image: Nursing Staff & Children Outside the Exhibition Building, Melbourne, 1919, Museum of Victoria Collection

# CONTENTS

# ACKNOWLEDGMENTS

Once again, a number of people supported my efforts to bring this story to life. My agent, Sarah McKenzie, seized on the idea early and believed that it was a story that needed to be told. Her enthusiasm is all that a writer could ask for from their agent. Thanks, too, to Andrew Swaffer and all at Woodslane Publishing, for their belief, support and professionalism.

My family always smile and nod politely when I reveal my next project, and then back me to the hilt. The leader in what may well be a conspiracy is Pamela who has walked beside me for many years and many miles, and who continues to inspire me every day of my life. Thanks are due as well to my niece Jacqui, her husband Matt and their beautiful girls, Kyla, Saraya and Tia for their love and support.

# INTRODUCTION

During the 20th Century, Australia would suffer through three events which would cause major losses of life and social dislocation, and which would leave the young nation in a far different situation after their occurrence than it had been beforehand. Two of these events were world wars, the first lasting from 1914 until 1918 and claiming in excess of 60,000 Australian lives while the second, running from 1939 until 1945, led to almost 40,000 Australian deaths. Those world wars, and Australia's casualties during them, have been the subjects of extensive research and review, both at the time and in the years since they ended. All Australians have a good idea of the course of both wars just as most Australian suburbs and towns have memorials to those who served and, particularly, to those who never returned.

The third event did not involve or invoke images of heroic young Australians — almost always young men — leaping out of trenches to attack an enemy whose very existence threatened their homeland, but the military analogy is a valid one. The third event, an outbreak of disease, offered the same threats to Australians as those presented by warfare, the threat of becoming a casualty, a victim of an unseen enemy. Those who did become casualties could also become fatalities, although at a lower rate than those in the frontline of military activity. Like the battlefield enemies, this disease came from overseas, the result of a complex interaction of naturally occurring phenomena.

1

Overseas, in Europe first and later in the United States, Africa and Asia, the disease struck at a time when the first of those world wars was coming to an end, inflicting further tragedies on already weakened people and societies, and it spread with a rapidity and a morbidity that almost put the suffering inflicted during the war into the shade. And it was coming, inevitably and inexorably, towards Australia.

Some would call this disease the *"Spanish flu"* while others would refer to it as a *"pneumonic plague"* and those who contracted the disease were often referred to as *"having been paid a visit by the Spanish Lady."* The most accurate was probably *"pneumonic plague"*, although history would come to know the events around the disease as the pneumonic influenza pandemic of 1918-20 (with a bit of hedging around the dates).

Like the arguments about its correct description and nomenclature, the origins of the disease remain a subject of debate. Whatever those origins were, within a few months of significant numbers of victims being found in the military bases and labour corps camps of Western Europe, the rest of the continent was being ravaged by a disease that paid as little heed to frontlines and national borders as it did to the selection of its victims. By the end of 1918, the Spanish Flu had spread to the Americas, Africa and Asia leaving Australia and Antarctica as the only continents not affected. Antarctica's climate would be its best defence, but Australia would have to provide its own.

Before then, though, the "War to End All Wars" had finished with an Armistice signed on 11 November releasing almost 100,000 Australian servicemen and women from their wartime duties, young men and women all keen to return home as soon as possible. They would need to be repatriated by sea, a long voyage that would require stopovers to refuel and revictual, stopovers at ports and in countries where the disease had either established a foothold or was already raging and out of control. In those circumstances there was a distinct possibility that some of those returning would bring the disease with them.

In Australia, a sometimes-fractious federation had held together during the war but would need to hold together a little longer. In what may have been a last gasp of wartime unity, State and Commonwealth governments and authorities came together to determine the best, most appropriate strategy to save the nation from the destruction being wrought by disease elsewhere in the world. That strategy involved, in the first instance, keeping those who carried the disease as far away as possible from Australia or, if they made it here, placing them in isolation, in a quarantine so strict that they could not escape it until they were no longer a threat to the wider population because either the disease had run its course — or they were dead.

Just like the Allied positions of the Western Front, second and third lines of defence were put in place behind that frontline. Those support lines involved the development of vaccines, the establishment of physical and organisational structures that could cope, should coping become necessary, with a nation-wide pandemic, and the agreement to observe certain protocols to keep their multilateral approach viable under the pressures that such a pandemic would bring.

The opportunity for a trial, a sort of pressure test of the system arose in November and December 1918 when pneumonic influenza broke out in New Zealand and the Pacific Islands of Fiji, Tonga and Samoa, all in Australia's backyard. Australia's response was swift and targeted: two Royal Australian Navy warships, loaded with medical personnel and medical supplies, were despatched to the South Pacific to provide assistance wherever that assistance was required. While they were doing so, pneumonic influenza arrived from the back yard when a number of returning Australian soldiers broke their journey in New Zealand. From the backyard it moved to the doorstep, as infected Australian returning home via New Zealand brought the infection with them. The isolation regime at Sydney's North Head Quarantine Station was put to the test in early December just as the Woodman's Point Quarantine Station outside Fremantle would be put to the same test by infected soldiers a week later. Both would survive the test — barely — but in doing so would highlight shortages in medical knowledge, medical supplies and medical personnel. The experience highlighted, too, the sometimes-irrational fears the general public had about contagion.

Worse was to come. Pneumonic influenza arrived in Melbourne and Sydney, Australia's two largest cities, almost simultaneously — as authorities had known it would — and immediately caused a breakdown in the established order. Among the very first things to break down was the agreement between the States and the Commonwealth to act in a coordinated and agreed manner, From late January 1919 it became every state for itself, and the devil take the hindmost. The disease would find its way into every corner of the continent, from Tasmania to the Torres Strait, from Broome to Byron Bay. Wherever people went, pneumonic influenza stalked them. The railways and roadways that had opened up the continent became the arteries through which the infection flowed.

By the time the last cases were identified on Thursday Island in mid-1919, more than 15,000 Australians had succumbed to the disease and few families in the nation were unaffected. The Australian pneumonic influenza pandemic piled layers of misery on top of the tragedy of the First World War. Its arrival was predictable and its ending inevitable. Between those two events, the best and worst of Australia was on display, both extremes providing lessons for the future.

The Spanish flu pandemic caused Australia's third greatest loss of life, its casualties only surpassed by the two world wars. It has received little more than a mention in Australian histories and narratives of the 20th Century, something perhaps attributable to the timing of its appearance. The lessons of the First World War informed the national debate for a decade or more, while those of the Second World War largely shaped the country into the shape it still holds. The lessons of the Spanish flu pandemic were largely ignored; it was the type of event that occurred once, perhaps twice, in a millennium. There were valid lessons there, though, cautionary tales about preparedness and prophylaxis, protection and response. A century on, and faced with the possibility that Covid-19 and other viral diseases are no longer one in a lifetime events, some of those lessons will need to be learned again.

*Note on currency*: in 1918-20 the Australian pound (£) was the official currency in Australia and had been for a decade. A basket of goods costing £1 in 1919 would cost approximately $80 in 2020.[1]

*Influenza quarantine camp set up at Wallangarra, 1919.*

John Oxley Library, State Library of Queensland.

# CHAPTER 1

# Incubation

The first indications of the coming storm were innocuous, like echoes of distant thunder suggesting someone, in some other place, is about to face weather conditions that will test both their preparations and their patience. Conditions that you hope they survive and hope, too, will not come your way. There were little hints in news items buried towards the middle of the major newspapers, relegated to the general, minor news section by the more momentous news from the battlefields of the Western Front, the Eastern Front and the Middle East:

> *"A mysterious epidemic is spreading throughout Spain, and causing alarm. Forty per cent of the population is stricken. The railways, tramways, factories, newspaper offices, schools and theatres have been seriously disorganised owing to the depletion of their staffs, and many have had to close. Military manoeuvres have had to be suspended. Some of the symptoms resemble influenza, but in many cases there are sudden fits. King Alfonso and several of his ministers are ill. There have been few deaths."* [1]

While this may not have been much of a report, it was one of the few that Australian newspapers received that had not been carefully edited by censors in Australia or elsewhere and, in reality, it was only a small part of a much larger story. The mysterious disease that was spreading rapidly through Spain, had dislocated society and killed a few people was, elsewhere in Europe, also raging like wildfire and killing hundreds and then thousands of people a day. The censors didn't want anyone to know that, of course, as it might be bad for the war effort. In suppressing news of the real state of affairs, that censorship guaranteed that the mysterious illness would be known forever after as the "Spanish flu."

—◦◇◦—

The disease that was being described was more correctly *pneumonic influenza* and it was something that had been a public health menace for centuries if not longer. The name "influenza" had itself originated in 15th Century Italy where upper respiratory infections — which it was — were believed to be "influenced" by the stars. The ailment had been known in the Mediterranean region for a considerable time before it was given its particular name and was recognised as a seasonal phenomenon, hence the reference to the position of the stars, but beyond that little was known of its causes. Even less was known about possible cures.

Influenza's appearance in a population was attributed to everything from the alignment of the planets and stars to sudden and extreme weather changes, until 1892 when a German bacteriologist named Richard Pfeiffer isolated what he thought was the bacteria behind the infection. Pfeiffer had more than enough material to work with; in 1889-90, Europe was swept by a wave of influenza that took many lives and caused considerable social dislocation. Because this wave came out of the east and moved inexorably west, it became known as "Russian flu." [2] Clinically, scientists believed that Spanish flu was identical to Russian flu although it appeared to be a more virulent strain. Australia had, in fact, experienced the tail end of the Russian flu in 1892 when an epidemic moved across the country; more virulent than the previously experienced types of seasonal flu, this epidemic claimed the lives of over 2,000 people in Victoria and New South Wales, the two states hardest hit. However, compared to what they now began to learn about the situation across Europe, the Australian experience of influenza epidemics had been mild indeed.

Literally, within days of that first report from Europe, additional reporting was beginning to suggest that the Spanish flu was unlike anything Europe had experienced since the great plagues of the Middle Ages:

> *"The mysterious epidemic is increasing. Hundreds of thousands of people have been attacked in Madrid, and the telegraph offices are closed and the theatres are closing. Two hundred doctors are ill."* [3]

By early June, there were reports of over 700 dead in Spain, thousands more expected to die and a disease so virulent that it could impact, eventually and directly, millions of Spaniards.

Then, in the blink of an eye, the disease was reported in the United Kingdom. Within a month of the initial accounts of the outbreak in Spain, similar accounts published in Australian newspapers were originating in London. They gave graphic details about how the type of influenza which had recently attacked thousands of people in Spain had spread to England, exclaiming that hundreds of cases were being reported each day. Bland, general reporting quickly became:

> *"Spanish influenza is spreading in London. It is very infectious and the*

*immediate isolation of sufferers for five days is essential when lassitude, aching limbs, headache and catarrh begin. Huts for patients are being erected in some districts where the hospitals are crowded."* [4]

It soon became apparent that hundreds of victims were now dying every day in England. It also rapidly became apparent that Spanish flu knew no borders and respected no alliance. In quick succession, news was received that Romania was seeking enormous quantities of disinfectants and medical supplies from her ally Germany because the country was in the grip of a full-blown epidemic of Spanish flu and whole regions were being decimated by the disease. Neutral Holland reported that around 1000 industrial districts in that country — stretching across its territory and then into North Germany — had been severely affected by the epidemic. It was believed that up to half a million German soldiers had contracted the disease and that it had killed 800 schoolchildren in Berlin alone.

Spanish flu was also in the process of crossing the world's oceans. A Norwegian vessel arrived in New York with four dead crewmen and another 10 seriously ill with the disease. New York health authorities had taken steps to protect against the spread of the disease but, on the basis of reporting from all across Europe, stopping the march of Spanish flu might be well-nigh impossible. [5]

---

Suddenly the focus switched to Melbourne. A number of disturbing reports from the Broadmeadows Army Camp on the city's northern outskirts appeared almost simultaneously in the city's major newspapers. These reports detailed how, towards the end of the first week of August

1918, small numbers of troops began to report that they were ill with what some of them were convinced was Spanish flu. At first, it was just two or three soldiers a day, but within10 days the total had exceeded 150 and seemed to be heading rapidly towards 200. Most cases were admitted to the Broadmeadows camp hospital while the more serious cases were then transferred to the army's base hospital in St Kilda Road, Melbourne.

Detailed descriptions of the symptoms were provided to readers. The ailment, whatever it was, began like an ordinary cold but was soon followed by feverishness and severe headaches. There were often severe coughing fits during which a number of men had fallen into unconsciousness. In several cases, those attacked had also developed pneumonia but, fortunately, no-one had yet succumbed to the disease.

There were also reports that the illness had spread to the Laverton Army Base, but in a much milder form, and that at least 30 to 40 cases were being treated at the St Kilda Road base hospital. As well, some of the precautions being used to limit the spread were detailed for the public. At Broadmeadows, the YMCA huts, the Lady Stanley Concert Hall, and the Methodist and Salvation Army huts had been closed until further notice while, with the exception of the camp's guard force, all the men were being given daily leave from 4 p.m. until midnight while their accommodation huts and ablution blocks were being fumigated.

This particular Spanish flu scare then disappeared more rapidly than it had appeared. The Defence Minister, Senator George Pearce, who had an obvious interest and an equally obvious responsibility in the matter, issued a press release and gave a press conference addressing the situation on the morning of Saturday 17 August. Pearce revealed that he had sought and received a report on the matter from Colonel Alfred Sturdee, the Principal Medical Officer of the Victorian District. Sturdee's conclusion was that the various newspaper reports had been much exaggerated. He had assured the minister that outbreaks of influenza were not unusual in the winter months and that the current outbreak centred on the Broadmeadows camp was just ordinary, seasonal influenza, in no way different to the influenza currently also affecting numbers of civilians. The Broadmeadows outbreak was certainly **not** Spanish influenza and none of the patients currently in hospital was seriously ill.

Sturdee's report said that the newspapers were accurate with some details — upwards of 200 men had been affected — and that the mitigation processes they described were accurate. As soon as a soldier developed a full set of influenza symptoms, he would be sent by ambulance to the St Kilda Road base hospital. None of the patients admitted had reached anywhere near a life-threatening malignancy, and a visit to the isolation ward at the base hospital suggested that there was no uneasiness among the patients, most of whom seemed to be rather happy about resting in bed.

The average duration of the complaint, Sturdee had reported, was not long, just a few days at most. Meanwhile, all the huts and buildings at the Broadmeadows Camp had been thoroughly disinfected and a possible closure of the camp was something that had never been considered by authorities. That should have been the end of the story, but it wasn't.

Two days later, the Melbourne *Age* raised an important aspect of the situation that had occurred in an article under the sub-heading *"Official Secrecy."* The writer suggested that the public were being asked to accept a lot at face value. Two days earlier, the army's Principal Medical Officer had assured journalists that the outbreak of influenza was nothing out of the ordinary and that no-one should be uneasy about it. He said he believed there had been about 200 cases in total but was unable to give an exact figure. When asked if there had been any fresh cases, Colonel Sturdee had been unable to provide an answer, stating that the relevant reports did not come to him. Yet, at the base hospital, responsible officers were very apologetic but also could not provide any information. If they wanted questions answered, journalists were told, they would need to ask the Principal Medical Officer.

Was something really happening, and being kept secret, or were army medical authorities on the borderline when it came to competency?[6]

—⚬⚬⚭⚬⚬—

By the end of September, there were claims that the Spanish flu epidemic had spread almost completely across war-ravaged Europe. An official statement from Berlin detailed how a fresh outbreak of the disease was sweeping through the German army which now had 180,000 of its soldiers as patients while Hungarian newspapers were reporting 100,000 cases in Budapest alone. Even neutral Switzerland was not immune; there, hospitals were over-burdened and many schools and churches had been closed.[7]

While it would have come as no surprise to anyone that the disease would reach the United States, many people expressed shock when it did. In the first week of September a number of reports suggested that Spanish flu had broken out in three US army camps in three different states, with several deaths resulting. Its appearance in major population centres along the eastern seaboard was of more immediate concern, and even sparked conspiracy theories about the vector that carried it there. The news agency Reuters, normally an objective observer and reporter of events, distributed an alarming report:

*"A message from Washington says that the widespread appearance of Spanish influenza along the Atlantic coast has caused new official warnings to be issued stating U-boats are probably responsible for spreading the germs. The Chairman of the Health Section of the Shipping Board said today that it was known that men landed from*

*German submarines, and it was quite possible that germs had been*
*released in theatres and churches. It is recalled that influenza was*
*prevalent in Spain immediately after a visit of U-boats."* [8]

As in Europe, when Spanish flu hit the United States the numbers
infected almost literally exploded. The north-east was an early epicentre,
with the city of Boston and the state of Massachusetts particular hotspots.
Within days, more than 100 deaths had been reported, and preliminary
moves to close all schools, churches and theatres in the state had begun.
There were a number of military camps in Massachusetts, many others in
neighbouring states and even more in other states bordering the Atlantic
Ocean. In a week, in those camps full of soldiers waiting to be shipped
across to Europe, the official figure tracking those who had been infected
began to jump by thousands a day while deaths rose by hundreds a day.
All new drafts for the army were immediately postponed until the disease
had run its course. [9]

Both Europe and the United States were a long way from Australia
and were in a different hemisphere as well.

———◦◊◦◊◦◦———

The Union of South Africa was not only in the same hemisphere as
Australia. It was part of the same empire and shared links forged through
the Boer War at the turn of the century and, some would say more
importantly, through the Test cricket rivalry that had commenced during
the southern summer of 1910-11. It was more of a shock to Australians,
then, when the first reports of an outbreak of Spanish flu in South Africa
filtered through towards the end of September. Those first reports were
not particularly alarming, though; a gold mine on the Rand said that
some 300 of its native mine workers were affected by influenza and at

three other mines a number of Europeans seemed to have caught the illness. However, none of the cases seemed to be life-threatening. [10]

Within a week, the situation had changed dramatically, with a reported 10,000 cases among mine workers on the Rand. The South African Chancellor of Mines made light of it, saying it should have little effect on output because there were plenty of remaining miners and recovery from the ailment appeared to be quite rapid. He could not comment on reports that the epidemic had broken out in Durban and other major cities in the country. [11]

Within two weeks, the situation was out of control. Cape Town was described as resembling a city of the dead with all business practically at a standstill. Most of the city's cafés and restaurants were closed, public service departments were barely operating, and tram and train services had been cut by at least 50%. Reports came through of 230 burials conducted in a single day in the city's cemeteries. In the Kimberley diamond mining area business had been suspended for all enterprises except selling food and medicines. The native workforce was so decimated that the giant De Beers diamond company shut down all its mining operations at the end of the first week of October. The gold mines of the Rand fared no better, crippled when 20,000 of their workers were struck down by the disease. Collieries all across the Transvaal were closed and authorities noted that the mortality rate among South African natives was significantly higher than it was among Europeans. They also believed that the disease had been brought into the country by a shipload of returning native labourers who had been working as a civilian construction battalion behind the front lines in France. [12]

In among the reports of the spread of the disease through Europe, the

United States and South Africa, a much smaller story told how the Spanish steamship *Alfonso XIII,* carrying 1200 passengers and crew between Spain and the West Indies, found they had aboard a number of people infected with Spanish flu. Before they made landfall, 19 people had died and dozens, perhaps hundreds more were infected. Ships carrying large numbers of people in confined spaces were proving ideal sites to incubate the disease.[13]

Such reports attracted the attention of the various levels of government in Australia and from early October 1918, questions began to be asked and actions began to be taken. South Australian premier, Archibald Peake, was the first politician to raise the question of Spanish flu when he rose to answer a question in the South Australian Parliament on 8 October:

> *"…the government would communicate with the Federal government regarding Spanish influenza…and ask the Commonwealth authorities to take prompt and, if possible, effective steps to prevent its introduction to this state."* [14]

As good as his word, on 10 October, Peake sent a telegram to the acting Prime Minister, William Watt:

> *"Strongly urge precautionary measures be taken to prevent introduction of Spanish influenza into this state."* [15]

Peake's appeal was followed two days later by a similar appeal from Western Australia's premier, Henry Lefroy, who also despatched an urgent telegram to the acting Prime Minister:

> *"In view devastating outbreak Spanish influenza Cape Town would be*

*glad your assurance for publication that Federal Quarantine authorities are*
*taking every possible precaution against possible introduction disease here.*
*Understand Spanish influenza not present quarantinable disease."* [16]

By then, the Commonwealth had acted, both privately and publicly. In a statement released in Melbourne on 9 October, the Commonwealth Government revealed that it had already introduced a number of measures to prevent Spanish influenza from reaching Australia, with quarantine requirements being the obvious first step in the process. For some time, quarantine medical officers in all major Australian ports had been instructed to be especially vigilant for any cases of influenza, whether they considered it to be of the Spanish variety or not. Troopships bringing Australian soldiers home were of particular concern, and new procedures were about to be introduced for them.

In future, returning troopships would be thoroughly inspected by each port's senior medical officer, at sea and between 24 and 48 hours before the ship was due to dock. This would result in a more searching examination of those aboard than was previously possible. Anyone on the ship, passenger or crew, found to be displaying the symptoms of any infectious disease, including all forms of influenza, would be isolated and their quarters disinfected. If a substantial number of cases were found aboard, the ship would receive "special treatment." Similar arrangements would be put in place for the arrival of civilians at Australian ports [17] and particular attention would be paid to ships arriving from what were considered to be infected ports.

Those same quarantine authorities were also engaged in beginning prophylactic measures to address what the nation could face if the disease gained a foothold here. The department was liaising via telegram with relevant authorities in South Africa and had requested specimens of the germ cultures made from the organisms responsible for the disease then ravaging their country. When those specimens arrived in Australia, they would firstly be compared to a number that had already been isolated in Australia, such as those from patients infected at the Broadmeadows Army Camp. It had been reported that a vaccine had been developed and tested in South Africa, with satisfactory results. These two factors might prove decisive in Australia's defences.[18]

These actions, and much of what would be needed in both policy and practice should Spanish flu reach Australia, would be the responsibility of Australia's Director of Quarantine, John Howard Lidgett Cumpston, and in John Cumpston Australia had a man uniquely qualified for that task. The Melbourne-born and educated doctor had specialised in public health after graduation and had studied and researched public health in locations as far apart and different as London and the Philippines. Cumpston had joined the Commonwealth Quarantine Service soon after it was established in 1909, working as a senior quarantine officer in Western Australia, Victoria and Queensland. In mid-1913, he was made Director of Quarantine after acting in the position for several months. Well respected by his peers, colleagues and staff, Cumpston, and the rest of Australia, were given the opportunity to study an outbreak of Spanish flu up close in late October 1918.

---

The first reports of the incident in Australia were somewhat vague and imprecise as to what had actually occurred. Towards the end of September oblique references were made to Spanish flu, New Zealanders and deaths at sea. Over the first two weeks of October the true story became clear.

The steamship *Niagara* was part of the Canadian Pacific Line and in late September departed Vancouver for her regular run to Sydney, with stopovers at San Francisco, Hawaii, Suva and Auckland. Among her more than 600 passengers and crew were several who could legitimately claim to be VIPs, including the Prime Minister of New Zealand, William Massey, and his Finance Minister and deputy, Sir Joseph Ward, both returning from an Imperial Conference in London. An otherwise uneventful voyage took a sinister turn the day after the *Niagara* departed Hawaii for Suva when one of the junior stewards went down with "something or other" which soon developed into an ailment with all the symptoms of Spanish flu.

The stewards aboard the ship shared a common messing and accommodation space, and within a few days that one case became several and then dozens; eventually, among the 130 stewards the ship carried only seven would show no signs of infection. The illness, widely accepted as Spanish flu by the stewards who believed it had been brought aboard by a passenger, soon spread to other members of the crew, firemen and deckhands in particular. The increasing number of sick people aboard turned the voyage from something of a pleasure cruise into a joint effort to keep the ship sailing its charted course while keeping all aboard in reasonable health until they reached Auckland, the first port that offered the range of facilities they would need to deal with the outbreak.

The worst leg was the passage between Suva and Auckland, when more and more crew were affected. Women passengers organised themselves into a support service to replace all the stewards incapable of work, assisted by a number of male passengers who waited on the tables and helped cooks, cleaners and the like. The smoking saloon and two sections of cabins were turned into a temporary hospital during this time and the two doctors — Bartlett and McKenzie — and four nurses who were aboard took charge of that facility.

By the time *Niagara* docked at Auckland's Queen's Wharf on 12 October, several passengers were also displaying influenza symptoms of the ailment. By then, three of those who had contracted the disease were dead. The ship arrived on Saturday morning and was immediately placed in quarantine while public health and quarantine officials went aboard to conduct a thorough examination of the ship and all those aboard. While they did so those considered most seriously ill were taken by ambulance to an isolation ward at Auckland Hospital. With almost a hundred cases still on the ship, a call went out for volunteer doctors and nurses.

Those who were or had been ill were questioned extensively by the health officials. The sufferers reported a lot of common symptoms, including a high fever and severe headaches, a sore throat and a persistent cough with strong pain in the back of the legs and in the back itself. Most also reported great difficulty in getting out of their beds because of a general feeling of debilitation.

The Auckland waterside workers were in absolutely no doubt about what the *Niagara* was carrying and refused to unload or work the boat in any way. The New Zealand health officials who made the inspections on board were not so certain. Late on Sunday, they announced that any passengers who wanted to disembark at Auckland would be able to do so, after they and their baggage had been fumigated, from Monday morning. For years afterwards there would be persistent rumours that the decision was made, not on public health or quarantine grounds, but because the prime minister and his finance minister wanted to go home after an absence of several months; those rumours were never substantiated.[19]

---

On the Monday morning, William Massey and Sir Joseph Ward and their entourages, a small number of passengers and some 70 officers and crew left the *Niagara*, most of the latter having made successful recoveries from whatever the mystery ailment had been. Even so, they were not allowed to disembark until they had undergone a fumigation that left them clammy but clean. For good measure all the mail the ship carried, including that bound for Australia, was also fumigated. Among those who disembarked at Queen's Wharf were two Australians who then travelled almost immediately to the Auckland Railway Station where they caught a train to Wellington. There, they boarded another steamship which took them to Sydney. One disappeared into the general population there while the second caught a train to Melbourne where he, too, disappeared.[20]

---

On 15 October, in Auckland, Sir Joseph Ward spoke to the press about his recent experience aboard the *Niagara*. He outlined how the illness had struck quickly and how most of the ship's stewards were almost immediately incapacitated. He spoke, too, of how the illness spread through the ship, impacting passengers and crew alike, and paid tribute to the manner in which the women passengers rose to the occasion, taking over the work and responsibilities of those who had fallen by the wayside. He also spoke of how the passengers recognised the dedication of those crewmen who were not prepared to let disease interfere with the ship's normal workings and schedule. After they had arrived in Auckland, the passengers had all gathered together and, with one of them presiding over the meeting, passed a vote of tribute to the captain and his officers for their efforts on behalf of the passengers during what had been a difficult trip. On a more practical level, the passengers also donated 250 pounds to be distributed among the crew. Ward concluded by saying that 109 of the crew and nine of the passengers had been afflicted by the disease and that five of those had died, including the boatswain's mate. And that was the end of the conference.[21]

---

While Sir Joseph was addressing the journalists in Auckland, aboard the *Niagara* doctors and nurses were working hard to help sick crewmen recover to the level where the ship would be able to resume its voyage to Australia. Among those helping was a young Australian nurse who, if she hadn't been utilising her professional skills among the sick, would have been preparing to board the ship as a passenger. Her name was Sister Irvine Crossing and those who knew the 24-year-old described her as bubbling and bright. Irvine was from Sydney, where she completed her nursing training at Sir Alexander McCormack's private hospital, The Terraces, in Paddington (later known as the Scottish Hospital, The Terraces is today a retirement home.) After graduation, Irvine moved to New Zealand where she nursed firstly at the Gisborne Hospital before taking up a position at a private hospital in Auckland. In mid-1918, she had booked a ticket on the *Niagara* to visit Sydney for a holiday and to visit relatives.

Irvine Crossing was one of the first volunteer nurses and was still working aboard the *Niagara*, and preparing to sail for home, when she herself became ill. Rushed by ambulance to Auckland Hospital, her condition gradually deteriorated and she died there on 26 October; by then, the *Niagara* was in Sydney.

---

The rumours about the *Niagara* had arrived well before the vessel herself. The horrors of the disease and the number of fatalities were both wildly exaggerated but, unlike the broader Sydney public, the quarantine and public health officials chose to act on what they knew rather than what they imagined. They knew that 155 of the ship's crew and passengers had contracted the influenza-like ailment and that five of those who had caught the disease on the trip had died. They also knew that both those figures were higher than the rates normally associated with seasonal flu. They knew, too, they should not take any chances.

When *Niagara* arrived at Sydney Harbour on 25 October, three days later than scheduled, a yellow flag signalling sickness aboard was flying from her masthead. Rather than proceed up the harbour to her normal berth, she was ordered to anchor just inside the harbour entrance off the North Head Quarantine Station. The station had been prepared for the ship's arrival; its previous residents — returned soldiers suffering from tuberculosis — had recently been relocated to a vacant ward at the Royal Prince Alfred Hospital. The passengers would be ferried to the quarantine station where they would be held in quarantine for not less than a week. The steamship, after being fumigated and disinfected by quarantine authorities, would be handed back to its owners four days later. It could then be moved to Darling Harbour to be unloaded. [22]

After that, everyone would wait to see what developed.

*Vaccine Bottle - Spanish Influenza, 1919*

Museums Victoria

# CHAPTER 2

# Prophylaxis

Any sense of complacency that acting Prime Minister William Watt may have felt dissipated when he was given his personal copy of a coded telegram that had been received from the Governor-General of the Union of South Africa, Earl Buxton. Date-stamped 2.50 p.m., 12 October 1918, Buxton's telegram read:

"In view of the terrible experience through which South Africa is passing as a result of a violent outbreak of so-called Spanish influenza with highly pneumonic characteristics, the Prime Minister...considers it advisable to draw your special attention to the extreme seriousness of the malady with a view to possibility of timely measures being taken by your government to prevent its introduction from overseas.

The malady is infectious in the highest degree and produces extreme prostration with an appalling death rate among coloured persons and natives while among Europeans after a week's experience there is now distinctly increased seriousness in the character of attacks. At Kimberley yesterday fifty Europeans died, at Cape Town a still larger number while coloured persons and natives at these cities are dying daily in hundreds.

Prime Minister is anxious that your country should be spared a *similar calamity and accordingly takes this step to give you timely warning."* [1]

It is also obvious that Watt took his duties seriously. He might have been an acting prime minister but that did not prevent him from both contemplating and then taking decisive action. He received Buxton's telegram the day after it had been sent from Pretoria and, after discussions with those most relevant to the issue, wrote on the bottom of the telegram:

1. *Ask C.O.S. to thank P.M. of South Africa.*
2. *Send to Minister of Customs and request him to have report prepared immediately by Director of Quarantine for submission to me indicating precautionary measures being taken as proposed.* [2]

That important decisions had been made was obvious almost immediately. On 17 October, three proclamations by Australia's Governor-General, Sir Ronald Munro Ferguson, were gazetted. The first declared South Africa to be a place that contained a quarantinable disease, namely influenza. The second declared influenza itself to be a quarantinable disease, while the third declared Fremantle, Adelaide, Melbourne, Sydney and Brisbane to all be first ports of entry for vessels arriving from South Africa.

On 19 October, the prime minister's private secretary, Malcolm Shepherd, wrote to Munro Ferguson with the suggested wording of a telegram the prime minister would like him to send to Earl Buxton in Pretoria:

*"Your warning greatly appreciated; definite action on stringent lines has been taken. Admiralty asked to give instructions to troopships carrying*

*Australian troops that no person leave or board ship in South African ports. Immediate application this measure would be appreciated. Health Department Pretoria asked supply further information nature organism producing fatal results also other medical details. Quarantine measures will be imposed on all vessels arriving here from South Africa."* [3]

By then Federal Cabinet had approved a number of stringent quarantine measures and, moreover, were keeping the public up to date with what they were doing and why they were doing it. The new measures were prominently reported in all major capital city and regional newspapers. Prominent articles detailed how servicemen and women on Australian troopships would not be allowed to have any communication with the shore or board any other vessel while their own was in any South African port. Any person who, inadvertently or otherwise, breached this regulation would be immediately placed in quarantine upon arrival in Australia for a minimum of seven days. While in quarantine the detainees would be disinfected, with particular attention being paid to their throats and nasal passages.

In addition, all quarantine offices had been directed to keep a strict lookout for anyone displaying symptoms associated with influenza, irrespective of whether they were soldiers or civilians, on any vessel arriving in Australian waters. The closest possible scrutiny would be applied to any person, and any vessel, that had travelled to Australia via South Africa.

The government was also taking steps to build a second line of defence in case the quarantine wall was breached. South African government officials and scientists had been asked to provide as much detail as possible about organisms associated with Spanish flu and forward those details to their counterparts in Australia who had already commenced work on trying to find a vaccine for the disease. Within days of these reassuring announcements, the nation's biosecurity was challenged in one of the most unlikely locations.[4]

—◦◦◦◦◦—

The Burns, Philp & Co. steamship *Mataram* sailed into Darwin Harbour on Friday 18 October, outward bound from Singapore and with several more stops planned before she reached her destination port of Sydney. As well as a mixed cargo, *Mataram* carried in excess of 70 passengers, 50 of whom were now displaying symptoms of Spanish flu. There had been no deaths on the ship to date, but eight of the cases were considered to be seriously ill. Darwin quarantine authorities immediately acted in accordance with the new directives. *Mataram* was placed in quarantine and the passengers who were disembarking in Darwin, or whose lives were considered to be at risk, were taken from the ship and placed ashore at the Channel Island Quarantine Station. Senior quarantine officials in Melbourne were notified of the *Mataram's* arrival, the disease aboard and the actions taken.

The majority of the passengers aboard *Mataram* were bound for Thursday Island, which suited quarantine authorities as disembarking on an island provided an additional layer of security. *Mataram* sailed for Thursday Island on 21 October and disembarked most of her passengers into quarantine there. By then, there were 61 cases aboard and one of the early patients had died. However, no new cases had appeared after the vessel left Darwin, and the stops at Townsville and Brisbane, under strict quarantine, were without further incident.

When *Mataram* arrived at Sydney on 1 November, there were only five persons left aboard who had contracted influenza and they were all convalescent. Ship, crew and passengers were placed in quarantine and during the seven days of that, the ship and all aboard were fumigated and

disinfected. There was also a frisson of excitement when a small fire —
quickly extinguished — broke out on the vessel. Just a couple of days
after the *Niagara* was released from quarantine, so was the *Mataram*; the
system seemed to be working.

———◦◦◦◦◦———

The relative calm in Australia was not reflected elsewhere in the world.
The disease still appeared to be out of control in Europe. By early
November, outbreaks had been reported throughout Scandinavia while
in Vienna, capital of the vanquished Austro-Hungarian Empire, 1753
people had died in a single week. There, the supply of coffins had run
out and some bodies were reportedly packed in ice for several weeks
before being buried in paper sacks. Conditions in the United Kingdom
remained dire. In London, 1300 Metropolitan Police Force officers
had contracted the disease and 1000 telephone operators were off duty
through illness. Ambulances cruising the streets were picking up 25 or
more bodies every day.

While the epidemic in South Africa appeared to be abating, it was
still cutting a swathe through neighbouring Rhodesia (Zimbabwe). The
slowing down in the South African infection rate allowed authorities
there to begin to assess the disease's impact. They estimated that the
death toll in Cape Province was 7,400, 75% of whom were natives or
coloured. Elsewhere, the death toll in the Kimberley was estimated to
be 5,000 with a national total well in excess of 20,000. Those figures
were being matched by India, where the first epicentre was Bombay
(Mumbai). By early November, there had been 13,394 deaths in Bombay
alone while it was believed that upwards of 5,000 people were dying in
India each week.

Two countries with close links to India were reporting significant losses to the disease. In neighbouring Ceylon (Sri Lanka), the situation was so bad that the country's governor contacted the Australian governor-general directly, asking him to advise the acting prime minister that:

> *"Influenza is endemic in Ceylon at this time; suggest it would be advisable to prohibit for the present landing at Colombo of troops proceeding to and coming from Europe."*

Spanish flu had also reached the Federated States of Malaya, home to tens of thousands of Indians who had either moved their permanently, predominantly for work on the rubber plantations, or who lived there as indentured labourers in either the rubber or tin-mining industries. There was a regular and consistent movement between there and India. A number of Australian companies also had financial interests in Malaya, and it was through those companies that some idea of the scale of the problem became apparent. In late October, the general manager of a group of companies operating Australian-owned tin mines reported that the mines now had just enough labourers for the dredges to operate in daylight hours only and that he expected to soon have to close down all operations completely. [5]

Australia was still an island at the bottom of the world, enjoying all the protections that being surrounded by sea on all sides offered. Increasingly, though, the last ports of call for vessels sailing to Australia were cities or ports in the grip of Spanish flu. Increasingly, too, those vessels were not just carrying passengers, crew and cargo, they were carrying disease as well.

---

In preparing a second, prophylactic line of defence, the government would rely heavily on the ability of the Commonwealth Serum Laboratories (CSL) to develop vaccines that could stop or slow the spread and impact of the disease. CSL had been established in an office and laboratory complex in the inner Melbourne suburb of Royal Park in 1916 to address and alleviate the disruption to Australia's pharmaceutical supplies caused by the war. As soon as they learned of the outbreak of Spanish flu, CSL scientists began planning the direction their research and experimentation should take based, in part, on Australia's experience during the 1892 Russian flu pandemic. That research was given added urgency — and additional opportunities — when some of the Spanish flu victims arrived in Australian quarantine stations. Medical science was unaware of the existence of viruses but well aware of the presence of "germs", or bacteria, in the spread and effects of diseases. Though not aware that the pneumonic form of influenza could be caused by either bacteria or viruses, CSL chose to address what they believed was the causative agent, the germs behind Spanish flu.

The first step in CSL's process of developing a Spanish flu vaccine was to collect samples of the actual disease causative agents or organisms, and to this end CSL sent a doctor to Sydney. There, he was able to isolate and collect material from the nasal and lung passages of sufferers who had arrived on the *Niagara* and who were being held at North Head. For both comparison and additional material, a request was sent to quarantine authorities in Western Australia, asking for similar material from patients who had contracted the disease aboard the *Charon* (see below).

Then cultivation began, a process and a description not for the fainthearted. Spanish flu, or pneumonic influenza, was a mixed infection in that it attacked different parts of the body in different ways, so the strains used by CSL scientists in developing a vaccine were the influenza germs. Firstly, streptococci were taken from septic patients and were cultured in a broth prepared from ox heart muscle and pentone, a digested meat.

The common cold germs were cultivated on agar, a jelly produced from a variety of Japanese seaweed. The agar was made soluble and placed in a flask where it could be mixed with horse blood and allowed to set again.

The various germs collected from Spanish flu sufferers were then placed on these preparations and stored in a room kept at a constant heat of 37° Celsius — body blood temperature — for 24 hours. In that environment, a single germ would divide into two 'daughter' germs in 20 minutes, meaning that within those 24 hours hundreds of millions of the germs could be produced. The figures were mind-boggling, especially as the influenza bacillus was the smallest organism the CSL scientists would ever deal with; it was very delicate, and it was 1/25,000$^{th}$ of an inch in size.

The next step in the process was the collection or harvesting of the material, undertaken with the use of syphons. The collected material was placed in separate containers where the germs were killed by treatment with a chemical called trieresol. After sterilisation, portions of the sample were diluted in a sterile salt solution, and that solution became the vaccine, ready for bottling and suitable for inoculation. The process ended when all dishes and bottles were thoroughly sterilised, and the agar and broth, which lose their nutrients after being sterilised, were destroyed.

The product, which CSL would call the Coryza vaccine, was produced in two strengths labelled Coryza A and Coryza B. The A vaccine contained "only" 25 million influenza organisms while the B vaccine contained 125 million. Both were administered, but a week apart, allowing a person's body to become accustomed to the weaker vaccine before the injection of the stronger, B vaccine. The vaccines were manufactured at CSL's Royal Park facility and from 15 October 1918 when the process commenced, until 15 March 1919, when the initial run was completed, CSL produced three million free doses of the vaccine for the Australian people. [6] Even if the vaccine did not kill outright the pneumonic influenza causative agent, the scientists were confident it would prevent the disease's more serious complications.

———◦◦◦◦◦◦———

Acting Prime Minister Watt was also aware that Australia had been a somewhat fractious federation, a point reinforced when he and his department received a telegram from the head of the Department of Customs and Trade on 14 November. The telegram asked the prime minister to authorise the despatch of a telegram to all state premiers as soon as possible. That telegram read:

> "May I invite your attention: serious form epidemic influenza prevalent New Zealand. Vessels arriving from New Zealand have had extensive epidemics. Disease presenting features unusual virulence and fatality. Suggest facts justify careful consideration of advisability State Governments making adequate advance preparations against possibility epidemic within Australia. If Commonwealth can render assistance glad you would indicate early what direction assistance likely." [7]

The telegrams were despatched that day.

———◦◦◦◦◦◦———

It is impossible to know whether a specific incident prompted the head of Customs and Trade to contact the Prime Minister but the fact was that the states' and Commonwealth approach to an impending crisis was both piecemeal and unco-ordinated. A good case in point had recently taken place. On 24 October, the New South Wales Health Minister, John Fitzgerald, had written to Defence Minister George Pearce seeking military tents that could be placed in the grounds of the Coast Hospital, Sydney's isolation hospital at Little Bay to the south-east of the city.[8] The minister's office had replied on 28 October, saying the NSW request was under "urgent consideration" but nothing further had been heard.

The 14 November telegram prompted further action, and the following week NSW Premier William Holman wrote directly to the prime minister asking what had happened to the request. Watt annotated the premier's letter and sent it on to George Pearce with the message, *"Please arrange for supply of tents if necessary."* Soon after, the commanders of all military districts in Australia were informed that any tents not required for military purposes could be loaned to civil authorities.

Things moved slowly in South Australia, Western Australia, Queensland and Tasmania. On 17 October, the South Australian government declared Spanish influenza to be an infectious or notifiable disease under the state's Health Act. At the end of that month, to reassure nervous South Australians, Dr. Hone, the Chief Quarantine Officer at Port Adelaide, stated that his office had in place, or had ordered, enough supplies of the Coryza vaccine to meet any foreseeable emergency.

Perhaps realising that what they had done really wasn't very much, on 21 November a Bill was brought before the South Australian House of Assembly without prior notice and was passed as an urgent measure. Amending the state's Health Act, the new law gave greater powers to South Australia's Central Board of Health in the matter of medical isolation. Now, should an outbreak of Spanish flu occur in the state, the Board would be able to stop traffic, control entry and exit from buildings, and prevent or limit the carriage of persons in any vehicle.

The Queensland government said that it, too, was cooperating with Commonwealth authorities, and on 24 October announced that it was waiting for supplies of influenza vaccine from the south to guarantee the health of its citizens. That appears to be about all it did, in the early days at least, for a month later Brisbane's main newspaper was expressing the opinion that the Queensland government seemed to be somewhat indifferent to the possibility of an outbreak of Spanish influenza. The paper spoke to the state's Home Secretary, John Huxham, who said that he was optimistic that the state would escape the disease but added that there would be full cooperation with Commonwealth authorities if and when it was needed.[9]

Hardly any attention, publicly at least, was paid to the issue by the Tasmanian government, a fact that prompted a letter to the editor of the Launceston *Examiner* on 5 November to ask what the government would actually do if there were an outbreak of Spanish flu in the state. It was a similar story in Western Australia although there, to be fair, both state and Commonwealth authorities were looking closely at quarantine requirements and facilities for the expected return of thousands of soldiers from the battlefields of the First World War.

In Victoria, which was where the Federal Parliament also sat and where many Commonwealth departments were located, the state government seemed determined to bring the people along with them. Dr. Edward Robertson, chairman of the Victorian Health Board — and who also had a background in epidemiology — told journalists that as soon as the board learned of the outbreak of Spanish flu at Cape Town, it had contacted the Commonwealth Quarantine Department. The board had asked whether the department had any current information from South Africa and/or whether they planned to establish contacts there.

Dr. Robertson added that he had received information that very day indicating that Spanish flu was similar to ordinary, seasonal influenza but was complicated by the advent of a catarrhal organism. The deadly effects that were being reported were produced by the combination of three organisms: the influenza bacillus, the micrococcus catarrhalis and an unnamed variety of streptococcus. The combined toxins of these three organisms produced the form of the disease and its often-fatal outcome.[10]

A week later the Victorian Health Minister also spoke to journalists, saying that every precaution was being taken to prevent the influenza epidemic from reaching his state. Reports his department had received showed that picture theatres and other entertainment venues, where numbers of people congregated, were prime sources of contagion. He noted that authorities in England had banned children under 16 years attending such venues. He could not say what might happen in Victoria as decisions would be made according to circumstances. At the present, his advice to parents would be to keep their children away from gatherings where conditions might be favourable to the spread of disease.[11]

Soon afterwards, Dr. Robertson announced that his department had produced a pamphlet dealing with Spanish flu and said it would be circulated widely throughout the state. The pamphlet, a small booklet really, would be of great value should an outbreak occur. It began with a brief outline of how the disease worked, stressing that the infecting organisms were contained in discharges from the mouth and nose. For those who were either sick or convalescent, those discharges had to be destroyed. Equally, carriers of the disease needed to be sought out and disinfected.

To carry out that sort of disinfection on the scale that an epidemic would require, the Health Department recommended the use of an "inhalatorium." Despite the somewhat unusual nomenclature, an inhalatorium was simply a room that could be completely sealed and into which a steam jet containing a concentration of 1% zinc sulphate could be injected under pressure. Such appurtenances were now being widely adopted, Robertson explained, and Dr. Cumpston, the Federal Director of Quarantine, had erected an experimental inhalatorium at Royal Park. If it proved as successful as was hoped, it should be the role of local councils to have inhalatoria erected in their jurisdictions. Some people, he also noted, suggested that they should be attached to schools.

Dr. Robertson said he was convinced that handkerchiefs should be used in all instances of coughing or sneezing, but the difficulty would be inducing people to adopt their use, a particular issue with children. For individuals who seemed to have contracted influenza, douches, sprays, gargles and inhalants could be used. Robertson, and his booklet, made the point that a vaccine had been developed and could prove to be very effective.

In the event of a widespread epidemic, and especially if it was virulent, improvised hospitals may need to be established. Local councils should consider this as a priority. They should now begin looking for available buildings and assess those buildings' suitability for conversion into a temporary hospital. Without identifying which building it was, the Victorian government had also selected a building that could be converted into a very large hospital if necessary. Finally, the Health Department suggested that local councils should ascertain the number of volunteer nurses available in their area and then put in place arrangements to have them trained in the treatment of influenza patients. [12]

New South Wales was also heavily involved in monitoring what was happening in and around the North Head Quarantine Station and in looking at what might possibly happen. In November, the State Cabinet decided to establish something they described as an "Influenza Council." It was to be chaired by Dr. Robert Paton, chairman of the NSW Board of Health, and 12 medical practitioners recommended by the British Medical Association, still the peak medical body in Australia. It was intended to meet as soon as practical to establish some form of state board to address emerging issues around Spanish flu. As well, the Health Department was supervising the development and production of an influenza vaccine, in conjunction with rather than in opposition to CSL's production of the Coryza vaccine in Melbourne.

The Health Department and the state government were also looking to prepare for worst-case scenarios. The Sydney City Council had already said it would make its town hall available for the voluntary inoculation program scheduled to commence in late November, and many local councils had also indicated that they would do the same thing. The NSW government was itself looking to bigger things and had opened discussions with the Commonwealth over quarantine facilities. NSW believed that the North Head Quarantine Station had too many drawbacks in terms of its capacity and its proximity to Sydney itself. Because of this, the state government was suggesting that the naval facilities at Jervis Bay be vacated by the military and turned over to quarantine authorities for redevelopment as a major quarantine station. [13]

———

The Commonwealth's second line of defence — prophylaxis — was critically dependant on a consistency of approach across all jurisdictions and by mid-November it was obvious that this might take some achieving. Victoria and New South Wales led the way in disease preparedness, but the laissez-faire attitude of some of the other states threatened to undermine all they had done. John Cumpston led the push to achieve some degree of unity and co-ordination, calling for a conference to be held in Melbourne, in private rooms at Parliament House, during the last week of November. Attendees would include health ministers from every state, the directors-general of their health departments and representatives of the British Medical Association. Almost immediately after he made the call, a political stoush erupted.

A week before the conference, scheduled for 26-27 November, the editors of the morning, evening and weekly newspapers in Sydney sent a delegation to the New South Wales Minister of Health to protest against the proposed venue of the conference, Melbourne instead of Sydney. If a conference was needed at all — and they didn't seem convinced on that point — they believed that it should be held in Sydney. They offered up a number of arguments in support of this claim. At a time of such crisis, it would be an act of folly to send the state's senior medical officers to Melbourne for a conference. Sydney in general, and the North Head Quarantine Station in particular, was now the epicentre of the influenza threat and, for what it was worth, conference delegates from Queensland would have to pass through Sydney to get to Melbourne.

The Health Minister took the plea from the newspaper representatives to State Cabinet where it was endorsed. A telegram presenting the New South Wales position was sent urgently to the acting prime minister, requesting a quick decision and reply. Urgency was the only part of the request that was acceded to, and the answer was no.

---

The conference went ahead as planned in Melbourne and despite all the naysayers, it was an outstanding success. By the time it was over, the Commonwealth had agreed to assist the states in a number of ways should pandemic pneumonic influenza — now the agreed descriptor — break out in Australia. Federal authorities would be responsible for proclaiming which states were infected as well as maintaining both maritime and land quarantine. The Commonwealth also undertook to supply vaccine to all states free of charge for free inoculations; supplies would be made available as well to the medical profession for private practice. Stores of vaccine would be held at the main quarantine station in each state and would be available to doctors at a reasonable cost. The

Commonwealth also undertook to assist the states by placing federal structures and facilities at the disposal of the states.

In return, the states would arrange emergency hospitals, vaccination depots, ambulance services, medical staff and public awareness measures. It was, however, a raft of recommendations that were unanimously agreed that would determine the impact on Australian society when and if the pneumonic influenza pandemic reached Australia. [14]

The very first resolution passed was that the disease would be formally designated pneumonic influenza. The conference then noted that the spread of the disease overseas suggested public travel was a facilitator of that spread. Therefore, on the outbreak of pneumonic influenza in Australia, public travel would need to be restricted until those restrictions were no longer effective. Doing so would allow unaffected states to complete their organisational preparations which would, in turn, hopefully diminish the virulence of any epidemic.

There was also agreement that as soon as a case of pneumonic influenza was detected in a state, that state's Chief Health Officer would immediately notify the Commonwealth Director of Quarantine; the Commonwealth would then take the necessary steps to proclaim that state to be formally and legally declared an infected state. When that process had been completed, all traffic with the proclaimed state would be suspended until another case was detected in a neighbouring state.

If interstate sea traffic was permitted, it would be subject to strict quarantine, and no person could travel from an infected state without a permit issued by the Commonwealth. The various movement restrictions would not apply to local interstate traffic among residents who lived within 10 miles (16 kilometres) of the border in a "clean" state or in other areas exempted by an agreement with contiguous states and the Commonwealth. In line with this, when a state was declared infected, the Commonwealth would take complete control of its interstate traffic, both land and sea; all states agreed to this and would offer both aid and co-operation. If there was an outbreak there would, however, be no restrictions on the interstate traffic of goods and mail provided that care was taken to prevent contact between the persons handling those goods and mail.

The conference also agreed that, to deal with any outbreak, there should be local district isolation and state quarantines. States that lacked the power to enforce such directions should quickly obtain it. It was also agreed that in the states, the heads of the quarantine and health departments should maintain close liaison to keep each other informed of the progress of the epidemic and of the actions each had taken.

Each state agreed to establish an Advisory Committee, comprising their Chief Health Officer and a limited number of doctors from the British Medical Association. As well, the conference also recommended that each state undertook a number of specific actions. These included establishing serum depots and special hospitals, and the organisation of ambulance transport and adequate medical and nursing assistance. States were charged with issuing advice and updates to local authorities through the press and the issuing of circulars. They should arrange, too, the supply of respirators to the public.

Looking at additional measures, it was agreed without dissent that, should an outbreak of pneumonic influenza occur in any state, all places of public resort within that state should be closed. This included theatres, music halls, picture shows, race meetings, churches and schools. All public meetings would also be prohibited while out-patient departments at general hospitals would also be closely regulated.

Finally, the conference recommended that the Commonwealth government immediately request the Defence Minister disband all military camps until the danger of an epidemic had passed. As well, the minister should be asked to retain all the military's medical and nursing staff in place so that, should an outbreak occur, those resources would be available for state authorities to utilise. The conference closed with those present agreeing that any repeal of the pneumonic influenza proclamations was to be a Commonwealth responsibility.

The following day the acting Minister for Customs, Mr. Massey Greene, announced that the Commonwealth would adopt all the conference's recommendations. Shortly afterwards, acting Prime Minister Watt also announced that the Federal government would supply free serum — the Coryza vaccine — in bulk to all states. Everything seemed to be in place, and it was now just a waiting, and hoping, game.

# CHAPTER 3

# An Ounce of Prevention

To be fair to the newspaper owners and editors in Sydney and the New South Wales Cabinet, their claim that Sydney was the hotspot for pneumonic influenza in November 1918 had the weight of scientific evidence behind it. On 7 November, the Union Steamship Company vessel *Atua* arrived off Sydney Heads and reported an outbreak of influenza on board. The ship was outbound from Fiji and had sailed to Australia via Auckland; passengers had been taken aboard at both Suva and in Auckland. There were 52 influenza cases aboard, mostly among the Pacific Islander crew, but there had been no deaths aboard the ship. The captain reported that the disease had broken out after the *Atua* had left Auckland for Sydney.

The deaths soon began to occur; within two days of *Atua's* arrival, three of her crew succumbed to the disease. Next, the ship's purser, a middle-aged man from Sydney, died on 11 November. By then, there were more than 150 patients from the ship in the North Head Quarantine Station hospital, several of whom were in a critical condition. The next day two of them, both ship's stewards and both from Melbourne, died from the disease and there were a further two deaths four days later, on 16 November. An engine trimmer and another crew member died during the evening of 19 November when four others from the *Atua* were in what was described as a "serious" condition; one of them, a Fijian coal trimmer named Michele Nau died the next day. Two more died on 22 November, at which point 57 of the vessels passengers or crew were being treated in hospital with some in a critical condition.

The very next day, Dr. Mitchell, the head of the medical staff at North Head, said that the *Atua* patients had reached and passed the crisis point and there was now a steady improvement among those who had been hospitalised. He also revealed that, apart from the *Atua* patients, the hospital held another 31 influenza sufferers. Recovered patients, including several from the *Atua*, had been released the previous day and allowed to return to their ships, including the *Manuka,* which had steamed in the day after *Atua. Atua* herself sailed at noon on 23 November and was due to return directly to Fiji. The partial clearing out of the quarantine station could not have come at a better time.

---

At the time of the signing of the Armistice on 11 November, there were a number of Australian troopships carrying Australian servicemen and women to Europe, the Mediterranean and the Middle East. Those troopships were ordered to return to Australia. The closest among them were in the Pacific, heading for the Panama Canal, when the recall order was received. The first to return would be the *Medic* due to arrive around 21-22 November, and it came as something of a surprise to quarantine officials when they received a signal from the ship stating that she had 100 cases of influenza aboard; as far as they were aware, *Medic* had not visited any other ports since departing Sydney.

The *Medic* was carrying almost 1000 soldiers to the battlefields of Europe; while most of them were reinforcements for Australian formations, she was also carrying a contingent of Italian reservists returning home from Australia to join the Italian army. Turning around in the mid-Pacific, *Medic* headed back to Sydney, calling in at Auckland en route, something not initially known to quarantine officials. More significantly, officers aboard the *Medic* were permitted to go ashore there even though the city was in the grip of Spanish flu. When they returned to the *Medic,* the ship continued its voyage. None of those officers had displayed flu symptoms when they returned to the ship.

*Medic* arrived off Sydney Heads during the evening of 20 November and entered the harbour the following morning. By then, the 100 cases the captain had originally reported had grown to 205 and would continue to grow to 439 by 25 November. They were originally treated at sea by military doctors aboard the troopship but would soon be taken ashore to join the 300 other patients now housed at the North Head Quarantine Station.

The sheer numbers, combined with the level of care many of the patients required, threatened to overwhelm the system. Daily reports were prepared for medical and quarantine authorities detailing the circumstances of the various ships in quarantine and the circumstances of those in quarantine ashore. The 9 a.m. report on 23 November described 10 of the patients taken off the *Medic* as "very ill," and reported that another of the *Atua's* passengers, a four-month-old boy, had died during the previous night. Four more passengers from the *Medic,* all soldiers, died on 25 November. By Wednesday 27 November, the total number of deaths at the quarantine station had reached 24, a figure that now included seven soldiers from the *Medic*. By then as well, there were at least 2,000 people being held in quarantine, many aboard ships, at or off North Head while there were 453 suffering from the disease being held at the station. [1] That was why the call for volunteer medical staff had gone out.

One of those who answered that call was 27-year-old Annie Egan.

Annie had commenced her nursing training at St. Vincent's Hospital in Darlinghurst in May 1915 and passed her final examination earlier that year, in June. Enlisted in the Australian Army Nursing Service, Annie was almost immediately posted to the North Head Quarantine Station hospital. There, she and the other volunteers were immediately struck by the scale of the problems they would face. With limited staff and limited medical supplies, the doctors and nurses did what they could to alleviate suffering and save lives.

As well as providing inoculations and general nursing duties, Annie and the other staff held what they called a thermometer parade every morning during which all the people in quarantine, at North Head and on the ships anchored nearby, had their temperatures taken to see if they were running a fever. The staff also operated the station's inhalatorium where lungs and airways were disinfected in a zinc sulphate steam. To disinfect clothing, luggage and bedding, more conventional autoclaves were utilised. Those patients with severe symptoms were given painkillers, bathed, cooled and fed, and generally made to feel as comfortable as possible.

To protect herself, Annie — like all the other quarantine staff — wore a protective mask while working. It was not enough, though, and by 26 November, Annie knew that she had also contracted the disease.

---

One of the New South Wales government's concerns in the lead-up to the medical conference in Melbourne had been the sheer size of the quarantine operation centred on North Head. Shortly after the *Medic* had anchored in Watson's Bay, another recalled troopship, the *Riverina,* had sailed into Sydney Harbour and, although declared clean, she was also placed in quarantine as a precautionary measure. *Riverina* brought the total number of ships riding at anchor in quarantine to 13. Aboard them were at least 1500 young men anxious to get home.

To alleviate some of the boredom those young men would be feeling, newspapers and other reading material was delivered to both the *Medic* and the *Riverina*, the material being organised through the Australian Comforts Fund and the Red Cross. Despite this, there were reports that some Manly ferries had been passing unnecessarily close to quarantined ships and that papers had been thrown to them. When apprised of this, the Chief Quarantine Officer said that any person or vessel communicating with those ships without authorisation would also be placed in quarantine.

If those casual transfers between Manly ferries and quarantined ships were actually going on, they were also illegal. A proclamation under the War Precautions Act prohibited other vessels from approaching within 200 yards (190 metres) of an area containing ships under quarantine. No boats or launches were permitted to move about Manly, North Harbour or Spring Cove between sunset and sunrise. The area would be guarded day and night by military personnel and water police. While their prime responsibility was to prevent anyone absconding from quarantine, they would also arrest anyone seeking to interfere with that quarantine.

The second point the New South Wales government had tried to impress upon the Federal government in the run-up to the Melbourne conference was that the North Head facility and offshore quarantine represented an ongoing threat of infection to Australia's largest city. Quarantine authorities had reassured the state government that every individual held in quarantine was clean — clear of infection — before they were released. This did not allay all fears, and many Sydneysiders expressed their opinion, publicly and privately, that it was inevitable that the disease would reach Sydney via North Head. One of the young men in quarantine would either be released prematurely, and bring the disease out with him, or another would be tempted by the bright lights of the city and would break out of quarantine to experience them. Either way, Spanish flu would be loose in the city and the genie would be out of the bottle.

It was these concerns, overcrowding and risk of quarantine failure, which prompted the New South Wales government to contact the acting Prime Minister on the eve of the Melbourne conference. The telegram they sent on 21 November read:

> "The holding of such large numbers in quarantine contiguous to Sydney has created great alarm here. In view of the serious position, our Cabinet desires you to urgently consider a proposal to have Jervis Bay evacuated by the military...with the contacts (those who have been in touch with infected persons) to be kept there. Even under military discipline, there are grave dangers of the contacts in Sydney."[2]

While the New South Wales proposal was rejected by the prime minister, the question of the quarantine stations, their positioning and their roles, were all problems that just wouldn't seem to go away.

⸺◇◇◇◇⸺

There was even less chance of the public losing interest in the question of quarantine stations when stories from within or about them seemed to pop up in newspapers every other day. After the Melbourne medical conference was over, and its outcomes had been widely reported, one of that city's major newspapers printed a letter written by one of the soldiers aboard the *Medic* in quarantine to his father. Reprinted in newspapers across the country, the letter caused a minor sensation. The anonymous writer described how the troopship had sailed from Australia but had been recalled when the Armistice was signed. Calling in to New Zealand on the way home, the young soldier wrote how nearly all the officers went ashore while the other ranks had to remain aboard the *Medic;* the outcome being predictable: *"The result was that some of the officers contracted influenza and the men, huddled together like mice, naturally caught it."*

The letter continued with descriptions of how the disease spread through the ship *"like wildfire,"* with up to 100 men reporting sick in a single day. The doctors and nurses aboard did a splendid job but were simply overwhelmed by the scale of the outbreak. He noted that the Italian reservists seemed to hold out longest against the disease, *"but when they caught it they went down like flies."* He also noted that, when they arrived in Sydney, the Italians threatened to burn the ship to the waterline unless they were taken ashore; that transfer was quickly arranged.

Aboard the *Medic,* the soldiers who remained were confined to the between-deck spaces. The canteen was closed, meaning they were unable to buy tobacco and matches. Books and newspapers from the Red Cross and the Australian Comforts Fund were one thing; living relatively comfortably while in quarantine was something else. The reports of exchanges between ships in quarantine and Manly ferries now had a more complete context. [3]

The Sydney newspapers also reported on the state of play at the North Head Quarantine Station each day, how many were in hospital and how many of those were dangerously ill or critically ill. It also reported on individual deaths — by the end of November there had been 29 of these — and gave the personal details of each patient who died. On 4 December, those newspapers reported that Nurse Annie Egan had died during the previous afternoon and another controversy erupted.

Annie's condition was one of those reported on from the time she was admitted to the quarantine station hospital. At first, she was reported as merely being "ill", but her condition continued to deteriorate while some of her patients, men she had really cared for, had succumbed to the disease. On 3 December, the newspapers noted that Annie's condition had been upgraded to "dangerously ill." A devout Catholic, and aware that the end was near, on that morning Annie asked if she would be able to see a Catholic priest; the request was refused on quarantine grounds even though the local priest at Manly was willing to see her or, at the very least, talk to her through the front gates of the station.

A compromise of sorts was reached. Later in the morning, Annie was allowed to talk to the priest by telephone. It was far from ideal but it allowed Annie to unburden her soul and to hear the priest respond by telling her she would not be travelling alone on her journey and that he would say a special Mass for her. Within a few hours, Annie Egan was dead, and within a few hours more she had been laid to rest in the quarantine station's cemetery. With no priest available, Annie's funeral service was conducted by a Catholic nurse. It was a full military funeral; a bugler played "The Last Post" as troops in full uniform fired a volley above Annie's grave. At the conclusion of the service, soldiers and quarantine station staff placed wreaths they had made from locally gathered wildflowers on her grave. The next day, a newspaper storm erupted.

It was not just that volunteer nurse Annie Egan had died; that was an occupational hazard and all the volunteers had known the risks they would be facing and the possible fate that awaited them. It was more the circumstances of her death — reaching out for succour in her hour of need and then being denied the solace of her religion. Newspaper editorials and letters to those who wrote the editorials were not especially sectarian; people of all faiths could seemingly identify with Annie in her last days, perhaps because she reminded them all of what could be their own fates.

The period covered by Annie Egan's brief service at the quarantine station coincided with another health crisis in small Pacific Island nations well out in the ocean to the east of Australia. On 21 November, the New Zealand government contacted the Australian government requesting assistance in addressing the influenza outbreak that had occurred in its recently acquired protectorate of Samoa. [4] It was suspected, and would later be confirmed, that the disease was brought to Samoa, and to Fiji and Tonga as well, by infected crewmen aboard the Union Steamship Company vessel *Talune* on its monthly supply run through the islands. When confronted later, the ship's captain would claim that he was not aware that influenza was a notifiable disease, but by then the damage had been done.

New Zealand, struggling with its own Spanish flu epidemic, could only offer limited assistance, hence the request to the Australian government, and that government was more than happy to assist. The issues raised by the arrival of the *Niagara* and the *Medic* had shown how vulnerable Australia could be to the introduction of Spanish flu from the Pacific. With a defence posture based on fighting enemies, whether human or bacteriological, as far from the Australian mainland as possible, Australia was prepared to act, and act quickly.

Two days after the New Zealand request arrived, the light cruiser HMAS *Encounter* sailed from Sydney after being loaded, in record time, with 100 tons of stores including 371 tents and 1000 blankets. [5] The next day, a second Royal Australian Navy (RAN) vessel, HMAS *Fantome* [6], carrying the main medical contingent for the expedition under the command of Surgeon Sydney O'Neill, also departed. The party included another RAN surgeon besides O'Neill, an Australian Army Medical Corps (AAMC) major and five other AAMC doctors, 33 medical orderlies, three RAN sick berth ratings and a New Zealand Army Medical Corps lieutenant. Also aboard were special medical stores and a supply of the Coryza vaccine, A and B strengths.

Almost as soon as they cleared Sydney Heads the doctors aboard *Fantome* began inoculating the ship's company with the Coryza A vaccine. Two days out, she relayed a message she had received from the *Encounter*, sailing somewhere ahead of her. Related to the situation in Samoa, it read:

> *"Serious epidemic continues. Approximately fifty deaths daily. Both islands affected but quite unable to assist outside. Regret delay. Encounter should proceed direct to Apia."*[7]

The information had originated in Suva as the Australian government had, on the recommendation of the Customs Department, tasked the High Commissioner for the Western Pacific, based in Suva, to provide regular updates for the Ocean Islands, Nauru, the Gilbert and Ellice Islands (Kiribati and Tuvalu), the Marshall Islands, Solomon Islands, New Hebrides and Fiji. These reports would be relayed to both RAN vessels.

Despite being asked to sail directly to Samoa, HMAS *Encounter* arrived at Suva late in the morning of 30 November and there learned that the situation in Tonga was now at least as bad as that in Samoa but that in Tonga there were no doctors and few medicines available for the Tongan people. Responding to this news, the ship's captain, Walter Thring, and the senior medical officer aboard, Surgeon Commander Grey, identified a team of doctors and orderlies from the ship's company, and they and a list of supplies were offloaded. A private yacht would be chartered to take them all to Tonga. Just six hours after she arrived at Suva, the *Encounter* was on her way again. Those aboard were somewhat reassured that the *Fantome* and her medical team were not too far behind.

*Encounter* arrived at Apia during the morning of 3 December, anchoring well offshore in the main harbour. An exchange of radio signals with authorities followed and from those, *Encounter's* captain and

Surgeon Grey learned that the blankets and tents they carried would not be needed. Samoan authorities also had enough fresh food for their people but were short of dry food and, more particularly, condensed milk. Those authorities were also having problems finding crews for boats taking much-needed food and medicine to the big island of Savaii and the smaller outlying islands. While the threat was diminishing on the main island of Upola, it was believed that Savaii was being especially hard hit. Volunteers for possible landing parties for Samoa and their next destination, Tonga, were called for; 80 officers and other ranks immediately put their names forward.

The local response to the unfolding disaster had been swift and encouraging. In quick time, the local European community had mobilised to assist the Samoan population with the delivery of food and water to Samoan homes, a critical issue when every member of a family fell ill. While the epidemic was waning when *Encounter* arrived, those volunteers were still able to offer some assistance. The ship's landing party, along with the local garrison of the New Zealand Army managed the difficult task of burying thousands of bodies as nearly the entire population was incapacitated. [8]

Other circumstances then intervened. *Encounter* was not carrying enough coal to allow her to make a side-trip to Savaii, while her anchorage in Apia harbour was becoming increasingly problematic as her anchors dragged. Her shore party was not needed in Samoa, on Upolu at least, and Surgeon Grey had received no indication as to whether or not the supplies they had brought from Australia and landed there were of any actual use. Knowing that the *Fantome* was a few hours behind her and sensing that he could achieve nothing further in Samoa, Thring decided to take *Encounter* directly to Tonga.

HMAS *Fantome* indeed arrived at Suva, just a few hours after *Encounter* had departed the port, and learned that all of Fiji was now infected and that many deaths had occurred. At Suva, another small medical party was put together to join those from *Encounter* on their chartered journey to Tonga to help with relief operations there. While the details of the charter were being finalised, the senior medical officers aboard *Fantome* held a conference with local medical authorities. That afternoon, *Fantome* sailed for Samoa. Once they had cleared Suva Harbour, all the on-board inoculations were completed.

On 2 December, one day out from Samoa, the *Fantome's* captain also called for volunteers for a shore party and, after medical checks, 77 officers and other ranks were selected. The ship arrived on schedule the next day and placed itself in strict quarantine while two boat parties ferried men and supplies ashore. Like *Encounter* before them, *Fantome* found that a lot of what they brought, hospital equipment in particular, was not needed while the locals now believed they were over the worst of the epidemic. Understanding there was little more for them to do in Samoa, *Fantome,* too, sailed for Tonga where they planned to drop off one medical officer and six orderlies to join the relief party sailing from Suva.

---

*Encounter* arrived at Tonga during the afternoon of 5 December. A small medical relief party was landed and soon reported back that a larger naval landing party would not be required. They also reported that the chartered yacht carrying medical personnel and supplies from Fiji had broken down and been forced to return to Suva. When the relief party returned to the ship several hours later, their senior officer reported that he had spoken to the British Consul in Nukualofa, and the two men had discussed the Tongan situation. The Australian learned that 97% of the Tongan population had been affected by the disease and that there had been at least 500 deaths. The Consul also noted that the situation seemed to be improving and believed that the country had enough supplies to deal with the situation.

With nothing further to do in the Pacific Islands, Walter Thring decided it was time to take the *Encounter* back to Sydney, with a stopover at Suva to get an update on the situation there and collect the Tonga relief party they had dropped off during their initial visit. En route to Australia, he wrote a mission report which he concluded with some observations on the influenza outbreak in the South Pacific:

> *"The weather conditions appear to have had a considerable influence on the epidemic. When we first arrived at Suva the outbreak there had not been very severe, the weather being fine and dry. At our second visit, heavy rains with hot steamy weather had set in and the influenza seemed to be considerably worse. Tonga was fine and dry but daily rains appear to be the norm in Samoa."[9]*

Authorities in Australia could make of it what they would.

———◦◦◦◦◦———

*Fantome* departed Tonga for Suva on 7 December. As the Tonga relief party had not yet arrived at the island, one of the AAMC doctors and the extra medical orderlies were left behind to see if they could assist in the country's outlying areas. Arriving at Suva two days later, *Fantome* anchored in the middle of the harbour, observing strict quarantine conditions as influenza was still virulent ashore. During the ship's stay this time, there was no interaction between ship and shore. Coaling was completed while *Fantome* sat at anchor in the harbour and after getting a clean Bill of Health from the Port Health Officer, *Fantome* sailed for Australia on 10 December.

Sydney O'Neill, the senior medical officer aboard *Fantome*, also wrote a report on the expedition as he sailed home. He noted that while *Fantome* remained influenza-free for the duration of the voyage, he could not say whether this was attributable to the Coryza vaccine or the strict quarantine conditions that were observed everywhere they visited. He also wrote that civil authorities in Fiji, Tonga and Samoa all believed that influenza had been brought to their islands by those aboard the steamship *Talune*.

In regard to treatments, medical officers in Fiji and Tonga advocated the regular gargling of antiseptic to prevent the infection developing into pneumonia. Dr. Lynch, the Senior Medical Officer in Suva, gave O'Neill an example of a successful intervention. All the students at a Suva boys' school, 80 boys aged between eight and 16 years, contracted Spanish flu. Lynch turned the school buildings into a temporary hospital and provided a suitable nursing staff. All the patients were seriously ill, yet only two developed pneumonia during their isolation and the disease was contained within the school.

As with Walter Thring's report, Surgeon Commander Sydney O'Neill was happy to submit his report and leave it up to higher authorities to take what they could from it. [10]

The Australia that HMAS' *Encounter* and *Fantome* returned to after three weeks in the Pacific was not significantly different to the Australia they had departed. The only cases of Spanish flu in the country were confined in quarantine stations and though there had been several dozen deaths these, too, had occurred in quarantine stations and the disease had not spread out into the general population. And, if anything, quarantine restrictions had been increased while they were away.

Because returning troopships had been especially problematic, additional requirements had been levied on them. New instructions issued to the senior medical officers on troop transport and the hospital ships that were also beginning to return from the various theatres of war stipulated that a "rigorous" inspection was now to be made of every person aboard the vessel. That senior medical officer would be held personally responsible for the inspection regime and was expected to become directly involved in the process himself. As well, he would be held personally responsible for impressing on his medical staff the critical importance of reporting all suspicious cases which occurred aboard the vessel. Finally, that officer must offer every assistance to the Port Quarantine Officer when landfall was made.

The administration of the quarantine stations themselves was also being tightened up. In Victoria, for instance, Major W. T. Conder, then officer in charge of the Langwarrin Army Camp, was appointed to take charge of all troops at the Portsea Quarantine Station at the entrance to Port Phillip Bay. While one of the reasons given for the appointment was to streamline communications between the quarantine station and military headquarters, a tightening of military discipline at the station was also a consideration. [11]

The following week, Defence Minister George Pearce also spoke of the additional precautions that had been introduced. He outlined how all State Military Commandants had been issued orders directing them to assist as far as possible the quarantine authorities through the provision of personnel and equipment. Military tentage had been placed at the disposal of quarantine officials as far as Defence requirements allowed that to happen. All Citizen Force (Reserve) training camps had been deferred to a future date when the probability of infection had ceased, and instructions had been issued to all military districts to construct inhalatoria, Pearce noting that some had already been completed. [12]

Finally, as well as the books and other entertainments provided to the North Head Quarantine Station by the Red Cross and the Australian Comforts Fund, the Defence Department was providing the station with additional medical officers, nurses, tents and mattresses as well as personal items to support the station in its work.

The quarantine barrier continued to hold into December, although there were some close-run occurrences. The voyages of the RAN ships *Encounter* and *Fantome* had been of limited value to both the Pacific Islanders they had been sent to help and to Australian authorities who hoped to learn more of the nature of the disease. They did bring back some good news, though, and that was that Spanish flu seemed to be playing itself out in the Pacific, thereby reducing the threat in the east. That was very apposite as the next crisis would emerge in the west.

# CHAPTER 4

# Woodman's Point

## I.

The unfolding tragedy of the North Head Quarantine Station was a clear pointer to what could go wrong with the quarantine system, and gave a clear indication of just what needed to be done to secure Australia's maritime border from the increasing threat of pneumonic influenza. Those pointers and indications were especially pertinent for Western Australia and its major port of Fremantle. There would soon be thousands, then tens of thousands of Australian servicemen and women returning from the battlefields and casualty wards of the Western Front and the Middle East and, just as Fremantle had been the last Australian port they saw when they departed, it would also be the first Australian port they saw when they returned. Both the Commonwealth and Western Australian governments recognised this fact and wanted to do something about it; they just weren't certain what that something should be. And, as it transpired, it was not as though they had not been given the opportunity for a kind of trial run.

On the morning of Monday 21 October 1918, the steamer *Charon* arrived in the roadstead in Roebuck Bay, just off the north-western Australian port town of Broome, having departed Singapore a week earlier. As well as crew and general cargo, *Charon* was carrying 120 passengers, mainly citizens of Perth whose port, Fremantle, was *Charon's* ultimate destination. She was also flying a yellow flag, the international signal for notifying authorities that there was infectious disease aboard. The small boat that set out from the main jetty carried a Customs officer and a policeman, and they would be joined shortly by a doctor who had been caught up on other business.

Discussions with the *Charon's* captain and sick bay officer revealed that there were several cases of influenza aboard, although all seemed to be relatively mild. However, with Spanish flu ravaging large swathes of Asia and Africa, the captain decided to err on the side of caution, hence the yellow flag and the discussions on the bridge. In that situation, the Broome doctor was the final authority and he instructed the captain to continue to Fremantle where he would be required to go into quarantine. Discussions over, the three officials returned to shore where they would prepare brief reports and notify authorities in Perth of what was coming their way aboard *Charon.*

In what was rapidly becoming a charged environment, those three officials' return to shore, and what they told people there, quickly developed a life of its own. A few minor cases of mild influenza suddenly became 39 cases of an *"extremely virulent"* form of influenza, with the underlying assumption that pneumonic influenza was now making its way down the coast of Western Australia.[1] *Charon* sailed from Broome on 22 October and on the 25th was reported to be between Geraldton and Fremantle. Those worried about the ship's imminent arrival were somewhat reassured when both state and federal authorities announced that appropriate arrangements had been made to use the quarantine facilities at Woodman's Point[2] to accommodate those aboard *Charon*.

Those facilities were now a lot more appropriate than they had been in 1886 when the quarantine station was established by the colonial authorities on an isolated peninsula over 10 kilometres to the south of Fremantle. Then, they had been used to isolating passengers arriving from interstate or overseas who were either suffering from, or had been exposed to, such diseases as smallpox, leprosy or any one of a variety of potentially fatal fevers. Federation in 1901 had seen an upgrade of what had been very primitive facilities but the 20th Century had also seen the growth of both Perth and Fremantle; what had been an isolated spot was now just beyond the southern boundaries of the growing metropolis. It should be more than suitable for the job it was now being asked to do, perhaps.

Despite the official reports from the authorities in Broome, rumours continued to swirl about what was actually aboard the *Charon*, and there was still doubt in at least one official's mind. As soon as he learned of the impending arrival of the *Charon* and its cargo of influenza-infected patients, the Western Australian Commissioner of Public Health, Dr. Everitt Atkinson, urged Federal authorities, notably the Quarantine Department, to appoint a Resident Medical Officer to the Woodman's Point Quarantine Station while patients were confined there. Atkinson argued that it should also be a full-time position and the incumbent should remain there until the current crisis was over. It was also reported in local newspapers that quarantine authorities were having difficulty in obtaining the requisite number of nurses to attend what was assumed to be quite a large complement of patients aboard *Charon*. Those nurses were quickly found, perhaps as a result of the Western Australian Health Department agreeing to undertake some analytical work at the station for Federal authorities.[3] A Resident Medical Officer, Dr. Roy Mitchell, was also found and took up his appointment immediately.[4]

*Charon* arrived off Fremantle early in the morning of Saturday 26 October and following directions from various immigration, customs and quarantine officials moved slowly to Owen's Anchorage, just off the coast and approximately halfway between Fremantle and Woodman's Point, where she dropped anchor and waited for those various officials to come aboard and/or issue further instructions. Those officials and instructions weren't long in coming. That afternoon, *Charon's* cargo was fumigated before being loaded onto lighters for the trip back to Fremantle while doctors examined all those aboard.

They did not find a disease-ravaged crew and seriously ill passengers, as some believed they would. Instead they found in semi-isolation around a dozen cases of what seemed to be quite a mild form of influenza, probably not Spanish flu. Most of the dozen or so cases involved Asian crew members although two of the European officers and two of the white Australian passengers also appeared infected. The *Charon* was therefore directed to sail to Woodman's Point where all passengers and crew would be placed in quarantine. Those suffering from the disease would be placed in the isolation hospital and all others in general accommodation from which they would be released after seven days if they had not by then shown any signs of influenza.

As an outbreak of a virulent, killer disease, the story of the *Charon* was very much an anti-climax. It did, though, prompt a lot of letters to editors of newspapers all around Australia asking (again) why ships with confirmed cases of influenza on board would be allowed anywhere near Australia's major population centres.[5]

—◦◦◦◦◦—

After the frisson of excitement generated by the arrival of the *Charon* had died away, Federal quarantine and Western Australian health authorities turned their minds to what was surely going to become their greatest challenge, the tens of thousands of Australian soldiers returning home from the battlefields of the Western Front and the Middle East to be demobilised and returned to civilian life. Again, there was an opportunity to pressure test the system before it was threatened by large numbers of troops, whether infected with pneumonic influenza or not and, this time, the authorities by and large failed that test.

The first of these returning soldiers arrived even before the war was over. On 6 November, two soldiers were admitted to the isolation facilities at Woodman's Point when they were found to be suffering mild cases of influenza. They were part of 140 Western Australian soldiers aboard a returning troopship, the remainder of whom were held at the facility for a week before being returned to Perth. A week later, there were 335 soldiers in quarantine there but, still, the original two were the only soldiers with symptoms of influenza. This was a point that State Premier Lefroy was at pains to make, especially given the public disquiet about a major quarantine station on the doorstep of Perth. For good measure, he also poured scorn on those spreading rumours that security at Woodman's Point was so lax that a number of men had broken out of the facility and made their way to Perth. Two weeks later, he may have regretted those comments.

During the war, the former White Star liner *Runic* was taken over by the Australian government for use as a troopship and it was in this capacity that she arrived off Fremantle on Sunday 17 November 1918 with 1300 returning soldiers, from all over Australia. Among those soldiers were two with mild cases of influenza, but that was enough to see all the Western Australians aboard transferred to the quarantine station at Woodman's Point. The numbers involved are not clear, but were likely to be substantial, perhaps 50 or more. What is clear, however, is that in that number were several — one figure given is eight, while another says10 — who were not prepared to wait out their seven days' quarantine. After dark that evening, they broke out of camp and made their way to the suburb immediately to the north of the camp, Coogee, where they went straight to the hotel and demanded service. A military guard was summoned, and after a brief clash the escapees were placed in custody and returned to Woodman's Point where they spent the rest of their quarantine isolated and under guard.

The breakout couldn't be kept secret as too many people had seen it directly or knew it had occurred, and it again prompted a flood of letters to editors pointing out the presumed folly of having quarantine stations adjacent to urban areas. This time there were also some positive suggestions, with both Garden and Rottnest Islands, just off the coast opposite Perth and Fremantle, put forward as preferred sites for quarantine facilities. Before anything concrete could be put in place, though, the war had ended, other large troopships had arrived, Woodman's Point had been overwhelmed and Australia experienced one of the few mutinies in its history.

---

Arthur Thwaites may not have known and, if he did know, may not have cared that he was one of around 900 soldiers who were on board the last ship to leave Australia carrying reinforcements for the units still fighting on the Western Front. Arthur was also in many ways an unlikely soldier. His official job title was "Dispenser's Assistant" and he worked for a pharmacist at Mudgee in western New South Wales, a long way from his childhood home in Liverpool on Sydney's western outskirts and an even longer way from France and Belgium. His occupation was one that made him exempt from military service but in October 1917, for whatever reasons, Arthur gave up his work and left his mother and brother behind when he signed up to join the Australian Army for the duration of the war (and, for good measure, four months afterwards). Two months later, at the completion of his two months' initial training, the 29-year-old was drafted into the Australian Army Medical Corps at the Liverpool Army Camp.[6]

Thwaites' first postings were all to army hospitals: the field hospitals at Liverpool and Menangle and then the garrison hospital at Liverpool. He was a good soldier, too, and when he and a large draft of infantry reinforcements boarded a train at the Liverpool camp at 1 p.m. on Friday 18 October, he was already an acting corporal, well-known and well-respected by the other men. Thwaites, amongst others, marched to the station carrying all their kit, plus an enormous sandwich comprising two very thick slices of bread and an enormous slab of rock-hard cheese. Most were still nibbling at its edges when their train arrived at Goulburn, where urns of hot tea and more sandwiches awaited them, a brief break in a journey that would end at the Broadmeadows Army Camp, just to the north of Melbourne, at 8 a.m. the next morning.[7]

The troops remained at Broadmeadows long enough to consume a substantial breakfast and, three hours later, an even more substantial lunch, so it may have been a relief when they again entrained and, after picking up a contingent of Victorian reinforcements in Melbourne, resumed their journey west. A short break at Ballarat was followed by an overnight trip to the Mitcham Army Camp, outside Adelaide, where they arrived at 8 a.m. on Sunday morning. Their camp was over three kilometres from the railhead and the troops all marched that distance in full equipment and carrying their sea kitbags. The men were granted several hours leave that afternoon but were also taken on a route march before breakfast the next day.

They entrained once more and travelled to Port Adelaide where the eastern states' reinforcements were now joined by a contingent of

South Australians. At 10.15 a.m. on 22 October, they began climbing the gangways to board His Majesty's Australian Transport (HMAT) A 36, the steamship *Boonah*.[8] *Boonah* sailed at 12.30 p.m. that day heading west into the Great Australian Bight for what proved to be a typically rough crossing. It was agony for most of the seasick men, but it did give them their sea legs and most felt like experienced sailors when they arrived at Fremantle on 29 October. There, a final contingent of 158 Western Australian reinforcements were marched aboard and at 2 a.m. on 30 October, lines were cast off and *Boonah* sailed west into the vast reaches of the Indian Ocean.

The transport was now carrying almost one thousand young men, most of them bound for an uncertain future in the trenches of the Western Front, and their officers and crew were certainly not going to let them dwell on what their future there might hold. In maritime terms, *Boonah* was a young boat, well-fitted and equipped and, apart from a slightly offensive smell from the bilges apparent on the lower decks, capable of a fast, safe and pleasant crossing to the first port of call, the South African port city of Durban.

The young men were not given a lot of time to dwell on what might or might not be awaiting them and a clear routine was established during their first day out from Fremantle. For the duration of the voyage, they were roused at 6 a.m. each day and led on a compulsory walk around the ship's deck. They would then clear and stow their hammocks, which were attached to massive hooks suspended from the deck above them, transforming their sleeping quarters into the ship's main dining room or one of the subsidiary mess areas. Breakfast was served at 7.30 a.m., lunch at 12.30 p.m. and tea at 4.30 p.m. Seventeen men would sit at each of the many tables stretched down the length of the dining room. Lights out was at 9 p.m. each evening. Between these mealtimes, there were physical training sessions twice a day while various working parties were formed for specific tasks each day. Working dress — military dungarees — was worn every day except Sunday, when full uniform was worn for the various church services.

When off-duty, there were books and games in the various lounges, most supplied by the YMCA, while two of the recreation areas also contained battered pianos, always popular for evening singalongs. Concerts and boxing tournaments were held at least twice a week, and at these officers would mix freely with the men. To those men, the overwhelming majority of whom were very young and very unworldly, the voyage across the Indian Ocean was like some kind of pleasure cruise or holiday, busy days interspersed with good meals and fresh fruit, with not a lot to either think or worry about. They even had their own daily newspaper, the *Boonah Boomerang.* The main complaint they might have had was the difficulty of falling asleep surrounded by the noises, bumps and groans of hundreds of men also trying to fall asleep.

As *Boonah* sailed west, the world changed. Just over halfway through the leg to South Africa, the Armistice was signed, ending the fighting if not the war. When the ship tied up to a buoy off Durban in the Bay of Natal at 8 a.m. on the morning of Saturday 16 November, no-one aboard, military or civilian, was certain what would happen next, and so they sat and waited for orders while the officers tried to keep the men entertained and employed. Durban, from the vantage point of an offshore anchorage, is a beautiful city and the troops were very disappointed that there was no chance of being given leave to explore the city and its surrounds. They knew, though, that much of the city was in the grip of pneumonic influenza and that hundreds of people were either dying or being hospitalised each day they sat there.

Even so, it was too much of a temptation for one small group of young men. On the second night there, a group of around eight soldiers lowered a life raft to the water and paddled to shore, planning to spend the night exploring and returning to *Boonah* before dawn in the hope that no-one would notice them missing. They would never know whether that plan would have worked because South African authorities, suspecting some of the Australians might try to do just that, had doubled the guard force along the seashore and wharves and the soldiers were arrested as they came ashore. They were charged and put in gaol awaiting a decision on how their breach of discipline would be handled. [9]

By then, the ship's future had been determined by Australian authorities; *Boonah* would return to Australia without discharging any the cargo and troops she carried. To do so, she would need to be revictualled and her bunkers would need to be topped up with coal. All this was to be achieved while the quarantine around the ship was maintained, something that may have appeared relatively simple for senior officials in Melbourne but that was a practical impossibility.

The re-coaling and re-victualling would be undertaken by South African labourers and stevedores who, along with food and coal, would be brought out to the *Boonah* each day to work until the task was completed. In theory, the workers, all South African natives, would have absolutely no contact with the Australian troops aboard, something that turned out to be impossible to police. Some would be left on board overnight, sequestered from the Australians, but required to carry supplies to various storage areas on the ship. When the soldiers learned that the South Africans earned about one-tenth of the wage they would have been paid in Australia, they began to sympathise with them. When they saw that their overseers carried heavy sticks, and were not afraid to use them, that sympathy grew. [10]

To begin with, too, many of those labourers brought with them small souvenirs, carved objects, handmade jewellery and the like, that they wished to sell or trade to the men on the boat. The trinkets found a ready market. As well, while the Australians considered them light-hearted and happy, they also considered that numbers of them were clearly underfed and would find ways to slip them scraps of food. Finally, the labourers brought something else with them, an illness that caused some of them to simply collapse to the deck, unable to work any further. Those who collapsed would not be seen again after they were taken back to shore.

With stores and coal aboard, *Boonah* departed Durban at 6.30 a.m. on Sunday 24 November. The next day, there was a medical emergency aboard when one of the troops developed acute appendicitis. Despite the rough seas and the absence of an operating theatre, one of the two AAMC doctors aboard successfully removed the infected appendix. The following day another minor medical problem appeared when one of the young soldiers developed symptoms, a sore throat and tonsillitis, that looked very much like pneumonic influenza. Another followed later that day, several more the next and then, in a trice, there were up to 30 soldiers presenting with influenza symptoms every day. The medical contingent aboard, two doctors and 30 medical staff, threatened to be overwhelmed but, with the assistance of the ship's captain and crew, were able to set up temporary isolation hospitals all over the ship.

Their endeavours were not helped by the sailing orders *Boonah's* captain had been given. Rather than a direct return to Fremantle, the *Boonah* had been instructed to skirt Madagascar and then sail some 800 kilometres to the south of the normal sailing routes to call in at a small dot in the ocean, St. Paul's Island, to check on an unmanned rescue station there. Not only did this add several days to the duration of the voyage, it took *Boonah* down into the Roaring Forties and what was, for all aboard, unseasonably and unreasonably cold weather, and this at a time when pneumonic influenza was being found in increasing numbers. That in turn meant that, to avoid the cold and the cutting wind, men wrapped themselves in blankets and congregated below decks, near the smell from the bilges but also near the various steam pipes and machinery that seemed to give off the heat they all sought.

By 2 December there were over 200 cases aboard the ship, including Sergeant Arthur Thwaites, who had thrown himself into the work of helping others before contracting a bad case of the disease himself. [11] Unable to assist any more, Thwaites became one of the dozens of patients placed into one of the temporary hospitals, his being located on the bridge deck. There, Thwaites was looked after by the two doctors, medical orderlies, volunteers from the troops aboard and ship's crew. The doctors checked him twice a day, the orderlies changed soiled bedding and bedclothes and the volunteers served him the food the doctors prescribed for all suffering with influenza, a diet composed mainly of hard-boiled eggs, fish, pudding, tea and, sometimes, an allowance of beef tea. Nothing, however, seemed to make a lot of difference in the majority of cases.

During the evening of 9 December, with almost 300 cases of pneumonic influenza aboard *Boonah,* Arthur Thwaites climbed out of his cot on the bridge deck, pulled a dressing gown across his shoulders, and went for a walk. Climbing down to the main deck, he walked past several soldiers who were either sleeping or try to sleep in nooks and crannies as their normal sleeping spaces had been allocated to the ill. One or two knew him and one of these, a private named Donald Foreman, asked Thwaites what he was doing, telling him the time and saying that the sergeant should be in bed; Thwaites said that was what he intended to do. Several of those who spotted him noted that sighting because it appeared to them that he was wearing a blanket wrapped around his shoulders and not much else.

Towards the stern of the ship, Thwaites stopped and looked down at Private Morgan O'Neill, who was trying unsuccessfully to sleep on the bed he had wedged underneath some rigging. O'Neill noticed his presence but assumed it was just another soldier making his way down the latrines near the stern, so he turned over and away from the man. Thwaites watched O'Neill for a few seconds more then made his way across to the ship's railings where he slipped the dressing gown from his shoulders. He then climbed the railings, balanced for a second, and stepped into space.

———◦◦◦◦◦———

The next morning, 10 December, the officer commanding Australian troops aboard, Major J. H. O'Halloran, convened a Court of Enquiry aboard *Boonah* to investigate the loss overboard of Sergeant Arthur Thwaites. The court heard evidence from several witnesses, including Morgan O'Neill, who all detailed the late-night perambulations of the sick man and any conversations they had with him. The enquiry also heard from one of the two AAMC doctors aboard, Captain Gilbert Brown. Brown testified that he heard about the man overboard incident soon after it occurred and immediately did the rounds of the ship's hospitals. During this, he noted that Sergeant Thwaites was missing from the bridge deck hospital and immediately informed the Officer of the Watch of that.

Brown knew Sergeant Thwaites well and told the court that he had been in hospital for around a week, very ill with influenza. The previous day, Brown had examined Thwaites, noting that he had a temperature of 104° Fahrenheit, but that he was not delirious. He did point out, however, that a person with a temperature that high could easily *become* delirious and throw themselves overboard without really knowing what they were doing. The doctor also offered his professional opinion on what would have happened to the sergeant:

> *"On entering the water at that temperature he would probably have taken a deep breath and fill his lungs with sea water. He would die almost instantly from shock and asphyxiation."* [12]

71

Brown added that he had examined Thwaites' belongings earlier that morning and had found no indications of contemplated suicide.

*Boonah's* captain, Allan Johnson, also appeared before the enquiry and detailed how the ship had been stopped as soon as the details about a man overboard had been received by the bridge. As the ship reversed its course and then steamed in circles, a number of lifebuoys with lights attached had been thrown overboard. *Boonah* had searched the area where Sergeant Thwaites had disappeared for approximately 45 minutes but could find no trace of the soldier, and so Johnson ordered that the ship resume its original course. Even at the time, he held no hopes for Thwaites' survival as he had entered the water just 20 metres from the ship's stern. At that point, his body would probably have been sucked into the ship's propeller and chopped into pieces.

At the conclusion of the enquiry, O'Halloran handed down his finding, which was that of accidental death. Arthur Thwaites had died as the result of falling or jumping from the ship's railing while in the grip of delirium. By then, O'Halloran himself was feeling ill and by day's end would be admitted to the ship's hospital with pneumonic influenza. The following day, Wednesday 11 December, *Boonah* arrived off Fremantle and awaited further instructions. The first of these was to steam south to a position approximately halfway between Fremantle and the Woodman's Point Quarantine Station, anchor there, and wait. By then, 298 of those aboard, crew and soldiers alike, were suffering from influenza and some were in a very serious condition. They could wait at sea, but they could not wait very long.

## II.

From 2 December, the radio operator aboard *Boonah* contacted army and maritime authorities in Perth each evening to detail the ship's progress as well as the increasing toll that was being taken by Spanish flu aboard the ship. The war was over, so the transmissions were in clear and could thus be picked up by other ships whose radio operators were listening. One of those ships was another Australian vessel, the *Wyreema*, and if *Boonah* had been the last Australian ship to sail for the conflict in Europe, *Wyreema* may well have been the second last. Aboard her was a contingent of Australian Army Nursing Service (AANS) nurses, a contingent that included Rosa O'Kane, a young nurse from Charters Towers in Queensland. Rosa, the other nurses and the entire medical contingent aboard *Wyreema* followed the developing disaster aboard the *Boonah* closely, knowing that the fate of the ill soldiers was now linked to their own.

—————◦◦◦◦◦◦—————

Rosa O'Kane's journey to the *Wyreema*, now sailing back to Australia, had been a very long one. Born in Charters Towers in 1890, Rosa and her two brothers were raised primarily by their mother, Jeanie, as their father had died when all three children were very young. Jeanie O'Kane had also travelled a long and difficult path in her life. Born in Ballymoney, County Antrim in Ireland, at 18 years of age she had travelled to Australia with her brother and sister to join another brother who had migrated to Queensland some years earlier. The family settled in Maryborough in Central Queensland where the young, determined and well-educated Jeanie immediately found work as a teacher in the Queensland state school sector. After three years in Maryborough, in 1879 Jeanie was posted to Charters Towers where she met John O'Kane.[13] The O'Kane's were very prominent there, John's father having started the *Northern Miner,* one of the more influential local newspapers, while John published and edited another newspaper, the *Evening Herald.*

73

The two O'Kanes, John and Jeannie, were not even distantly related but each fell in love with the other and, after a short courtship, married. After two sons, a daughter they named Rosa was born but, shortly after Rosa was born, John O'Kane died suddenly leaving Jeanie and the children alone in the world. Jeanie rose to the challenge, taking over the *Evening Herald* which she published, edited and wrote for every day for the next decade, looking after and watching over her children as they proceeded through the educational system. [14] From an early age, Rosa had wanted to be a nurse and at age 20 commenced training at the Townsville Hospital, completing that training in 1915. Two years later, she was a member of the Australian Army Nursing Service, a junior officer working at the Kangaroo Point Military Hospital in Brisbane. From there, in June 1918, Rosa sent a telegram to her mother saying that she would soon be leaving to join a transport ship and did not expect to return for at least six months.

That transport was the troopship *Wyreema*, [15] which sailed from Sydney on 14 October, stopping at Adelaide and Fremantle before it, too, headed out into the Indian Ocean. It carried more army reinforcements for the battlefields of Western Europe and it also carried a tranche of 45 AAMC nurses and orderlies whose ultimate destinations were the field hospitals of Salonica in northern Greece, where they would look after casualties from the ongoing fighting in the Balkans. Most of the voyage across the Indian Ocean was uneventful, but there were two exceptions. The presence of 26 nurses among the hundreds of men on board made the ship's concerts that much more interesting, and the star performer in these appears to have been Rosa O'Kane. It was no surprise to those who knew her as, from childhood, she had performed in school, church and semi-professional plays and musicals in Charters Towers. The other exception was that the war they were sailing to was over before they could reach it.

*Wyreema's* stopover point in South Africa was Cape Town and when they reached the port city it, too, was being ravaged by pneumonic influenza. The quarantine imposed on *Wyreema* was more stringent and more effective than that undertaken for *Boonah* and when the ship departed Cape Town for her return voyage to Australia, there were no cases aboard. For the duration of that voyage, *Wyreema* sailed two days ahead of *Boonah*, but all aboard were aware of the issues plaguing their fellow troopship. Discussions were held aboard the *Wyreema,* and discussions were held between *Wyreema* and army and quarantine officials in Fremantle. These culminated in a meeting aboard *Wyreema* on 8 December 1918.

Assistance in nursing the men struck down by pneumonic influenza aboard the *Boonah* would be required in two days and there were simply not the requisite number of nurses currently available in Perth or Fremantle. The commander of all army personnel aboard *Wyreema*, Major P. M. McFarlane, had been asked to assist with this, and told the 26 assembled nurses that volunteers were needed to provide medical support to the doctors and staff in place at the Woodman's Point Quarantine Station. They would be required to nurse large numbers of very sick soldiers and the disease that had laid those soldiers low was extremely virulent, meaning that their own health would be put at risk. The major then asked for volunteers and all 26 nurses put their hands up. That was more than was needed, so all names were written down on paper and put in a hat before 20 names were drawn out.

The six girls who missed out were clearly disappointed but the 20 whose names had been read out were quietly satisfied that they would be given the opportunity to contribute in an area in which they had been trained. They would be given time to prepare everything they thought they might need and were dismissed to do just that. Rosa O'Kane was one of the excited 20.

*Wyreema* had anchored off Fremantle during the afternoon of 8 December, the nurses had drawn lots on 9 December and on 10 December, at 4 p.m. in the afternoon, longboats carried the 20 volunteer nurses, their belongings and their supplies to the jetty at Woodman's Point. As they stood on the jetty, watching the boat return to the *Wyreema,* they all felt suddenly very lonely and isolated, feelings not helped by the sounds of a furious argument in one of the station's administration buildings.[16] The nurses waited until the voices died down before reporting their arrival and having a look around. They were all hungry and tired from nervous excitement and were also soon disappointed as well. They found that, far from being ready to receive a large number of very-ill men, the quarantine station was suited to handle, at best, the small numbers that had come ashore from the *Charon.*

After being treated to a lot of luxuries aboard *Wyreema,* what they found at Woodman's Point suggested that local authorities had little if any idea of what a quarantine station actually needed to operate effectively as an army camp let alone an isolation hospital. They knew that around 300 patients would soon be brought ashore and found that there were nowhere near enough staff on site to cope with those numbers. There was a shortage of drugs, there was a shortage of dressings and there was a critical shortage of appropriate foodstuffs and pure water. The only drinks available in any quantity were aerated lemon drinks. One of the nurses, Susie Cone and her best friend Nurse Brady, walked back down to the jetty to look out at *Wyreema.* If they had not, both thought they might have broken down and cried.

Later, when there was time to reflect, it would become patently apparent that, despite a week's warning, local authorities, both state and federal, were simply unprepared to make the necessary arrangements. A generous interpretation would be that they simply did not understand the complexities of running a major quarantine station when it was filled to capacity, and beyond. A less generous interpretation would be that preparations were hampered by bureaucratic jealousies and an attitude that whatever happened it could always be made to look like someone else's problem.

Nurses Cone and Brady would have had a clear view of the *Boonah*, anchored out beyond the *Wyreema*, and would also have known that they did not have a lot of time to prepare for the arrival of their first patients, scheduled for the following morning. Out on the *Wyreema*, too, preparations were being made for that transfer with a number of decisions being made. The first was that the most dangerously ill patients would be put ashore first, followed by those whose illness was less severe, all the way through to those patients who had suffered pneumonic influenza but had now seemed to have recovered. Eventually, all sufferers, past and present, would be transferred to the Woodman's Point facility and the *Boonah* would continue its journey back to Port Adelaide.

---

The transfer of the most dangerously ill patients began at 10 a.m. the following morning and was an almost complete disaster from the start. The patients were to be transferred by a shuttle run between ship and shore, and that shuttle run was to be undertaken by the *Reliance,* believed to have been the smallest tugboat based at Fremantle. There was an attempt to steer cots down the gangway and onto the tugboat, but the sea was choppy that day and any attempts to move a cot from a large ship to a small boat were clearly inviting disaster. Patients were therefore carried on stretchers, itself a fraught process, and the size of *Reliance* meant that many trips would need to be made through the rough seas. On each trip, those aboard and in the open — the patients — would be soaked through by the waters breaking over the boat.

Ashore, the nurses waited for them to arrive. They were apprehensive as they had learned that the senior doctor at the station, Roy Mitchell, had requested 50 nurses to staff the facility but that, apart from the 20 from the AANS there were only a few civilian nurses available at Woodman's Point. The only positive they could find was that Red Cross volunteers had opened a post at Woodman's Point and stocked it with many of the items — sanitary and foodstuffs — that the officials had so clearly overlooked.

The nurses had all been up for several hours by then. They had been divided into teams with each team being given responsibility for one section of the camp. In Section W3, four nurses were in charge of a "ward" comprising a single hut containing eight beds and 10 tents, each of which could hold several patients if necessary. The hut was for the worst cases, those requiring the most supervision and treatment. Those less ill would be placed in the tents although, with daytime summer temperatures now starting to reach extremes, those tents were hardly ideal. Susie Cone was working there when the first patients were landed shortly after 10 a.m. and helped up to W3:

*"About 10 a.m. the boys began to come up from the jetty. Our tents and hut were soon full. Poor lads were in a terrible plight. Filth and dirt all over them, terribly sick; we had no drugs, no clean shirts or pyjamas to put on them. All we could do is wash them and get them as comfortable as possible."* [17]

Three of their patients brought ashore died that day, the first of many, many days of hell. It took three days to bring the 337 infected and recovering patients ashore and in those three days 10 of them would die and new infections would appear aboard the *Boonah*. Worse, pneumonic influenza began to appear among the medical staff treating the ill. Eventually, some 20 of that staff — including Roy Mitchell — would contract the disease and be laid low. Eight of those 20 would die, including four of the nurses, three from the AANS and one civilian volunteer. The first to die would be Rosa O'Kane.

Rosa's death shook the others to their core. She died in the early hours of Saturday 21 December and was buried in the Woodman's Pont Quarantine Station cemetery with full military honours at 4 p.m. that afternoon. One of the other nurses, Sister Morris, wrote a letter describing what happened:

> *"Between 2 a.m. and 3 a.m. on a beautiful moonlit night, four sailors carried the body, wrapped in a winding sheet of the Union Jack, to the mortuary out in the scrub. Later in the day the burial took place at the quarantine station. The nurses made little wreaths from West Australian wildflowers, which were placed on the coffin with the Union Jack. I did not leave the graveside until 'The Last Post' was sounded."* [18]

Rosa would soon be joined there by her fellow army nurses Doris Ridgway and Ada Thompson and the civilian nurse Hilda Williams as well as another four medical orderlies and all those young men from the *Boonah*.[19] Rosa was the first, though, and it was all so sudden at the end. Her friend Susie Cone noted that, *"Poor old O'Kane died early this morning, one can hardly realise that she is gone; everyone very depressed about it."*[20] That night, only nine of the *Boonah* nurses were fit for duty.

Within two weeks, there would be over 600 patients, ill, recovering and recovered at the facility, at least three times more than it had been designed to hold. Along with the eight medical staff, 26 of the patients had died, and the entire system was stretched so close to breaking point that it was a miracle of sorts that a revolution did not break out alongside the epidemic at Woodman's Point. The day after the first patients arrived,

Susie Cone had written in her diary that, *"Boys all very ill. Very little food to feed them on. Drugs scarce. This place is Hell!"* The next day she noted that the death toll had reached 10 and then, for a while at least, her entries dried up as the work took over completely.

There was a breaking point, however, and that point came very close. Disgusted at the lack of preparation before they arrived and desperate for all those things they and their patients needed in the way of foods, medicines and support, the *Wyreema* nurses wrote several formal letters to military, civilian, Commonwealth and state authorities about the real conditions at Woodman's Point and, when there was no official response to any of those letters, took the bold decision to write a letter detailing all their complaints to the main Perth newspaper, the *West Australian*. In it, the nurses asked for more skilled medical attention and for adequate supplies of drugs, milk and medical supplies to help reduce the deaths and suffering at Woodman's Point, which they believed was primarily caused by simple neglect. That certainly did prompt a swift response.[21]

The letter was never published as it was intercepted by military authorities. Sometime soon afterwards, the AANS nurses were called together and had the Military Act read to them. They were told that if they had been English nurses in England, they would have been court-martialled and punished severely but that they were to be let off with a stern warning. As well as that warning, a sentry was placed alongside the quarantine station's sole telephone to monitor their calls, all their letters were seized and examined before they were posted and they were not allowed to nurse the ill from their own ranks, that duty being handed over to civilian nurses. The military guards who patrolled the perimeters of the quarantine station were also warned that some of the nurses might try to escape in an effort to draw attention to conditions at Woodman's Point.

Those conditions remained in place whenever there were AANS nurses at the station. They were draconian, given the true circumstances there, but to the military they were necessary; necessary because a very short distance away, members of the Australian Army had staged a mutiny over possible detention at Woodman's Point.

## III.

At dawn on Friday 13 December, as the doctors and nurses at Woodman's Point struggled to cope with the 400 plus patients they were now responsible for, another troopship, the *Port Lyttleton,* dropped anchor off the North Mole at Fremantle. Carrying between 800 and 900 returning soldiers from all around Australia, the vessel had just completed a two-month voyage that had started in the English port of Southampton. Included among those returning soldiers were roughly 100 Western Australians, many of whom had slept briefly if at all during the preceding night. Kits were packed and repacked, buttons and belts polished and shined. [22]

It had been a long and somewhat dreary voyage home. The *Port Lyttleton* was a good enough vessel and, at the beginning at least, both the food they were served and the daily activities they took part in were fresh. By the time the ship stopped at Cape Town both had started to lose their initial allure. Cape Town, too, was a disappointment. With pneumonic influenza cutting a swathe through the local population, the troopship was put in quarantine, a situation explained quite clearly to the men by their officers. The men fully endorsed the decision and indicated that the sooner they could set foot in Australia the happier they would all be. Without any physical interactions in South Africa, *Port Lyttleton* continued her homeward voyage.

But, around the time the men expected to be going ashore to meet the friends and relatives waiting on the main wharf, the anchor was again weighed and the *Port Lyttleton* turned her bow to the open sea. This was a much shorter trip than the previous, though, and the ship was soon at anchor off Rottnest Island. The men aboard were told that this was to comply with quarantine regulations and most of them accepted that as an explanation. For the Western Australians, it was a temporary impediment to their setting foot on the land they could see sitting on the horizon and for those from elsewhere, it was a slight delay in a voyage that seemed to have been filled with slight delays.

*Port Lyttleton* sat at anchor off the coast for the rest of Friday and all day Saturday until, early on Sunday morning, the soldiers aboard learned that this was to be more than a slight delay; their ship had been once more ordered to get underway but this time they would be sailing to Melbourne. This, they were told, was related to the influenza pandemic and the need for the strict enforcement of quarantine regulations. It was a direct order to the ship's captain, and it was also a tipping point for the Western Australians aboard. They had been prepared to wait an additional two days to get ashore but a voyage to Melbourne would add several weeks to their return journey and they were not in a mood to accept that.

What made the decision to sail away even more galling was that the *Port Lyttleton* was a "clean" ship. In the two months since they departed Southampton, there had been no illness aboard, no bouts of seasonal influenza, no spreading of the common cold. The only admissions to the ship's sick bays had been a handful of victims of minor accidents, most due to shipboard sports or general skylarking. There had been no suggestion of anything resembling pneumonic influenza and even though they had sat off Cape Town when the disease there had been at its peak, quarantine had held and there had been no sign of an infection in the three weeks since they had departed South African waters. They decided to act and in this were supported by all the other ordinary soldiers aboard.

Meetings were hurriedly organised and a corporal was elected spokesman for the disgruntled soldiers. A plan was also hastily put together. That plan would see the 100 Western Australians take four of the ship's lifeboats and row to the mainland, coming ashore at Cottesloe beach. There they would contact the local police and ask for transport to be arranged to take them all to the Woodman's Point Quarantine Station where they expected to be placed in quarantine for seven days. The men unanimously rejected taking any actions which could frighten or threaten the civilian population.

That decision made, the spokesman corporal approached the senior army officer aboard, a colonel from the eastern states, and asked him to contact authorities ashore and, as an opening gambit, to arrange for tugboats to be sent out to the *Port Lyttleton* to ferry all the Western Australians to shore. Unless this was done by dusk, the soldiers would make their own way to shore. The only response to this request was a reiteration of the order for the ship and all the soldiers aboard to proceed to Melbourne. It was at this point that discontent turned into disobedience.

The corporal then made his way to the bridge where he told the captain of what he and the others intended to do, first asking permission to take the lifeboats. That permission was refused, the captain saying it was his intention to raise steam, weigh the anchor and depart for Melbourne as soon as possible. In a brisk exchange, the corporal said that those plans would not yet come to fruition and he had a thousand men prepared to stop them. The corporal — never identified in any of the reports — issued instructions which led to the engine room stokers being called up to the deck while the forecastle was picketed and the windlass surrounded to prevent the anchor being raised.

The standoff continued until late afternoon when the Western Australians put their plan into action. Once again, kitbags were checked and stowed aboard one of the four lifeboats they would take, and those lifeboats were filled in an orderly fashion before being winched down to the choppy waters below. Those among the soldiers who had been at the original Gallipoli landing joked among themselves about starting the war in a lifeboat and now ending it in another. Most were just nervous, though, and if they spoke it was in a burst of nervous energy.

It soon became obvious that soldiers and sailors possessed different skill sets. The last lifeboat lowered, the one that the corporal boarded after all others, had far fewer men than the three others. It was also filling with water, something they found was caused by the boat's drainage plug not being properly in place. This meant a considerable delay before they could set out for shore as the plug had to be seated properly and the water sloshing around their feet bailed out before they could commence rowing. By the time all this was completed, it was dark and the seas seemed to be rising even more. As the men in all four boats began to worry about the others, and about how they would ever make it to shore, the sky was lit by a number of flares.

Those flares, and the occasional Verey light, were fired from one of the Fremantle tugboats, the *Albatross*, and were being used to illuminate the sea as the tug rounded up the lifeboats and transferred their occupants to her own deck spaces. Had she not done so, it seemed apparent that the lifeboats would be swamped, and their occupants lost in the now stormy seas. Those occupants seemed happy to be rescued, none more so than those in the fourth lifeboat, found last of all and still filling with water. Its occupants were quickly taken aboard the *Albatross* but the lifeboat, now very low in the water, was not tethered to the tugboat like the other three.

Despite pleas to be taken ashore, the *Albatross'* captain followed the orders he had been given and sailed back to the *Port Lyttleton* sitting well off the much larger vessel until some kind of transfer could be made when it was daylight. Again, this was never going to happen while the hundred soldiers outnumbered the tugboat crew by a factor of ten to one. Shortly afterwards, another tugboat arrived from Fremantle. It was the little *Reliance* and it carried a number of senior officers from both the army and the Quarantine Service. It came to a halt and, using a megaphone, one of those senior officers ordered the soldiers aboard *Albatross* to return to the *Port Lyttleton* where they were to board to allow the troopship to resume its journey to the eastern states. This suggestion was roundly rejected by the Western Australians. Next, the officer with the megaphone asked to speak to the officers among the men. There were officers among them, two majors and two captains who sympathised with the plight of their men, but the shouted response from the *Albatross* was that those officers were in detention and would not be allowed to speak.

The seeming standoff was broken when the *Reliance* moved away, across to the *Port Lyttleton* where it seemed hundreds of soldiers were now lining the rails to watch the entertainment below. As the tug pulled up to the ship's gangway, those troops started pelting it with missiles, anything that came to hand but primarily potatoes and lumps of coal. The officers aboard the tug crouched behind whatever cover they could find while the *Reliance* made a hasty retreat. As it moved out of range, a number of Verey lights and flares were fired at its rapidly shrinking silhouette. *Albatross* remained where it was for the night. The soldiers aboard stood guard in shifts to make certain they were neither boarded nor moved. Those not on watch slept wherever and however they could.

Shortly after dawn the next morning, *Albatross* crossed the water to the *Port Lyttleton* where some of the soldiers called up to their comrades watching from the ships' rails. They asked for breakfast, and within minutes a supply line of men were bringing buckets down the gangplank to the tugboat. Some contained a thick beef stew and others carried freshly brewed coffee; both were received gratefully.

Aboard *Albatross*, an agreement had been reached with the boat's captain and with the authorities ashore. After the men had finished breakfast and sent the empty buckets back to the *Port Lyttleton,* the tugboat raised its anchor and started its engine. Within a few short minutes, it was making its way to the Woodman's Point Quarantine Station where the men aboard would spend a week in strict quarantine. Shortly before it tied up at the station's jetty, any of those aboard who looked back at the *Port Lyttleton* would have seen smoke coming thickly from her funnels and, if they were eagle-eyed, would have noted that her anchor had been raised. As the men and their kitbags were deposited on the Woodman's Point jetty, their troopship slowly moved away from where she had been moored and, turning south, started her long-delayed journey to Melbourne.

At the end of their week in quarantine, the Western Australians were marched down to the jetty again and this time they boarded another tugboat which carried them to Fremantle and to their waiting families and friends. No formal action was taken against them, beyond all having their pay docked to pay for a replacement lifeboat for the fourth boat which was not recovered. Any breach of the Army Act was tactfully ignored.

One of the Western Australian soldiers who took part in what was legally a mutiny, wrote to the Perth newspaper, the *Australian* shortly after the events took place, detailing what had happened and why it had happened. Signing off as *"A Private from the Port Lyttleton,"* the otherwise anonymous writer said that he had served in the frontline for the past four years and felt that this service should have counted for something. He ended his letter on an ominous note: *"I warn the authorities that they will strike serious trouble unless they show more consideration to the homecoming Diggers."* [23] The authorities, not just in Perth but in the eastern states as well, were now on notice.

# CHAPTER 5

# Hiatus: December 1918-January 1919

f the Commonwealth's call for a medical conference in late November, and the conference itself, were meant to be reminders to the states that what they were facing would affect all if it affected one, that call worked. From late November onwards, the other states fell into line behind Victoria and New South Wales and the Commonwealth itself in their efforts to, firstly, prevent Spanish flu from entering their territory while also laying down the groundwork for a vigorous and effective response if it did. In the short term at least, the measures seemed to work and there grew a feeling that the new year of 1919 might be disease free. Those most directly involved in the areas of health and quarantine knew that continuing vigilance and discipline would be the keys to success and that the keys to vigilance and discipline were the ongoing support of political leaders and the ongoing belief among the general public that the measures which had been introduced were necessary. Unfortunately, neither of these could be guaranteed.

---

Western Australia sprang into action early, perhaps stung by the implicit criticism in the invitation to join with the other states and the realisation that theirs' was one of the states most directly in the firing line. On 26 November, the opening day of the Melbourne medical conference, Western Australian Premier Henry Lefroy wrote a detailed note to the Prime Minister's Department outlining the actions his government had already taken to address the possibility of an outbreak of Spanish flu in his state.

On 28 October, the state government had initiated an awareness campaign by distributing an introductory pamphlet on Spanish influenza to all local government authorities. They had also taken a number of more concrete and practical measures. For example, Dr. Cumpston, the Director of Quarantine, had been contacted and asked to provide samples of the nozzle and inhalation apparatus — the inhalatorium — that he was then trialling at Royal Park in Victoria with a view to also trialling it in the west. Given the developing situation in New Zealand, authorities there had also been contacted and asked for any advice they could offer the state based on what they were experiencing and what they had learned.

Lefroy went on to outline the additional measures his government was preparing to take. They had already held preliminary discussions with local military commanders, and had an agreement with the state's Principal Military Medical Officer that, should an influenza epidemic occur, the military would make available to civil authorities ambulances, medical officers, nurses and medical orderlies. The state's Public Works Department had been asked to prepare both plans and specifications for temporary canvas hospital wards and had also been asked to prepare similar documentation for the construction of inhalatoria.

At the municipal level, local health authorities were again being contacted and asked to select sites, adjacent to existing hospitals if possible, on which temporary hospital accommodation could be placed in case existing facilities were swamped by the sheer number of patients requiring treatment. A draft poster outlining health and hygiene measures was being prepared and would be ready for printing and distribution throughout the state whenever that proved necessary. Finally, all District Medical Officers had been contacted individually and advised of the current situation and of the measures that would be taken should that situation change.[1]

As Lefroy had foreshadowed, during the first week of December a number of new regulations were gazetted by the Western Australian government. Under those regulations, the state's Health Minister, or his deputy, were given the power to prohibit any or all public meetings or public gatherings. Any or all places of public entertainment could be ordered to close, as could any other premises where the public could congregate *"for business or pleasure."* The Minister could also close any or all churches, schools or colleges, and regulate and control the outpatient departments of all general hospitals.

While the planning appeared to be very good, the incidents involving the *Boonah* and the *Port Lyttleton* put a considerable dent in the Western Australian public's faith in its government. Even before the *Boonah* dropped anchor in Gage Roads, the mayor of Fremantle had written to all local members of state and federal parliament asking them to beg Premier Lefroy to not allow anyone from the ship to set foot on the mainland because of the danger of them spreading infection. The mayor, William Wray,[2] believed, on the basis of medical advice he had received, that his community would be endangered if the men aboard *Boonah* were landed on the mainland. Wray urged that the ship be refuelled and revictualled offshore and then sent on its way to the eastern states where the men aboard could be treated in isolated hospitals well away from population centres.[3]

Wray's calls attracted considerable publicity and were soon followed by similar requests from the Perth City Council to the state government asking for the Western Australian primary quarantine station to be moved from Woodman's Point to either Rottnest Island or Garden Island. It was a cause taken up by Perth's most popular and influential newspaper, the *West Australian*. In an editorial in its edition published on 11 December, the newspaper described the decision to allow infected soldiers to be landed at Woodman's Point as *"reprehensible in the highest degree."* It went on to claim that, *"there is no reason why the contacts (those who have been in contact with influenza sufferers) should be detained here…Isolation of the patients at Garden or Rottnest Island only will satisfy public opinion."*

One complication, though, was the state government's unwillingness to hand over Rottnest Island to Commonwealth authorities because of the considerable tourist revenues the island generated. It was a topic and an argument that would continue into 1919 and beyond. And it was probably just a coincidence that the day after the *West Australian* editorial was published, as dozens of very sick men were being ferried ashore at Woodmen's Point, public inoculation depots were opened at the Perth Town Hall, the Leederville Town Hall and the North Perth Town Hall.

———

South Australia, too, was prodded into action, and in the wake of the Melbourne conference its state government moved to reassure all South Australians that it was prepared for anything that Spanish flu could bring. Through press releases, it reported that the South Australian branch of the British Medical Association had reassured the government of its willingness to act on all the recommendations that came out of the Melbourne conference and that it was also preparing to nominate three of its members to the state's main health body. That body, the Central Board of Health, had also recommended that all the Melbourne resolutions be accepted, and the South Australian government had committed to do just that.

Other bodies were also being brought into the broad-based planning process. The Board of Management of the Adelaide Hospital had recently become involved with the Board of Health. It had agreed to arrange for isolation facilities to be established on a larger than normal scale and to undertake bacteriological examinations while also providing medical and nursing services for the first cases identified plus any sent from other hospitals. The state's Railway Commissioner had agreed to make ambulances available for both narrow and broad-gauged railways and would also arrange for the disinfection of railway carriages if necessary. The cooperation of the military had also been sought for the possible utilisation of military buildings.

Finally, the premier had scheduled his own medical conference for 5 December. That conference would include representatives of all the city and rural Boards of Health and would place the Melbourne conference's resolutions into a South Australian context. The state government was also buoyed by news that one of the state's largest employers was also coming onside to help protect the state. Broken Hill Propriety (BHP) announced on 7 December that, among other measures, the company was building an inhalatorium at its Port Pirie works. While waiting for that facility to be completed, 300 of its employees there would be inoculated with Coryza vaccine.

---

The centrepiece of South Australia's defences would be the Torrens Island Quarantine Station as, like their neighbours to the west, South Australia was putting most of its faith in its ability to keep Spanish flu out of the state. A quarantine station had been on Torrens Island, in the Port River estuary several kilometres from Adelaide, for decades and since Federation in 1901 had been considerably upgraded using

Commonwealth funds. It would be the primary reception point for returning South Australian servicemen and women, including those who had been aboard the *Boonah,* and before those troops arrived, journalists were given a tour of the facility in the hope that their reports would help to reassure an increasingly nervous South Australian public.

The reports those journalists wrote were impressive. One described in some detail how the first arrivals in quarantine would also be the first to use a new, state of the art ablutions block that had recently been installed by the Quarantine Department. Within that block, 36 men at a time could avail themselves of 36 hot or cold showers or a plunge bath. Refreshed by the experience, the men could then be directed to one of the 12 new cottages, each of which was designed to accommodate 12 residents, or one of the nine older and smaller cottages, each designed for six residents. Without saying that in all probability most of the cottages would be reserved for officers and women, the journalists were then shown two large dormitories that had been divided into *"cosy cubicles."*

The journalists were also told that most of the permanent buildings at the station had recently been renovated and the accommodation areas equipped with new bedsteads and bedding and a number of conveniences had been installed to engender a home-like feeling about the place. That feeling could be expanded, too, if the numbers demanded it. The station had adequate tentage for an additional 150 people, each of whom would be provided with good mattresses and bedding.

There were two dining rooms at the facility, each of which could accommodate 120 people at a sitting. There were also two large marquees stored onsite, waiting to be erected for use as reading and recreation rooms. Another building had been set aside for use as a Red Cross Depot where stores and medical comforts could be kept. For recreations more active than reading and relaxing, the station had adequate supplies of cricket and football equipment, a piano and a gramophone and large numbers of puzzle books and indoor games. When the men needed a break from all that activity, cake, fruit, sweets and cool drinks would be made available for them. When their quarantine period of seven days was almost over, on each of the last three days the men would undergo inhalation treatments for10 minutes.

Authorities expected that a number of returnees would be carrying infections, possibly including pneumonic influenza, and they too would be accommodated at the Torrens Island facility. Referred to as the Isolation Block, the area reserved for infectious patients was actually a group of buildings quite apart from the normal quarantine area. A light rail track extended from the landing stage to this area allowing patients on stretchers to be taken directly to the isolation hospital without having to pass through the general grounds. In the isolation area, too, there was an observation ward for suspicious cases, located in a separate building in a distant corner of the block.

Also within that area were what authorities described as *"convenient and well-appointed quarters"* for the medical and nursing staff who would be working in the Isolation Block. The hospital there was also convenient and well-appointed, each ward containing just eight beds. Should that prove inadequate, a dozen tents could be placed nearby for additional cases if required. A large marquee was also available for use as a recreation area. The state government hoped that this facility, and sensible precautions in the general populace, would be enough.[4]

---

Despite the fears of some newspaper correspondents, the Tasmanian government was taking the threat of Spanish flu seriously. In early December, Dr. Clarke, the state's acting Chief Health Officer, told journalists that preparations were well underway to address the possibility of pneumonic influenza breaking out in the state. Arrangements were then being put in place to establish vaccine depots in all the major population centres across the state, while a special advisory committee was being formed by the Department of Public Health in conjunction with the Tasmanian branch of the British Medical Association. Regulations dealing with measures to stop or limit the effects of an epidemic were being drawn up by that department and would be published shortly.

Clarke had attended the Melbourne medical conference and spoke quite glowingly about its outcomes. He described how the Director of Quarantine, John Cumpston, was enthusiastic about what the Coryza vaccine offered Australia. Cumpston had told the conference that before the vaccine was used, 13 nurses had caught pneumonic influenza, but after it was used no more members of staff at the particular institution caught the disease, something Cumpston found to be very encouraging.

The Director of Quarantine had also told the conference that one of the ships currently in quarantine had initially reported 100 new cases a day. Within two days of the Coryza vaccine being given to the ship's crew and passengers, that number had dropped to 20 and finally to four. As well as acting to prevent the disease, Cumpston believed the vaccine, when used as a treatment, led to patients suffering a milder form of the disease.[5] Dr. Cumpston's words had reassured Dr. Clarke and he wanted to use them to reassure his fellow Tasmanians.

A week after Dr. Clarke's encouraging words, the main Tasmanian newspapers were reporting that John Cumpston had expressed his opinion that the period of greatest danger from pneumonic influenza was certainly over, although he did also warn that constant watchfulness would still need to be exercised.[6]

Tasmania pushed ahead with the recommendations Clarke had agreed to in Melbourne. By the middle of December, an inoculation depot had opened in Hobart's City Hall and across the state there were reports suggesting that most inoculations were actually being given by family doctors. Those reports tied in with Cumpston's upbeat assessment of Coryza, and there was an expectation that the vaccine would give immunity for a period of six to 12 months and partial immunity for even longer.

During the last week in December, the Tasmanian government gazetted the regulations that Clarke had brought back from Melbourne as recommendations. The new regulations mandated that, unless a doctor had attended an individual, anyone suffering with the symptoms associated with pneumonic influenza was required to report all their details to the local authority. That person would then be isolated and the personal details of all those with whom they had been in contact would be noted. Those who knew they had been in contact with a suspected sufferer were also required to notify the local authority. Doctors, too, were to notify the Chief Health Officer of all cases that came to their attention.

Finally, no-one who had contracted the disease or who had been in contact with someone who had, was to enter any public building or conveyance, or any other place where numbers of people congregated. Breaching of any of the regulations would attract a fine of £20. Most Tasmanians thought that these regulations, and a diminution of the threat on the mainland, would be enough to see their state through the trying times ahead.[7]

---

In Queensland, also thought to be lagging behind the more populous states, the state government acted in early December in the wake of the Melbourne conference. Through their Health Department a pamphlet along the lines suggested at the conference was issued to all local municipal authorities for onward circulation. It was a very practical document, containing lots of hints of the "go to bed and call a doctor" type. There were a number of observations and directions about personal hygiene, an explanation of the hows and whys of disinfection and a suggestion to spend as much time as possible in the open air. The messages the pamphlet contained were reinforced by senior health officials at a series of public meetings and presentations.

Those messages were also backed up by a series of practical measures. The state's first vaccination depot was opened in the Brisbane Town Hall on Friday 6 December. Over 100 people were inoculated there that first day and the following week a second depot was opened in South Brisbane. In support of their operations health officials wrote to all major newspapers in Queensland lauding the reliability and effectiveness of the Coryza vaccine. It was a message that proved difficult to sell, however. The Brisbane Town Hall depot would operate only on Fridays and that in South Brisbane for two afternoons a week. Then, in the run-up to Christmas, state health officials announced that both depots would be closed for the festive season and would not reopen until 6 January 1919.

---

New South Wales was obviously focused on North Head and the potential threat it posed, but authorities did not lose sight of the bigger picture. Vaccination depots were opened in several town halls and, as Australia's most populous state, its health officials also commissioned the production of a regular supply of Coryza vaccine against the possibility that the CSL supplies would be interrupted or could prove insufficient for New South Wales' needs.

A similar situation prevailed in Victoria, where both state and Federal health and quarantine officials were aware of the risk but where the general public, lacking an example like the North Head or Woodman's Point quarantine stations, were slow to appreciate the gravity of the threat they were facing. Vaccination was a prime case in point. Inoculation with the Coryza vaccine had been recommended by the Victorian Board of Health but, as in Brisbane, there was barely a trickle of volunteers through the doors of the depots set up in town halls across Melbourne and in regional cities.

In Victoria, too, the Health Department used the state's major newspapers to push the vaccination message hard during the first half of December. Sensing that there may have been concerns about the public vaccination depots, the department explained that the Coryza vaccine could be purchased privately from the Quarantine Office at 51 Spring Street in Melbourne. The cost of each treatment with the A and B vaccines was two shillings and sixpence. An individual purchasing the vaccines could then be inoculated by his or her own doctor, and instructions for its use were given with the vaccine. The sequencing of the inoculations, and the reasons for that sequencing, were also carefully explained, and it was suggested that such inoculations could act as a preventative for up to six months.[8]

If the general public did not appear to be taking the threat seriously, the same could not be said for local organisations, voluntary and civic. In Bendigo, one of Victoria's largest regional cities, the local council took steps to procure a section of the Bendigo Gaol for use as an isolation hospital in the event of an outbreak of Spanish flu. The Defence Department had been using a section of the gaol as a detention barracks but that was now in excess of requirements. Bendigo Council believed it could easily be converted into a 100-bed hospital, complete with accommodation for staff; all it needed was an up to date kitchen.[9]

Elsewhere, and nationally, the St. John Ambulance Association indicated that it would be prepared to allow its trained students to assist local doctors and nurses should the anticipated outbreak occur. Then, out of the blue, it seemed that all the preparations may have been in vain.

———◦◦◦◦◦———

In Melbourne on 4 December, the Victorian Health Minister, John Bowser, stated categorically that no cases of pneumonic influenza had occurred in that state. At the end of the month, having just celebrated the first peacetime Christmas in five years and looking forward to a new year that should see the last of the AIF return home, an assessment was made of the impact of Spanish flu on Australia. It revealed that, between 1 October and 31 December 1918, approximately 1100 people had been diagnosed as having contracted pneumonic influenza. A further 20,000 people had been isolated and treated using a combination of inoculations and regular disinfectant inhalations. Just over 100 of those who had contracted the disease had perished. [10]

There was widespread speculation, supported at times by informed opinion, that Australia's quarantine system had stopped the disease in its tracks and prevented it from gaining a foothold in the country. John Cumpston himself acknowledged that some ships' captains had falsified records to avoid their ship and crew going into quarantine, but also seemed to suggest that he thought Australia's greatest threat had passed. In the first days of 1919, he went even further in a front-page article in one of Melbourne's leading newspapers.

It was something of a speculative piece in which the Director of Quarantine pondered what might have been had the pandemic reached Australia: *"on the experience of other countries, it could have been confidently anticipated that an extremely large amount of sickness and disablement and many deaths would have taken place with all reservations which must be made in the case of a hypothetical estimate, it is not unlikely that the number of deaths would have been somewhere in the neighbourhood of 20,000... It is certain that the critical period is over."* [11]

At almost the same time, Victorian health authorities announced that provision had been made for 500 Spanish flu patients, just in case. The patients would be accommodated at the Alfred and Fairfield Infectious Disease hospitals and at the Broadmeadows Army Camp.

---

During the evening and into the night of 22-23 January, several people reported to the Outpatients' Department at Melbourne Hospital complaining of feeling ill and displaying influenza-like symptoms. Bacteriological specimens were taken from each person who presented but, until the results were back, none of the medical staff could say with any certainty what the ailment actually was. One of those who presented and was admitted to the hospital was a stevedore who had recently been involved in unloading a ship that had just arrived from New Zealand.

---

Around the same time, at the Red Cross Rest Home at Wirth's Park, across the Yarra from Melbourne's CBD (and where the Arts Centre is now located) eight men, returned soldiers, suddenly developed fevers and the range of symptoms usually associated with influenza. They were immediately isolated before being taken by ambulance to the Caulfield Military Hospital where they were admitted to an isolation ward. By the next morning, rumours began to circulate suggesting that the eight affected men were all soldiers who had recently returned to Australia aboard the troopship *Leicestershire* and were at the rest home awaiting transport to their home state of Tasmania. There was no mention that the *Leicestershire* had also carried a number of passengers who had arrived originally on the *Boonah* and who were taken from Adelaide to Melbourne.

The officer in charge of the men at the rest home, Captain J. A. F. McLean, vigorously denied all those rumours the next morning. He was quoted as saying: *"We have one man affected who landed from the transport yesterday. All the patients are discharged men, many of whom have been home as long as two years. Whatever the disease may be, it was contracted in Melbourne."* McLean also said that as soon as he was made aware of the outbreak, he had the ill men placed in a separate ward with guards at the gate to prevent any of the other 200 soldiers who were in the building leaving the home and possibly spreading the infection.[12] Which was all very well of course, but didn't answer questions like why veterans who had been back for two years were living in a rest home and why the seeming panic in the middle of the night. Plus, of course, hadn't there been some trouble with learning the truth from the military just a couple of months ago, when there was an outbreak of something at Broadmeadows?

Because of the nature of the ailment, a number of top-level health and quarantine experts were called in during the morning of 23 January, John Cumpston among them. After listening to reports from those who had been involved the previous evening and examining the clinical data, the experts came to a conclusion. It was that the illness which had struck several people the previous evening was in fact a form of seasonal influenza, very similar to the form that struck the Broadmeadows Army Camp two months earlier. Because of this, no objection was raised to the men from the Red Cross Rest Home being granted leave. The expert group did note that the temperatures of several of those who were admitted had dropped by the morning and that none were considered to be dangerously ill. And, as an additional precaution, those admitted to Melbourne Hospital had now been taken to the isolation ward at Caulfield Military Hospital.

The experts then paid tribute to two groups of people. The first was the volunteers working at the Red Cross Rest Home at Wirth's Park who had remained on duty and gone about their work as if nothing had happened. The second was the matrons and nurses at the Melbourne and Caulfield Hospitals, also all of whom went about their work with care and compassion even though they knew that, had the illness been pneumonic influenza, they could all having been putting themselves at mortal risk.

———∞∞∞∞——

Later in the day, as the rumours continued to swirl and somehow grow in the process, the experts were again trotted out. When interviewed, John Cumpston tried to reassure the public by saying that there was no need for alarm at present. He explained how he and a number of officers from the Customs Department had spent a busy morning undertaking a range of investigations but that now — he was speaking around the middle of the day — it was too early to make a pronouncement one way or the other as to whether the patients who had presented at the Melbourne Hospital were suffering from pneumonic influenza. He did know, though, that his quarantine officials were preparing for every possible outcome; not because this could be the Spanish flu, but because it was their job to do so.

Still later in the day, Lieutenant-Colonel Arthur Sturdee, in his capacity as Principal Medical Officer for Victoria, was also interviewed. He, too, was quite reassuring and stated that no other outbreak of influenza from any military camp or hospital in Victoria had been reported to him. He also stated quite emphatically that every precaution would be taken to see that the men who had been transferred to the Caulfield Military Hospital remained effectively isolated. [13]

———∞∞∞∞——

John Cumpston was again on the front foot with reporters the following day, telling them at the outset that there had been no developments since he last spoke to suggest that what they were witnessing was an outbreak of pneumonic influenza. Nothing had changed in the last 24 hours and there were no indications that a widespread epidemic was looming. He noted that events were being carefully monitored and, of course, other decisions would be made if and when circumstances changed. There was no more reason for alarm today than there had been yesterday and he, with all the other scientists and doctors, would know more when the results of the bacteriological examinations were received from CSL. These results would be made public as soon as they were known.

Cumpston told the reporters that he took some comfort from reports he was receiving from overseas, which suggested that the virulence of the disease was declining. Even if it now reached Australia, it would most probably be in a comparatively mild form. Australia had coped well to date and with the benefit of the experience in other countries, there was no real cause for alarm. The Director of Quarantine closed with more words of reassurance; if Spanish flu came to Australia, "…*it may not affect us more than a severe outbreak of that form of influenza with which we are familiar…*"[14]

Immediately below Cumpston's words of reassurance were several other reports that would have given the careful reader much food for thought. That morning, at the Melbourne Hospital, a new patient was admitted and two nurses fell ill with an influenza-like ailment. There were now 45 patients in Melbourne displaying similar symptoms, and four of them were nurses.

By lunchtime, there were several new patients awaiting examination at Melbourne Hospital and authorities there were taking no chances with the outbreak. Doctors and nurses were required to wear white overalls and gauze masks covering noses and mouths; those masks were also provided to all attendants who came into contact with patients displaying influenza symptoms. Two isolation wards had been set up and all who had been in contact with influenza patients were also being isolated. Hospital authorities were not seeing any discernible pattern in where the patients had originated either. Some were the only admissions from their district while other areas — North Melbourne, Albert Park, St Kilda, Port Melbourne and Brunswick — had each provided several patients.

The day ended with another reassuring message from Dr. E. Robertson, chairman of the Victorian Board of Health. Robertson was hopeful that what they were seeing was just a more virulent form of the seasonal influenza they experienced each year. He did concede, though, that they were keeping an eye on a cluster of cases which had occurred that day in Hawthorn.

---

The next day there were reports from Sydney that a soldier with influenza-like symptoms had been admitted to the military hospital at the Randwick Barracks. It was believed that the soldier had recently returned to Australia aboard the troopship *Sardinia*. [15]

---

On the morning of 27 January, the New South Wales Board of Health notified the Commonwealth that pneumonic influenza had been confirmed in cases outside of quarantine and asked that the state be declared infected. Appended to the request was a report submitted by the sub-committee of the British Medical Association that had been investigating recent cases admitted to the Randwick Military Hospital:

> *"We find that the patients are suffering from a similar disease to that which existed on the Medic and the Sardinia, of which ship two of our number have experience. In each case the disease was contracted in Melbourne or from contact with those cases, with the exception of one mild and doubtful case. In our opinion, the disease is what in this country is known as pneumonic influenza."* [16]

The Board also announced that the state government had decided that schools, theatres, picture shows and places of indoor public resort within the Sydney metropolitan area should also be closed for the present.

Even that afternoon, Victorian Premier Lawson was still telling reporters that the influenza outbreak in Victoria was not pneumonic influenza. This was based on medical advice, he said, and that advice in turn was based on the low mortality rate in the present outbreak. He also pointed out that there seemed to have been fewer presentations at public hospitals since he and the state's senior health officials downplayed the sometimes-sensational claims and rumours. [17]

---

On the morning of Tuesday 28 January, a conference of Melbourne's senior medical practitioners was held in the rooms of Dr. A. V. Anderson in Collins Street. As well as hosting the meeting, Anderson would be representing the Alfred Hospital, and he was joined by Dr. E. Robertson, chairman of the Public Health Board, Dr. McMeekin, Superintendent of the Melbourne Hospital, Dr. Ramsay Webb, President of the British

Medical Association, Dr. A. J. Wood from the Children's Hospital, Dr. A. Lewens from St. Vincent's Hospital and Dr. G. Lorimer from the Fairfield Infectious Diseases Hospital.

The men met for almost two hours and at the end of their meeting issued a statement, read to reporters by Dr. Anderson: *"we considered the evidence which we had collected for some days past and the conference declared Victoria to be infected with pneumonic influenza. Beyond that, I have nothing to say except that it is a matter now for health authorities to take such further action as may be deemed by the Government."*[18]

The eminent doctors were very, very right, but they were also very, very late.

*John Davidson and Christina Norrie wearing face masks during the*
*Spanish Flu pandemic, Killara, New South Wales, February 1919*

National Library of Australia

# CHAPTER 6

# Public Policy, Private Pain

The outbreak of pneumonic influenza in Australia in January 1919 would present a challenge to not only the public health organisations at both Commonwealth and State levels, but to the political system that underpinned those organisations. In many ways, the Federation of almost 20 years earlier had welded together a number of disparate colonies whose economic, social and political priorities were not always aligned. The first flush of nationhood had papered over many of the cracks between the new states and the new Commonwealth and a decade and a half later the War to End All Wars added an additional layer to that paper. But Australia remained an admixture of different polities, and the pneumonic influenza outbreak would reveal why some states considered themselves more "advanced" than others. It would also show where the power to resist the advance of the disease really was, and that was rarely in the private offices of those who held the reins of power through the exercise of democracy at either level of government.

That was all macro, big picture power games, and they were games that failed to attract or hold the interest of the men, women and children in the frontline and on the street. Their concerns were not public policy but private pain. They had read and heard about Spanish flu cutting a swathe through the undernourished and war-weary peoples of Europe, but that was half a world away. They had read and heard about the coloured masses of Africa and Asia dropping like flies when the disease struck, but those places, too, were a long way from Australia and their inhabitants were different (read lesser) than Australians and their lifestyles were in no way comparable to theirs.

The pneumonic influenza outbreak would test and expose all Australians to one of life's harshest realities. Fine words and noble intentions are rarely an adequate substitute for concrete actions based on the reality of the crisis that is being faced. And the antiseptic and anodyne words in a newspaper describing a raging disease overseas cutting down whole populations are meaningless when you are watching someone you love very dearly dying a truly horrible death.

⸻◦◦◦◦◦⸻

At the Commonwealth level, at times it was almost like there was a disconnect between the realities of addressing an outbreak of one of the deadliest diseases the world had known and the normal functioning of the body politic. On 22 January 1919, the Governor of Ceylon reported that the outbreak of pneumonic influenza in that colony was now over. After an exchange of minutes, memoranda and marginal notes, the Australian government agreed to allow passengers to embark there for Australia.

The diplomatic niceties would continue throughout the crisis. Two months later, Sir Ronald Munro Ferguson would receive a telegram from the Governor of the Straits Settlements in Singapore asking what the Australian experience of wearing masks to mitigate the pneumonic influenza epidemic had been. This was one of many requests which found its way to John Cumpston's desk. Cumpston's reply to the governor was characteristically polite and informative, suggesting that the Australian experience was that trained and competent persons wearing properly constructed and properly applied masks in isolation wards had proved effective. Otherwise, Cumpston suggested, ad hoc and casual use of the masks was of questionable value while adoption of masks by the general public for protection against infection was *"useless and even dangerous."*[1] The exchange was polite and dignified, unlike many of the other exchanges then taking place in Australian government circles.

Cumpston's home state, Victoria, was at the heart of many of those exchanges. The misunderstandings, disagreements and downright contrariness started early. On 28 January, the day after his state had been declared infected, the acting New South Wales Premier cabled William Watt:

> *"In consequence of outbreak of pneumonic influenza state government has taken action to close theatres, picture shows, etc. in accordance with arrangements suggested by conference of health ministers and officers... Picture showmen are now asking that moratorium be proclaimed in connection with rents, mortgages and unfulfilled contracts in connection with picture shows while they are closed, such moratorium to extend to rents of employees large numbers of whom will be temporarily thrown out of work. State government apparently has no power to act in absence of specific legislation. Can your government assist?"*

Watts' reply was sent the next day and it outlined how, following advice from the Solicitor-General, the Commonwealth was also apparently powerless to act in the circumstances. What it didn't say was that, if state legislation was needed, why were you asking the Commonwealth for assistance?[2]

New South Wales was acting in other areas, though, and acting with vigour. Believing that for reasons best known to the Victorian government that state had delayed notifying other jurisdictions that it had uncovered pneumonic influenza in Melbourne, the New South Wales government closed its borders when its status as an infected state was proclaimed late in the evening of 27 January. That action was in accordance with the various agreements that had been made at the November conference in Melbourne. When Victoria was also declared infected the next day their border, according to the same agreements, could have been reopened at certain places and under certain conditions; it wasn't. Queensland, too, immediately breached the November agreements by refusing free access to the state to any person living within 10 miles (16 kilometres) of its borders.

A week after New South Wales closed its borders, acting Prime Minister Watt wrote formally to the six state premiers acknowledging that the November agreements had now collapsed. In their place, Watt proposed a new suite of measures to control the spread and the economic impact of pneumonic influenza. The new measures would include limited maritime quarantine for interstate travellers but otherwise virtually no land border quarantine. States were free to implement their own health measures. The initial responses to Watt's proposals ranged from passive obstructionism to active resistance from all states except Victoria. In the face of this, Watt said that he would continue to seek co-operative solutions. If there was any blame to go around for the collapse of the November agreements — and there was more than enough for that — the Commonwealth would be able to sheet a large part of it home to Victoria, New South Wales and Queensland, the latter two playing their own games and Victoria simply paying little attention to anyone else. There would even be some left over for the Commonwealth itself.

———◇◇◇———

One area where the Commonwealth could continue to make a contribution was international liaison, especially in the areas of prophylaxis and treatment. There were still considerable numbers of Australian servicemen and women in the United Kingdom, at reinforcement depots or in hospitals, on secondment or on leave, and appropriate questions were directed to authorities over there. They may have been a bit discomfited by some of the responses.

The Australian interlocutors learned, for instance, that soldiers in AIF depots in the United Kingdom were not only inoculated, they were made to gargle Condy's crystals (potassium permanganate, then widely used as a disinfectant) in salt water twice a day. They also used the British Army's main weapon in its war on influenza, fresh air. All windows and doors in army huts would be kept open unless there was actually rain or snow blowing in through them. If the weather was fine, full advantage would be taken of it, with route marches undertaken every morning and every afternoon. For those who the regime didn't help, a special cemetery on Salisbury Plain was being extended. [3]

The Commonwealth also tried to bring as many of its military medical staff home as quickly as it possibly could, realising that their skills and experience would be invaluable in dealing with the outbreak of pneumonic influenza in Australia. They were scattered far and wide, in the United Kingdom and Western Europe, in the Mediterranean and the Middle East, and even in India where a sizeable contingent of Australian Army nurses would not be released until late in 1920. Perhaps 5% of Australia's doctors and nurses were actually not in Australia when the epidemic struck and those still overseas tended to be the youngest, fittest and most experienced in the type of medical treatment and nursing that would be most needed.

In many respects, nurses would be as significant as doctors in what was to come, and a lot would be placed on the inexperienced shoulders of many of those available in Australia. Across Australia at the end of 1918, nurses qualified for their profession by completing a type of apprenticeship. Most of what they learned was taught through on the job training, being told about the techniques and applications by senior nurses, while they also attended subject-specific lectures presented by their hospital's medical staff and experienced nurses. However, patients' needs always came before training and lectures, and it was expected that trainee nurses would only attend such presentations when they were off-duty.

Also at that time, the nursing workforce was almost exclusively female and almost overwhelmingly young and inexperienced. For instance, three years earlier in Victoria, it was estimated that over 80% of the nurses in the state hospital system were actually trainees.[4] Hospitals and nursing administrators knew that their young nurses were about to face a greater challenge than that faced by almost all those who had nursed in Australia before them. They would be working in what would be, literally, hothouses of infection where invisible germs swirled in the air and where failure to wear a face mask properly could result in a death sentence. Most of those nurses, and the doctors they assisted and medical orderlies they worked with, would be given a three-dose inoculation which would provide some physical protection. What they would see, hear, feel and smell would, however, require a lot more than that.

---

What the nurses, doctors, orderlies and other helpers would face was a particularly nasty disease. While most Australians would not contract pneumonic influenza, and most of those who did would have relatively mild cases, those who were hit hard suffered incredibly. It was something they would struggle to survive and something that would leave an indelible impression on them and on those who loved and nursed them. While every case was unique, there were soon enough common features for patterns to be discerned with the disease. For many, it struck very suddenly. After an incubation period that generally lasted one to two days, some could collapse in the street without warning while others could go to bed feeling well and then wish that they hadn't woken up the next morning. For most, though, the onset was marked by a sudden increase in body temperature, sometimes accompanied by alternating chills and shivering.

All of those attacked would experience headaches, sometimes very severe, and concentrated towards the front of the head. The pain was intense enough to cause giddiness and nausea and often prompted vomiting. Almost all would then report general muscular soreness and general lassitude; they simply did not want to get out of bed. At that point, it was not unusual for the sufferers to lose their hearing, sight and sense of smell. Other symptoms could include running eyes and nose, a dry, hacking cough and what was described as a "general malaise."

At this stage, the illness was identical to normal, seasonal influenza and would generally be treated as such. Then, as now, the usual treatment was aspirin to relieve the headaches and bodily pains, a lot of bed rest with protection from the cold plus nourishment. Simple advice from 1918 was, *"rest in bed, free movement of the bowels and a light diet are the most important measures."*[5] With such a regime, the majority of sufferers would show signs of improvement within a week, two at most. Their temperature, which may have risen to as high as 105° Fahrenheit (40.5° Celsius) usually began to fall between the fourth and 15th day and they would recover without further complications. The bodily aches and pains, and generalised weakness, could persist for weeks or even months.

If the influenza was pneumonic, additional symptoms would appear around three to four days after the initial diagnosis. It was now that secondary, bacterial infections set in and it was these that would carry off the patient. It was common for the ears, sinuses, all air passages and the lungs to be infected simultaneously or in sequence, with additional complications for both the cardio-vascular and central nervous systems. The face usually became flushed, the eyelids heavy and drooping and the eyes glistening. Blood could haemorrhage through mouth and nose or sometimes even the eyes. Teeth and hair would often fall out.

Towards the end of the battle between the disease and the body's immune system, the patient's skin would display cyanosis, the bluish discolouration due to low oxygen levels in the blood. Coughing would become dry, harsh and irritable while any sputum the patient coughed up would often be streaked with bright red blood. As their condition continued to deteriorate, the patient's skin sometimes took on a lilac or lavender hue. They would give off a peculiar smell, described by some as resembling musty straw. In their time of greatest struggle, sleep was denied them as insomnia now became a symptom[6] For those at this terminal stage, the air leaking from their ruined lungs would create tiny air pockets just below the skin, pockets that would rupture as they moved, voluntarily or otherwise, and there would be a succession of small popping sounds, something like a breakfast cereal.[7] Some would sink into delirium and would be thankfully unaware that their lungs were filling with blood and other fluids, that their chest was distended and that they would soon drown in their own bodily liquids.

The disease would run its course, one way or the other, in around two weeks. Those with pre-existing heart or lung conditions who survived pneumonic influenza had their life expectancy further shortened. Permanent damage to internal organs was always a possibility while those who survived the disease faced a long and sometimes complicated road to recovery. Many, unfortunately, would never truly recover from what they had lived through.

---

Those who contracted pneumonic influenza would need to be nursed, whether that nursing occurred in a large city hospital or a small suburban worker's cottage, and that nursing would prove to be a very difficult task:

*"What with twenty-four hour linseed poultices (mixed at high speed in the day-room where the bottle of boiling water was and rushed at the double), brandy, rum, egg-flips, sponging and morphia — even those with the brightest prospects required constant hard nursing while delirious ones had to be coaxed into subjection and persuaded to remain in bed...Pneumonic patients were kept sitting upright, tied, by means of a pillow under the knees, to the back of the bed to maintain position. This was not easy. They were usually big, solid men, they were very sick and they slipped easily or sagged over to one side."*[8]

Not only was physically demanding and constant nursing required for many patients, the threat of catching the disease was ever-present. It was a threat exacerbated as they helped their patient cough up thick, acrid phlegm which had to be deposited in the spittoon the nurse held. The patients required constant movement and constant assistance in the simplest of actions — eating and their normal bodily functions. If it was hard for trained nurses in well-appointed hospitals, it would be so much harder for women caring for sufferers at home, especially if they had children and other responsibilities on top of that nursing. Nothing they had read in newspapers could prepare them for the reality they now faced.

———◇◇◇———

William Watt would have been forgiven for thinking he had chosen the short end of the stick when he agreed to become acting Prime Minister when Billy Hughes went off overseas. Less than a week after the country's two most populous states were declared to be infected with pneumonic influenza, he was in a stoush with several other states and seemed to be looking down the barrel of one of the most significant industrial disputes since Federation. It was no accident that several of these issues were inter-related.

On 31 January, 11 members of the crew of the Australian-owned steamship *Arawatta*, then anchored in Moreton Bay off Brisbane, gave the requisite 24 hours' notice of impending industrial action to the ship's agent, saying that when the time came they would simply walk off the *Arawatta* and hitch a lift to shore. The men did suggest to the agent that, because of the real risk of catching pneumonic influenza in both Sydney and Melbourne, they would not be signing on again to sail anywhere with the ship or the line that owned it. If, however, that line — the Sydney-based Australasian United Steam Navigation Company — offered them the same conditions that the New Zealand-based Union Steamship Company had recently offered its crews they would be more than willing to reconsider their position. The Union Steamship Company's sailing conditions now included a significant pay increase, death insurance for pneumonic influenza and normal pay for time spent in quarantine. Australasian declined to match their New Zealand counterpart's conditions, and industrial action was on.

That maritime industrial action would later spread to different ports for different reasons and in different disputes and would ultimately lead to major disruptions in Australia's interstate maritime commerce. It would, by mid-March, force the Commonwealth to allocate shipping tonnages on the major routes and by then it would be obvious, too, that those Commonwealth allocations were favouring New South Wales and Victoria, thereby giving William Watt another staunch enemy, Tasmania.

What had been an annoyance in March had become discontent a month later and would soon turn into defiance. In late April, the Commonwealth asked Tasmania to reduce its period of maritime quarantine from seven to four days, allowing a faster turnaround of shipping and loosening up trading conditions that little bit more at a time when shipping and commerce were suffering. Should Tasmania not accede to the request the Commonwealth said that it would be prepared to withdraw all the shipping it controlled from the Bass Strait trade. Tasmania, government and people, was singularly unimpressed. Their tourist trade had been decimated and they had looked on impotently as the coal they needed for their own industries was instead diverted to Victoria.

This latest demand, though, also opened up Tasmania a little bit more to the threat of pneumonic influenza while prompting a vigorous response. One member of Tasmania's House of Assembly wrote to Premier Walter Lee urging that State Parliament be urgently recalled so they could petition the King to suspend the Australian constitution. If that wasn't enough, the member believed that all Tasmanians should pray for deliverance from the Federal government. The local papers took up the cudgels, too, one calling for all Tasmanian federal parliamentarians to withdraw their support for Billy Hughes' Nationalist government. Some called for joint action with Queensland and Western Australia, who had also been given the same ultimatum on maritime quarantine. In the end it wouldn't matter; the various industrial disputes morphed into a long and nasty national maritime strike, and there would be no real winners anyway.

---

There would be big disputes and there would be little disputes. In early February, just over a week into the epidemic, Queensland clashed with the Commonwealth. Unhappy about some aspects of the Commonwealth's powers, they sought an exemption. When that was refused, the Queensland government mounted a challenge that would go all the way to the High Court of Australia (see below). A month after that, it was a pinprick rather than a wounded elephant.

On 10 March, the New South Wales' Premier's Office contacted the acting Prime Minister to say that the Superintendent of Police at Albury had recently reported that there was real trouble in enforcing the quarantine restrictions on the New South Wales/Victoria border. The superintendent had learned that a group of around 35 soldiers at Springhurst, a small town between Wangaratta in north-eastern Victoria and the border, had marched north from the town and that three of the group had allegedly tried to cross into New South Wales on 1 March. Not knowing whether or not the group was travelling with the approval of Defence authorities, New South Wales Premier William Holman would like to know if it were possible for all returning soldiers bound for his state to travel by sea.

The Prime Minister's Departmental staff seemed to be both confused and bemused. The soldiers referred to were certainly soldiers returning home to New South Wales, but they were returning to their home bases and not from overseas service but from leave. Did New South Wales expect all soldiers returning there from leave to travel by sea?[9]

There were little hiccups and there were little wins. Despite it being completely surrounded by New South Wales — declared infected on 27 January — it was not until 4 March that the Australian Capital Territory, administered by the Commonwealth, even gazetted pneumonic influenza as a notifiable disease. [10] Where it could help, the Commonwealth sometimes chose to do so. In the early days, from late January through to early March, there was an enormous demand for protective masks, with clear signs of both profiteering and hoarding. When apprised of the situation, the Commonwealth flexed its muscles. Using powers granted to help it prosecute the war, the Federal government declared that both butter muslin and gauze, the two materials most commonly used in masks, were now "necessary commodities" within proclaimed areas. This meant that the maximum prices charged for those materials could not exceed those charged on 24 January 1919, and anyone doing so would be prosecuted.

It was a small gesture, but it was something, a nod towards the spirit that had attached to the November medical conference in Melbourne. The unity of vision and purpose engendered there were now increasingly lost, and it would soon be every state for itself in the race to keep its citizens alive.

*City of Sydney staff during the influenza pandemic, c.1918-19*

City of Sydney Archives

# CHAPTER 7

# New South Wales: The Heart of the Matter

He would only ever be known to history as *"Soldier S.L."*, the first identifiable person who brought the disease to Sydney, to New South Wales and, possibly, to the Australia that existed beyond the fences of the quarantine stations. While his name would not be known to history (his name was withheld and is now lost), his movements certainly would be.

Soldier S.L. was a returned serviceman, a New South Welshman who had started the final leg of the journey back to his home state in Melbourne where he had disembarked, perhaps from the troopship *Leicestershire* or perhaps from the train from Adelaide where he may have spent time at the Torrens Island Quarantine Station. It wouldn't really matter in the end because on Monday 20 January, S.L. boarded a train at the Spencer Street Railway Station for the rail journey to Sydney. It was a journey interrupted at Albury for the changeover of gauges and trains and one that terminated at Central Station. For a significant part of that journey, S.L. shared a compartment with a civilian who had been quite ill. The man told S.L. he was running a temperature and that he had aches and pains all over his body. The soldier would also recall how the civilian was coughing and spluttering and certainly did seem to be quite sick.

Two days later, at his new home at Randwick Army Barracks in Sydney, S.L. developed symptoms identical to those described by the civilian on the train.[1] S.L. felt his condition start to deteriorate and on 23 January visited the Randwick Military Hospital where doctors considered his condition serious enough to warrant admission. On 24 January, the medical staff at Randwick contacted the New South Wales Health Department to report they had a *"suspicious case of illness"* in their military hospital. Before the department had time to respond, that suspicious case had been joined by seven others, all returning soldiers and all of whom developed the illness within two days of departing Melbourne.

The response of the Health Department was to put together an expert team of doctors, headed by the Director-General of Public Health, Dr. Robert Paton, and comprising in all seven very highly qualified medical specialists. The panel examined all eight soldiers plus three members of the hospital staff who had subsequently developed the same symptoms. These three, a doctor, a nurse and a medical orderly, had all been involved in treating the ailing soldiers. Upon admission to the military hospital, all eight soldiers had been given the generic diagnosis of "seasonal influenza," but the expert panel said what they found in the patients went beyond this. They had a much more virulent strain of influenza than the common, seasonal form and, with the experience of the North Head Quarantine Station behind them, Paton and his team had no hesitation in determining that the No. 4 Military Hospital at Randwick was now housing an outbreak of pneumonic influenza.

Shortly after 10 p.m. on the evening of Monday 27 January 1919, a special edition of the Commonwealth Gazette was issued. It contained a declaration that, due to the presence of pneumonic influenza, the entire state of New South Wales was declared both an infected state and a quarantine area.

## I.

Although the declaration was not something that New South Wales had looked forward to, it was something the authorities had prepared for and prepared very carefully. As soon as the declaration of infection and quarantine was gazetted, the New South Wales government undertook a number of actions, the first of which was to close the border with Victoria and declare an absolute prohibition against persons entering New South Wales from Victoria by land. Details consequent upon that decision were announced in the following days. The government also activated two groups it had established in November 1918: the Consultative Medical Council, consisting of senior medical practitioners nominated by the New South Wales branch of the British Medical Association; and the metropolitan citizens' Influenza Administrative Committee (IAC), which would operate out of the Education Department building.

The IAC was first off the mark in providing advice to the state government and on 28 January that government issued a proclamation covering the City of Sydney and the rest of Cumberland County which directed the immediate closure of all *"libraries, schools, churches, theatres, public halls and places of indoor resort for public entertainment."* This initial edict was followed on 30 January by a trifecta of proclamations announcing additional restrictions. Now, all people would be required to wear a mask covering their nose and mouth whenever they were in trams or on trains, in public spaces or shops and offices that were frequented by the public. The congregation of people in public spaces was also not allowed while further restrictions of persons travelling from Victoria to New South Wales were also announced. For good measure, one proclamation also declared that people living within 10 miles of the Victorian border should also wear masks in public.

The state government closed out the month of January with some additional restrictions. All racecourses in the County of Cumberland were ordered to close forthwith, all public meetings — for any purpose and whether indoors or outdoors — were banned, while the sale of liquor within the county was also banned. Medical practitioners were given the power to restrict the movement of individuals, especially of those who had come into contact with infected patients. Personal breaches of any of these new regulations could lead to a fine of at least £20.

The Consultative Medical Council also entered the pneumonic influenza debate in those first few days, issuing a press release recommending that, as the best natural resistance to the disease was continued exposure to fresh air, any form of outdoor activity was to be encouraged with the proviso that it was conducted away from crowds. The state government also ended that first week with the announcement that the restrictions it had put in place in Sydney and surrounds would soon be expanded to cover the entire state.

---

Most New South Welshmen, from the Premier down, blamed lax Victorian authorities and slipshod Victorian doctors for allowing a person, and then persons, carrying pneumonic influenza to leave their state and enter another. They said that, *"Our precautions have been in vain, our vigilance stultified and our hopes frustrated by Melbourne's failure to be sufficiently on her guard."*[2] The draconian response involved the complete closure of New South Wales' border with Victoria, something which came as a surprise to the Victorian government. When their state was also declared to be infected, they also believed the border would be reopened. After all, the states were both contiguous and infected, and the November agreements allowed for open borders in those circumstances. For New South Wales, Victoria's inexcusable delays in identifying and notifying the presence there of pneumonic influenza had already shattered those agreements.

A blanket ban on travel between the two states was never going to work, especially when Victorian authorities chose not to impose any travel bans of their own. The border was also simply too long, with too many potential crossing points, for any total prohibition on crossing to work. So, within 36 hours of it being imposed, the ban was modified. Quarantine stations were established at key crossing points along the border, and those wishing to enter New South Wales required to stay in them for four days and then pass medical checks before they could proceed. The same restrictions applied to all Victorians who travelled to New South Wales by sea.

The impossibility of total protection and prevention, post-facto, shutting the gate after the horse had bolted, was illustrated by the spread of the disease along the southern border of New South Wales. The border towns of Albury and Deniliquin, just inland from the border to the west of Albury, both reported their first confirmed cases of pneumonic influenza on 8 February. They were soon followed by the towns of Corowa, Culcairn and then Wagga Wagga, Junee and Holbrook in the southern Riverina. A barrier may not have been successfully erected in the south, but the government hoped to do a lot better in the north.

---

The proclamation of infection in New South Wales effectively closed all the state's borders, something the Queensland government decided to enforce immediately. The night after the border had been ordered to close, the Brisbane mail train pulled into the station at Tenterfield on its way north from Sydney. At the time when each state had a different railway gauge (the distance between the rails), Tenterfield was the spot where passengers and locomotives and carriages switched from the standard gauge of New South Wales to the narrow gauge of Queensland. This night there would be no switching of trains and tracks, however, and the 350 passengers aboard the mail train were told that, for them, this was the end of the line. Twenty kilometres short of the border, they were now effectively trapped between two states.

After remaining on the train while accommodation was hastily arranged for them, the passengers were then moved into that accommodation, a tent city hobbled together at the Tenterfield Showgrounds. While they were moving there with their few belongings, the mayor of Tenterfield was sending an urgent telegram to the New South Wales Health Minister saying that his town's resources were already being sorely tested and would be stretched to breaking point if the trains weren't stopped. But the trains kept coming and the next day, 29 January, there were 450 residents at the temporary camp with another 150 en route. Two days later, there were around 800 Queenslanders camped at the showgrounds; Tenterfield resembled a town under siege and supplies of just about everything were running out.

There, the stranded Queenslanders remained, victims — to all intents and purposes — of the ongoing wrangles between state governments and between those state governments and the Commonwealth. Those governments argued and bickered over what was to be done with the stranded passengers and, more importantly, who was going to pay for whatever was done.

On 6 February, the residents of Tenterfield passed a resolution, without a dissenting voice, protesting against the quarantine camp that had been set up in their town. While the townspeople said that they had immense sympathy for the travellers stuck in quarantine in a makeshift camp, they had their own lives and families to consider and the camp represented a possible source of infection for them all. Moreover, there did not appear to be an end in sight. In that at least, they were only partially right for, as they were voicing their protests, a purpose-built quarantine camp was under construction or, more correctly, its site had been selected and building materials dumped there.

That site was the small border settlement of Wallangarra. The quarantine camp was built in New South Wales, on the western side of the railway yards there, and its perimeters patrolled by New South Wales policemen, but in all other aspects it was controlled by the Queensland government. Some thought obviously went into its planning and construction. The site was divided into two compounds, one for new arrivals and the other for those awaiting the end of their four-day period of quarantine. The two compounds were separated by a seven-metre-wide strip of ground that would become known, not unsurprisingly, as "No Man's Land."

On 17 February, the first Queenslanders marched into their new quarantine camp at Wallangarra, welcomed by a selection of lively airs played by the Ipswich City Band. Anyone looking for a welcome from a representative of the Queensland government would have been disappointed because none of them chose to make the journey. The Queenslanders who marched in that day and those who followed them in the months ahead found a camp where conditions were primitive and distinctly uncomfortable in inclement weather, but which were survivable. [3] There were some rough edges to be knocked off — it was rumoured that it was only the intercession of the Anglican archbishop that secured separate toilet facilities for females — but now they were living in timber and corrugated iron rather than canvas.

At Wallangarra, the food was reasonable and the accommodation acceptable, while the only requirements levied on its residents were that they be inoculated, attend the specially constructed inhalatorium three times a day for10 minute sessions breathing in zinc sulphate fumes and pass a medical check at the end of their four days in quarantine. They had a plethora of free time in which to play games, put on concerts, produce a camp newspaper or just sit around gossiping. All seemed to share one complaint, though: the fact that the Queensland government expected them to pay for their own incarceration. That payment was calculated on a sliding scale ranging from the equivalent of about $70 a day (in today's values) for a married couple and $50 a day for single adults to half that amount for children aged between two and 12 years; children under two years were not charged. Everyone was supposed to pay the amount due before they were discharged but, because this was rarely feasible, they were allowed to depart when they signed a formal undertaking to repay the monies within three months.[4]

There seemed to be many more Queenslanders in New South Wales than the Queensland government had expected or prepared for. A system had to be put in place, and quickly, and so it was. In Sydney, the Queensland government had established an office known as the "Queensland Intelligence and Tourist Bureau," and it became the central point in the system. There, Queenslanders wanting to go home applied for a permit and made their travel bookings, then took a train to Wallangarra or a ship to Coolangatta or the large quarantine station at Lytton outside Brisbane. When all that had been done, the Queenslander could pack his or her bag and make his or her way back, slowly, to their home district. Behind them, in New South Wales, they left a state and a population grappling with a problem that seemed to grow bigger each passing day.

## II.

Within a few days of the correct diagnosis of soldier S.L. and the declaration of New South Wales as an infected state, scattered cases of pneumonic influenza began to appear among the civilian population of

Sydney. The earliest notified cases mirrored the military experience in that they were people either newly arrived from Melbourne or associates of such people. Slowly at first, and in ever-widening circles, the disease spread across the city until by the middle of March an average of 40 to 50 patients a day were being admitted to hospitals with symptoms of the disease. Every public hospital in Sydney had by now set aside isolation wards for those patients, and five emergency hospitals had also been opened. By then, 50 of those patients had died.

After the initial outbreak in Sydney, the disease spread throughout the state from different points and in different directions. Within two weeks, it had appeared in many towns downstream from Albury and Wodonga at about the same time as it spread to the west of Sydney. There, it was first reported in Penrith on 10 February, followed by cases diagnosed in Liverpool and Millthorpe and, to the north and west, in Lithgow and Orange. It was also reported in the far north of the state, near the Queensland border, on 10 February but the spread seemed to slow the further north and west it travelled. Cases reported in Lismore were followed by cases diagnosed in Murwillumbah until the last outbreak in the state was reported from Kyogle and the last individual case was diagnosed in Dorrigo on 27 September.

The story of how pneumonic influenza came to Newcastle and the Hunter region provides a case study for its spread throughout the state, as there was no infection in the district until late February.[5] On 25 February, a 28-year-old sailor was admitted to the infectious diseases area, D Ward, at the Newcastle Hospital; the sailor had been aboard the steamship *Ooma* which had arrived from Melbourne earlier that day. The surgeon aboard *Ooma* had examined him and diagnosed his ailment, an assessment supported by his wife, who was also a doctor. On arrival at Newcastle, the sailor was also examined by the acting Port Health Officer, who supported the two doctors' diagnosis and recommended that the sailor be admitted to Newcastle Hospital. There, resident medical staff also diagnosed the illness — as typhoid fever.

After his admission to hospital, the sailor's health declined quite rapidly. He soon became cyanotic and on the evening of 2 March the possibility of pneumonic influenza was raised for the first time; the sailor died later that night. Within 24 hours of his death, five nurses, two medical orderlies, one of the honorary medical staff and six patients in D Ward were all displaying influenza-like symptoms. A post-mortem conducted on the dead sailor found no signs of typhoid fever; it did, however, reveal pneumonic influenza.

---

It was not Newcastle or Kyogle, Albury or Lismore that posed the greatest threat to New South Wales. It was and would remain Sydney, and if the disease could not be controlled there, the impact would be so devastating that what happened elsewhere would be practically irrelevant. A Sydney decimated like the South African cities of Cape Town and Durban would mean a death toll in the tens if not the hundreds of thousands. In the early days at least, there had not been the explosive outbreak seen in South Africa, Europe and the Pacific Islands. It was more of a drip effect — a few here, a few more there — with numbers of infections, admissions and deaths steadily increasing as January became February and February became March. People were being admitted to hospital and people were dying but the public health system was being given the opportunity to respond under less pressure than had been expected, and it responded well.

### III.

The experience New South Wales had gained from the North Head

Quarantine Station's ongoing battle to identify, treat and contain the disease now proved invaluable. The members of the Consultative Medical Council had their own and their colleagues' hands-on experience available and made use of that from the time the infection promulgation was gazetted. Charged with providing medical advice to the New South Wales Health Department, one of their first pieces of advice was that the state should produce its own form of Coryza vaccine rather than relying on an ongoing supply from the CSL. The Commonwealth had promised that there would always be enough Coryza for all those who needed it but promises from the Commonwealth no longer carried the cachet they once had.

That vaccine was produced under government licence in the medical laboratories of the Royal Prince Alfred Hospital, which had developed an experimental vaccine in December 1918, spurred on by what was happening at North Head. At the end of December, they had on hand enough vaccine to inoculate up to 5000 people; midway through February 1919 that had increased to 40,000 single doses or 20,000 double doses available for distribution. In the first days of the outbreak these were given, free of charge, to the city's medical practitioners. [6] As well as organising the production and distribution of the influenza vaccine, arrangements were made with a number of manufacturing firms to provide a predetermined number of gauze masks and respirators for the public, and to also have raw materials and available machinery for the rapid supply of those products for the entire population of New South Wales should that ever prove necessary. [7]

The New South Wales government then took a half step back. In Sydney itself, it encouraged the work of the Influenza Advisory Committee and handed the day to day operations over to them. Under the auspices of the Committee, the city of Sydney was divided into 13 districts corresponding to the city's wards. In each district, the IAC appointed a district co-ordinator and provided that co-ordinator with a staff. In each district a suitable site for a central depot was also found, fitted out with telephones and given the stores and supplies necessary for it to become the district's hub in the fight against pneumonic influenza.

As well as a central depot, neighbourhood depots were established across the city. Known as Influenza Relief Depots, they were generally located in town halls and public schools and worked as local community hubs to assist residents whose lives and livelihoods had been affected by the disease. The majority of the staff at these neighbourhood depots were volunteers, assisted by some of the 1200 schoolteachers who chose to spend their unscheduled holidays helping others. The central depots, and the larger neighbourhood depots, also had on-site or visiting medical advisors available. The Red Cross was heavily involved in this; two of its nurses were based at the central depots, supported by members of the Voluntary Aid Detachments (VADs), trained volunteers, while there were always doctors on call. At some depots, assistance was provided by final year medical students from Sydney University.

The tasks undertaken by the depot staff were many and varied. One of the first of these was to distribute what became known as "SOS cards." Large, and made of stiff cardboard, the cards had "SOS" printed on one side and "FOOD" on the other and were to be placed in the front window of a residence if those within required some form of assistance. Depot staff visited homes whose residents had been affected by the disease and, if necessary, arranged for the removal of those found to be seriously ill to hospital. If necessary, they would also provide in-house nursing assistance and would also supply homes with such necessities as food, bedding, towels and clothing.

There was often also a financial aspect to their work. Where the primary earner in a household was struck down, and that household had no financial reserves to fall back on, the depots could either make direct relief payments to the family, pay their rent for them or make purchases on their behalf. The depots' financial operations soon expanded to involvement in the selection and furnishing of the emergency hospitals that were springing up in the suburbs. Finally, volunteers would stay in the family home where there were multiple cases present or where the sufferer was the household's primary carer. Again, if required, children were fostered out until their parent or carer recovered.

To assist the depot staff in their endeavours, motor transport was provided where possible. Motor cars — some volunteered, some hired — were the primary means of transport, while some 95 motorcycles with sidecars were used to rush doctors and nurses to hotspots around Sydney. Some idea of the scale of the operation can be gained from the statistic that 79,313 applicants asked for some form of assistance through the official application process; the actual number assisted was probably double that. The successful operation of the depots, central and neighbourhood, allowed the New South Wales government and its departments and instrumentalities to focus on the bigger picture items, and there were plenty of these.

---

Overseas experience suggested that large numbers of people would fall ill when the epidemic was at its peak, and the government set out to try to make certain it could cope with the hundreds, perhaps thousands, of extra patients who would require short-term hospitalisation. The state's main infectious diseases hospital, the Coast Hospital at Little Bay, was 16 kilometres from the city centre, and the roads between the two points were generally bad. There was, however, a light rail running from the city to the coast near the hospital. When approached by the Health Department, the state Railway Commissioners, who were responsible for the line, agreed to provide the use of two large ambulance tramcars and a receiving station at the terminus near the hospital. New sheds, rooms and other facilities would also be provided by them. Not to be outdone, the Tramways Department, with laudable ingenuity, fitted out several of its own tramcars as mobile inhalatoria, capable of being used at any point on the city's tramways.

All the city's major hospitals established isolation wards, if they didn't already have them, but projections suggested that even that might not be enough. Determined to increase capacity to 2,500 beds, the Health Department and the Influenza Advisory Committee oversaw the establishment of 12 emergency hospitals in Sydney and its suburbs. While most were relatively small, between 50 and 100 beds, and were established in vacant state schools, some were much larger and were carefully planned and fitted out. One of these was set up in the Royal Roller Rink in Moore Park and another, a 500-bed facility, was established down the road in the main grandstand at Randwick Racecourse. In a relatively short time, 2,500 beds were conjured into existence. Unfortunately, 500 of them — those at the Randwick Racecourse — would never be used, simply because there were not enough nurses available to service them.

To take patients to those hospitals, Sydney needed an integrated ambulance system rather than the hodgepodge of private service providers it had at the beginning of 1919. The dozens of autonomous services were brought together in February 1919 and a new organisation was formed to co-ordinate efforts, the Civil Ambulance and Transport Brigade. The new organisation worked closely with the IAC and the local depots and, in the process, became a completely motorised service. Ultimately, though, its direction and operations were at the behest of the Health Department.

What happened in Sydney — the structures and their functions — quickly became the template for the rest of the state. Outside the metropolitan area, similar organisations were established, country influenza committees whose activities were co-ordinated by bodies set up by the state government, the Country Influenza Administrative Board and the Newcastle Influenza Administrative Board. Both were in constant contact with the state's Health Department. There was also some tweaking of the models in April. Most of the local committees established additional services based on their experiences up to that time. Some set up home meal and counselling services, others opened street canteens while female volunteers took over full-time responsibilities for household chores and child-minding where the mother was ill. Across Sydney, eight homes were set up to house children whose mothers had been hospitalised.

The local committees were able to do this because the outbreak seemed to have a mind of its own. It had gone into some kind of hiatus and may even have been over.

IV.

There were some contemporaries who believed that, between 1918 and 1920, four waves of pneumonic influenza swept across New South Wales, the first commencing in late 1918 and the last ending in early 1920. A century on, that assertion is hard to either prove or disprove, but it seems more likely that the first and last of those waves were actually manifestations of normal seasonal influenza. However, what is indisputable is that there were two clear waves of infection between those start and end dates, the first of which reached its height around the middle of April 1919 and which was the more virulent of the two. Part of the problem in recognising waves is that pneumonic influenza, especially if it presented in a mild case, was often diagnosed as seasonal influenza. Even if it presented in a severe form, like the sailor from the *Ooma* in Newcastle, it could be diagnosed as something else entirely.

In its official assessment of the pneumonic influenza epidemic, the New South Wales Health Department would concede that, at the beginning of the outbreak, by only making "pneumonic influenza" a notifiable disease, many of those milder cases slipped through. This would have two effects. The first was that it let a number of disease carriers through to continue to spread the disease and the second was that it led to disease statistics that might be serious underestimates. [8]

Realising its mistake, the department sent circulars to all registered doctors and placed advertisements in the major newspapers urging both the medical profession and the general public to notify them of any cases they regarded as suspicious. Those cases would be visited by departmental medical staff who would make a diagnosis. All patients who, through this process, were found to be suffering from any form of influenza would be immediately removed to hospital, compulsorily if necessary. The premises from which they had been removed would be placed under quarantine for four days and other residents there confined to them for that period. Those quarantined residents would be visited each day by health officials who would bring a portable steam spraying apparatus. Residents would be offered a sulphate of zinc inhalation. There does not seem to have been much of a take-up of the opportunity to report by either general practitioners or the general public.

The misdiagnosis of cases very early in the epidemic may have been partly responsible for the mixed messages that were sent about restrictions imposed on public behaviours. The New South Wales government went early and went hard, closing churches and schools, banning all forms of public congregation and insisting on the wearing of masks at all times in public. But, when the figures did not suggest a coming apocalypse, it backed off. For three weeks, hospital admissions were in the dozens rather than the hundreds that had been predicted. The daily death toll, if anyone had succumbed in the previous 24 hours, was a single figure and usually a low single figure at that. The general public tired of the restrictions and the voices of special interest groups were increasingly clamorous.

The wearing of masks was extremely unpopular among most segments of society, the one exception being health professionals, again with one or two exceptions. On 15 February, the regulations on wearing masks in public were relaxed; it was no longer compulsory for them to be worn in the open, in groups of less than three people, in families, or for men working more than two metres apart. On 27 February, with an increase in infections, the regulations were tightened again only to be relaxed once more on 28 March when their wearing became compulsory only in ferry boat cabins, trains, trams and public lifts. In private spaces, they were compulsory in university classrooms and in work areas where more than five people were employed, except where that employment involved hard manual labour.

Church services, too, came back from the recesses to where they had been sent. From being banned outright because congregating — and therefore congregations — were not allowed, their restrictions were modified at the same time as those on the wearing of masks in public. From mid-February, church services were again permitted, albeit under certain conditions. The clergyman was required to stand at least six feet (1.82 metres) from his masked congregation, who in turn had to be at least three feet from each other. The service itself was to last no more than 30 minutes (later extended to 45) and was to be conducted in the open air.

There were changes towards the other end of the saints-and-sinners spectrum as well. While racecourses would remain closed, hotels were permitted to resume their trade but, like the churches, there were certain conditions attached. Customers were not allowed to mingle and could not remain inside the hotel for more than five minutes at a time. Theatres and picture shows were allowed to open again and for around two weeks from mid-March it was almost possible to pretend that things were back to normal. But in early April, it all suddenly changed again.

Hospital admissions, and deaths from the disease, began to move on a significantly upward curve from 17 March and, at the same time, there was a significant rise in cases in rural New South Wales. The two facts would become inter-related. Much of the early advice around pneumonic influenza had stressed the importance of fresh air, the value to one's health of being out of crowded city streets and in the unpolluted country air. As the disease started to strike much harder than before in Sydney from mid-March, this flight to the country was something that many Sydneysiders aspired to. Their country cousins feared they would bring the disease with them.

On 4 April, after representations from a number of country towns, restrictions were imposed on people travelling from Sydney to rural areas.[9] From that day, those travellers were required to sign a declaration stating that they had not knowingly been in contact with someone diagnosed with pneumonic influenza at any time during the past two days. They also needed to have been inoculated within the preceding three months and to have completed an inhalation treatment within the previous 24 hours. Finally, the traveller was required to produce a doctor's certificate from within 24 hours of the time of intended travel saying that the traveller had been examined and was showing no symptoms of pneumonic influenza. Bureaux were quickly set up near Central Station and near the wharves and elsewhere in Sydney to facilitate the obtaining of the medical certificates by those intending to travel; the examinations and the certificates were given free of charge.

The numbers continued to climb steadily until the week of 12 April. That week, the daily average number of admissions to Sydney's metropolitan hospitals was 146 and there were some 1700 patients with the disease being treated in 25 permanent and emergency hospitals; five of the latter had just opened to take the overflow from the former. That week, in metropolitan Sydney, there were 233 deaths that were registered as attributable to pneumonic influenza; 162 of those deaths occurred in the hospitals.

The hospital figures represented full capacity and perhaps a little more; the constraints being personnel and not physical capacity. The period of the most acute shortage lasted for less than a fortnight, from 9 until 18 April, but it was a period that brought home to Sydneysiders in particular just how fragile public health systems could be. It was a period that also marked the peak of the first wave. Between 19 March and 27 May, when hospital admissions hit a low point, 1542 residents of New South Wales would succumb to the disease. It was also a period that saw the first restrictions reimposed and a renewed preparedness to voluntarily adhere to them.

To help the general public cope, Sydney Hospital issued a circular, printed in red and full of general information designed to assist ordinary men and women cope with the surge in infections. Among the hints: *Masks should be made of four thicknesses of gauze or butter muslin...persons in contact with influenza patients should wear goggles — motor goggles are a good pattern...personal cleanliness...regular exercise...in case of a sudden onset of illness, call in a medical man immediately."*

The Royal Prince Alfred Hospital also joined the public health support functions with some gusto, albeit in a slightly different direction. There, they used the opportunity to combine public service with the hospital's operating capital by establishing a mask sterilising room in central Sydney where, for the sum of twopence, a face mask would be sterilised onsite, an initiative which proved to be an instant success.

There remained active resistance to the wearing of masks, however. In Sydney, one medical practitioner was arrested for failing to wear a mask in public. Brought before a police court, he accepted a short term of imprisonment rather than wear a mask which he claimed was of absolutely no value. His resistance was trumped by an insurance company who touted, at the height of the first wave, that all people really needed for protection was an inoculation, a veil and the purchase of an insurance policy.

---

From around 19 April, both hospital admissions and deaths attributable to pneumonic influenza began to decline. It was a trend that continued, in Sydney at least, for the next six weeks and as it did, the restrictions that had been reimposed were progressively lifted until all those remaining in place, with one exception, were removed on 16 May. That exception was the raft of requirements put in place for travellers leaving Sydney for country and regional areas, where new cases were still being reported. Those requirements remained in place until 8 July. The blanket, state-wide restrictions would not be replaced; instead, bans on individual activities would be imposed on a town, city or regional basis.

After the week ending 24 May, hospital admissions and influenza-related deaths both began to rise again, quite steeply this time, reaching a peak in the seven days between 20 and 26 June. This was the second wave, and it would almost bring Sydney to its knees. While doctors and epidemiologists found the second wave to be less virulent than the first, they also found it to be far more contagious, helped, no doubt, by the easing of restrictions on public and private behaviour.

For two months, on either side of the peak, large parts of Sydney resembled a ghost town, once busy streets now empty and once busy shops now closed. Those who went out now did so in masks, the mounting numbers of dead and infected being far stronger incentives for their use than any newspaper advertisements or government directives. It was a period characterised by the phrase, *"masked faces in quiet streets,"* and it was a period that snatched firstly hundreds and then thousands of people away from their loved ones.

In Sydney, the drop-off from the peak was rapid at first before slowing to a trickle and gradually tapering even further until there were no further cases by the end of September. There were still flare-ups in country areas, hotspots that suddenly appeared, flared up and then slowly faded away to leave nothing behind except sadness and regrets. They, too, had to be addressed and addressed with whatever resources were available in July-August 1919. A group of nurses, with all the requisite clearances, travelling from Melbourne to Brisbane were taken from their train in Sydney and asked if they could possibly help with a sudden outbreak of pneumonic influenza at Wangat, an isolated gold-mining town on the Williams River in the mid-Hunter region. They agreed to the request and entrained for Wangat. As they were working there in a makeshift hospital, another flare-up of the disease occurred in nearby Dungog. Several of the nurses were despatched to the emergency hospital set up in Dungog's town hall. The nurses' side-trip occupied five weeks and saw them tend to 180 patients, losing just one. It was that kind of battle in the bush.

30 September is a good date to claim as marking the end of the pneumonic influenza epidemic in New South Wales. It is the heart of springtime, the cold, wet winter is a rapidly receding memory and the days are growing noticeably longer and warmer. There were at least 5,844 New South Welshmen, women and children who would not enjoy the coming summer because they had not survived the epidemic; 4,302 of them had succumbed during the second wave. There would never be an accounting of the lives cut short by the after-effects of the disease, nor would there ever be an accounting of the misery and dislocation pneumonic influenza left in its wake.

New South Wales was the Australian epicentre of the worldwide pandemic, with Sydney at its heart. More people would be infected and would die there than in any other part of Australia. There is some irony in that fact as New South Wales has been considered the most efficient state in its preparation for the epidemic and the most effective state in its response. Had it not been so, the death toll, high as it was, would almost certainly have been worse, very much worse.

# CHAPTER 8

# Victoria: A State of (some) Denial

There were no photographs taken so, a century on, it is hard to know whether or not the principal speakers had straight faces or not. Either way, and in a total about-face, during the early afternoon of Tuesday 28 January 1919, the Victorian Premier, Harry Lawson, told a gathering of journalists called to his offices in Spring Street, Melbourne, that his government had taken all the actions necessary to have Victoria quarantined and formally gazetted as a state infected with pneumonic influenza. Almost as an aside, he made the point that the situation had been much more serious that morning than it had been the previous evening.

Premier Lawson went on to explain what the accompanying quarantine regulations would mean to the people of Victoria. Theatres, picture houses and music halls would have to close that night, if the quarantine proclamation was issued in time, and the next day if it wasn't. In ordinary times, state schools would have reopened after the summer holidays on the following Monday, but these were no longer ordinary times and all State schools would remain closed until all danger of infection had passed. Schools other than State schools would also be kept closed.

The state's Health Minister, John Bowser, then added to the premier's comments. The overnight change that the premier had alluded to, Bowser said, was due to the result of a post-mortem examination undertaken on one of the influenza patients who had died in hospital. That examination had shown that the influenza was of the pneumonic type although, he added, they were still unable to say definitively whether or not it was the Spanish flu. Not that it now mattered anymore. [1]

---

If the progress of the disease in Sydney was a slow burn, in Melbourne it was an explosion along the lines witnessed in Europe and South Africa. The day that Harry Lawson and John Bowser explained how the disease had fooled them all and Victoria was now infected, 40 cases were reported in Melbourne's inner south-eastern suburb of Prahran, where the local town hall was hurriedly converted into an inoculation depot. A few kilometres to the north, 20 cases were reported in Fitzroy, where the town hall was also converted into an inoculation depot for residents from Fitzroy and neighbouring Collingwood. In that depot the previous day, Collingwood municipal health authorities, assisted by fifth year medical students from Melbourne University, had inoculated 250 people. Before the day was over, reports of clusters of cases would also come in from Caulfield, Hawthorn, Essendon, Richmond and Malvern.

By the next day, 29 January, 15 deaths had been recorded among the dozens of sufferers who had been admitted to hospitals all across Melbourne. Those hospitals had also begun to put their own restrictions and protocols in place. Most public hospitals set up extra wards for isolating pneumonic influenza patients; four such wards were established in Melbourne Hospital alone. There, as well, visitors were not allowed to enter *any* of the hospital wards. The only exception made was for close relatives of patients described as "dangerously ill" and considered unlikely to survive. Those visitors would be issued with masks, caps and gowns by the hospital. Other visitors were expected to provide themselves with gauze face masks which they were required to wear while they were within the hospital grounds. Finally, every patient in the hospital, irrespective of their reason for being there, was vaccinated.[2]

A quick tabulation was undertaken on 1 February, three days after the proclamation of infection. The official figure of identified cases in those three days was 912. Victoria's Chief Health Officer, Dr. Edward Robertson, was at pains to make the point that the majority of these cases were reportedly mild. Further analysis revealed that the overwhelming majority of the reported cases were from the city of Melbourne and its suburbs, although cases had also been reported from as far away as Beechworth, Dimboola, Hampden and Rutherglen.[3]

---

Three days later, although apparently still not convinced that there had been an outbreak of pneumonic influenza in Victoria, Health Minister Bowser recommended to the meeting of State Cabinet that the State government introduce a number of restrictions based on what all states had agreed to at the November medical conference. He was particularly keen that race meetings and cricket matches be banned and suggested that any outdoor activity which brought significant numbers of people together should also be outlawed. Bowser told his Cabinet colleagues that he had instructed both the Tramways Board and the Railways Department that they were to take measures to prevent the overcrowding of trams and railway carriages. Moreover, he had warned that failure to do this would result in "drastic action." Perhaps a bit abashed by Bowser, his Cabinet colleagues immediately supported his recommendations which were introduced post-haste.[4] The declaration of Victoria as an infected state triggered other declarations and movements, one of which was the activation of the Victorian Influenza Advisory Committee (IAC), as suggested at the November conference and as New South Wales had done as soon as it was declared infected. In that state, their Influenza Advisory Committee had moved seamlessly into the existing bureau-cracy and was in no small way responsible for the successes that would come. That situation would not be paralleled in Victoria. There, the acti-vation of the Advisory Committee immediately had one consequence; it monumentally upset the Melbourne medical establishment.

The main health oversight body in Victoria, the Board of Health, had its nose put well and truly out of joint when the State government announced that it had activated the Influenza Advisory Committee and that the committee would be the peak body advising them on what to do to address the threat of a pneumonic influenza epidemic. What made that even more galling was that the Board was not consulted before any of the announcements. Because of that, several Board members made quite open threats to resign. And, to rub salt into an already painful wound, most of the board members only learnt of what had happened through the newspapers.

The IAC itself went straight into action, recommending a range of restrictions to try to prevent the spread of the disease, measures that had been agreed in November. Schools and churches to be closed, theatres, picture houses and places of mass gathering suspended until further notice, and some individual precautions to be taken. It was a bare minimum, it was a little late and, lacking the on the ground structures that would emerge in Sydney, it would lead to a very ad hoc response.

---

Outside Melbourne, the promulgation of Victoria as an infected state was something of a shock, but the closing of the New South Wales border was an even bigger shock to those Victorians living on or near the Murray

River. At one of the main crossing points between the states, the riverboat town of Echuca, things quickly ground to a halt as traffic between there and Moama, on the other side of the Murray, simply stopped. There were no real issues within either town until a woman from the Victorian town of Kyabram presented herself at the Echuca Hospital and was diagnosed with pneumonic influenza. When they learned of this, the New South Wales police completely sealed the border.

The hard closure of the border left dozens of residents from Echuca and Moama trapped on the wrong side of the Murray. It was, in fact, a very hard closure when New South Wales police locked the gate at their end of the bridge spanning the river. A rope was placed at waist height halfway across the bridge to mark the stopping point. Anyone approaching that point and not wearing a mask was ordered to immediately return to Victoria. If nothing else, the border closure brought home to residents in the district just how seriously authorities were taking the outbreak of a disease they had heard so much about.

There were soon regulations requiring medical clearances and proof of vaccination and inhalation treatments before that border could be crossed, but until then the locals did what they could. On the morning of 4 February, hundreds of people began lining up at the Moama Public School for the first of their vaccinations. Across the border in Victoria, they were slightly ahead. Nearly 1000 people had already received their first vaccination and would be receiving their second that week.[5]

---

If the vaccinations at the border and the formal closing of the bridge over the Murray River suggested some kind of formal plan was being put in place in northern Victoria, the same could not be said for large parts of Melbourne. In Sydney, their IAC oversaw the establishment of a significant number of local influenza committees which in turn oversaw the establishment of more than 100 inoculation and relief depots. The system had its flaws, but it was in place early and, by guiding Australia's largest city through eight months of threat from a killer disease, was responsible for saving thousands of lives. Though I looked long and hard for it, I was unable to find evidence of any parallel system in Victoria.

There were several hospitals already prepared for a possible outbreak, and they were all quality hospitals in terms of their reputation and the care they provided. The Melbourne Hospital, the Alfred, St Vincent's, Fairfield Infectious Diseases and the Homeopathic Hospital (which in 1934 would be renamed Prince Henry's Hospital) were all clustered around the central hub of Melbourne and, in January 1919, all had isolation wards for patients suffering from communicable diseases. In the wake of the November conference, the Victorian government had also announced that it had decided on the site for an emergency hospital and with that emergency now on the doorstep, it came as a surprise to absolutely no-one when the government announced that the mystery location was actually the Exhibition Building in inner-city Carlton. The 600 plus beds authorities put in there brought the Melbourne total of available beds to more than 2000.

In the early weeks of the epidemic, that capacity was stretched by patient numbers; the Homeopathic Hospital's 98 bed isolation ward was crowded with 186 patients. The capacity would be stretched even further by the same shortage of nurses that would hamper treatment and relief operations all across Australia. The government did what it could to alleviate the situation. Nurses were offered a pay rate of four pounds and four shillings a week, more than twice the weekly wages for a matron before the war. The government also organised for 50 nurses from New Zealand to sail to Melbourne to help with the shortage. Sometimes, though, even the best-intentioned plans fell afoul of bipartisanship. When a proposal to use Catholic nuns as nurses in the new Exhibition Hospital was put forward, it was almost as quickly shot down by conservative Protestant powerbrokers who described the nuns as *"a sacerdotally trained band of anti-Protestants."* [6] It is unlikely that someone in the depths of pneumonic influenza would have been able to recognise that bias.

The Influenza Advisory Committee was renamed the Medical Advisory Committee and seemed to also assume the role of providing common sense advice to whoever would listen. It began reporting directly to John Bowser, the Health Minister, advising him on the imposition or easing of restrictions, advice he would share with his Cabinet colleagues before concrete decisions would be made. The Committee also formulated advice to be disseminated to the wider public:

*"Experience in America has shown that infection within the home is of great frequency, and can be minimised by the isolation of the patient and the proper ventilation of the room. Even mild cases of influenza should remain in bed for three days after the temperature has fallen to normal, and the patients should lead a quiet life for a further period of four days. The dangers of relapse and secondary infection should be remembered. All unnecessary visiting of the sick should be avoided."* [7]

That advice was promulgated primarily through Melbourne's newspapers who early on took a keen interest in both the outbreak and the course it followed. From mid-February, those newspapers provided daily updates of the numbers impacted by the disease. Concentrating on the city's main hospitals, they would issue updates like:

*"Exhibition: Since six o'clock last night, six patients died in the Exhibition Hospital. Three cases were admitted today and two patients were discharged. Among the 235 in hospital, seven are reported to be in*

*a dangerous and seventeen in a serious condition. The total mortality is now forty-two."*[8]

The newspapers also sought and published expert opinion. In early March, Dr. Robertson, in his capacity as Chairman of the Board of Health, released a statement looking at the official figures collected to that time while also offering some professional observations on how the epidemic was unfolding. As of 2 March, five weeks into the outbreak, there had been 9,318 persons infected with pneumonic influenza in Victoria, although Robertson believed that this was only a proportion of the true number of cases to have occurred in the state. This was because a large number of people were unaware of the nature of their illness or chose not to report it to authorities. Of the 596 deaths of patients in isolation wards and emergency hospitals described as being due to pneumonia, a number were actually due to the secondary effects caused by pneumonic influenza. By way of comparison, Robertson said that in 1918, the total number of deaths in Victoria attributable to seasonal influenza was 210. Readers were left as confused at the end of his report as they had been at the beginning.[9]

The city and suburban newspapers also devoted a lot of space to what was happening in local municipalities and suburbs because in Melbourne, as in Sydney, that was where the daily battles were being fought.

*"Yesterday, the Wilson Recreation Hall, Brighton, was opened formally as an influenza hospital. The nursing staff consists of a matron and twelve VAD nurses under the direction of Dr. W. McClelland, Health Officer of the town. There is accommodation for forty female and eighteen male patients. Mr. I. H. Taylor, the Town Clerk, has received reports of 86 cases of influenza and four deaths (in the City of Brighton)."*[10]

Most municipalities had good Health Officers to help them through the crisis, and some had senior medical officers who were very good. In the City of Prahran, they had Dr. Richard Fetherston.

—◦◦×◦◦—

Richard Fetherston brought a lot to the position of Health Officer for Prahran. He was a local, born in Melbourne in 1864 at the hospital that would later become the Royal Women's Hospital, his father being the Resident Surgeon there. Richard followed his father into medicine, specialising in gynaecology and obstetrics and, after postgraduate studies overseas returned to Melbourne, to the Women's Hospital and to a private practice in Collins Street. Fetherston was also interested in military medicine and in 1887 was gazetted as a captain in the Victorian Militia. At the outbreak of the First World War, the 50-year-old held the rank of lieutenant-colonel in the militia and immediately volunteered for active service.

Fetherston's request was refused and he was instead appointed Inspector-General of the Australian Army Medical Corps. Based in Melbourne, he was responsible for both raising and forming those elements of the corps who would serve overseas as components of the Australian Imperial Force (AIF). In that capacity, Fetherston travelled overseas in 1915, visiting Egypt, Gallipoli and England. In 1916, he was promoted to major-general and made Surgeon-General of the Medical Corps. Two years later, in late 1918, he undertook another overseas tour of inspection, visiting Europe as the first cases of influenza were emerging there before returning home via the United States, which was having a similar experience.

Fetherston lived in Prahran, where in 1919 he shared a small medical practice with his father. As well as his role as Health Officer to the City of Prahran, Fetherston was also a senior figure in the Victorian Branch of the British Medical Association. The experience he brought to Prahran as it faced a massive challenge would be invaluable.

---

Dr. Fetherston was at the centre of things from the day the epidemic struck Prahran. That day, 40 cases were reported in the municipality and that day, too, Fetherston was at the temporary inoculation depot established at the Prahran Town Hall. He was there at 9 a.m. and he would be there at 9 p.m., and in the three January days remaining he would vaccinate hundreds of Prahran's residents each day. The workload was such that he made public appeals for trained volunteer nurses to assist him in his endeavours. He asked that they contact him directly at the town hall which, for him, would become something of a second home in the weeks ahead. [11]

Fetherston addressed a specially convened meeting of the Prahran City Council on the evening of 31 January to outline what he had learned about pneumonic influenza and what he thought they could all do to protect their citizens from it. He told the councillors that on his recent overseas tour of inspection, the question of pneumonic influenza had been a consistent topic in most conversations; this was especially true of his conversations with medical professionals. From those professionals, he had learned that the most virulent form of the disease had been found in India, while that currently ravaging Switzerland was not far behind. In the United States, the key medical concern was to prevent patients with seasonal influenza coming into contact with those who had contracted the pneumonic strain.

Fetherston went on to say to the councillors that he believed that the current outbreak in Melbourne was indeed the Spanish flu that had been so destructive overseas. He also believed that the disease was spread by personal contact, or else by sputum or other discharges from those already infected. If any of those discharges happened to reach the nose or throat of others, they would then become infected, the onset of the disease then being rapid. Once contracted, it could be extremely virulent and it was not unusual for victims to die within two days of first displaying symptoms. The best way to avoid contracting the disease was to spend as much time in fresh air as possible while avoiding contact with groups of people.

Fetherston concluded his presentation by saying that there was a safe distance to observe between people, a distance he estimated at no less than two metres. He also observed that face masks were not generally worn in public in the United States; however, they were all worn by medical staff working with pneumonic influenza patients. [12]

---

The Prahran City Council acted quickly and decisively once Victoria was declared an infected state. The day of that declaration, Mayor Ernest Willis laid out an immediate battle plan to give Prahran and its residents the best chance of getting through the epidemic. The first action the council undertook was to send Richard Fetherston and John Romanis, the Town Clerk, to see Dr. Edward Robertson and John Cumpston to seek their professional advice and to commit to undertaking whatever steps those senior public health officials considered either necessary or efficacious. Willis, Romanis, Fetherston and John Ellis, the council's most experienced representative, then planned the next steps.

The council had agreed that the Alfred Hospital, located within the city's boundaries, was the most appropriate facility to house an isolation unit for pneumonic influenza patients, and Ernest Willis convinced the Alfred Hospital Committee to hold a special meeting at which he and other council representatives could argue their case. That case was that the Alfred Hospital use the (rarely used) pavilion it had established for meningitis patients as a pneumonic influenza isolation ward. The secretary of the Board of Health, who was at the meeting, agreed with the council's proposal and by the end of the meeting those present had agreed that all pneumonic influenza cases from Prahran and district would henceforward be taken to the Alfred Hospital.

The solution of that problem potentially created another. The takeover of the isolation facility at the Alfred Hospital meant that there was nowhere for patients with ordinary influenza to be held in isolation, while there was also a possibility of the need for an overflow facility or emergency hospital. A small informal sub-committee of the council was formed to consider suitable sites for such a facility; it comprised Mayor Willis, Ben Matthews, the chair of the council's Health Committee, and Richard Fetherston. Schools were an obvious first choice, as most were large and airy and were now empty. The three men inspected the Technical Art School and the Hawksburn State School before deciding that the Armadale State School in Northcote Road was the best fit for purpose. The tipping point which put Armadale ahead of the other sites was it had a fully equipped kitchen and infants' rooms that could easily be converted into nurses' quarters. That special meeting of the council concluded with the passing of a resolution:

*"That the action of His Worship the Mayor and the Chairman of the Health Committee, in conjunction with the Health Officer, in arranging for the public vaccination of its citizens, and the establishment of a temporary hospital at the Armadale State School for influenza patients be confirmed, and that all details in connection with the equipment and the maintenance of the hospital be left in the hands of His Worship the Mayor, the Chairman of the Health Committee, the Health Officer and the Town Clerk."* [13]

Prophylaxis, preparation and professionalism became the key words in the program Prahran Council embarked upon. At the next regular council meeting, Mayor Willis was able to report that the inoculation depot at the town hall had vaccinated 9,000 residents with the Coryza A vaccine and staff were preparing to start the second round with the B vaccine. The process had been greatly enhanced through the assistance of Red Cross volunteers who greeted nervous residents and prepared them for the vaccination. Willis was also able to report that 350 cases of influenza had so far been reported in the city of Prahran and that, in each case, a qualified medical officer visited the households and carried out vaccinations and any other procedures considered necessary. He added that the council had a staff of relief workers who attended households where assistance was necessary and who could provide medicine, food and other medical comforts.

Richard Fetherston had called a meeting of all doctors working in Prahran and that meeting had agreed upon a uniform system of isolation for Prahran. Contacts, those who had been in close proximity to those with influenza, should remain in their homes for three days after their last contact. Convalescents would be sent to the Exhibition Hospital.

When Fetherston identified the need for a dedicated ambulance, a city business provided a suitable vehicle which, under his guidance, was quickly fitted out to professional standards. When he later asked for a second vehicle, one was procured within 30 minutes. Fetherston was also instrumental in arranging equipment from the Red Cross to assist in furnishing the Armadale State School hospital. At the end of the special council meeting, after Fetherston had outlined what had been done and what needed to be done, the meeting closed with a small tribute to him, Mayor Willis saying that he *"was the most capable man to steer them through the epidemic outbreak with the minimum of risk. (Hear, hear!)"* [14]

The emergency hospital established at the Armadale State School would be — arguably — Richard Fetherston's greatest achievement during the epidemic. The hospital that was established differed in some respects to that which he had originally championed. The severity of the outbreak stretched the capacity of Melbourne's major hospitals from the outset. Rather than being for all influenza patients, allowing the Alfred Hospital to treat those with pneumonic influenza, Armadale was required to treat pneumonic influenza patients from the outset as the Alfred Hospital struggled to cope with the numbers arriving there.

Fortunately, Fetherston's design was eminently suitable for the task. Within the school, the main hall and larger classrooms all became individual wards. Each ward was then divided into individual cubicles by suspending screens from overhead wires, effectively isolating each patient. He was particularly insistent on this arrangement because of what he had learned about disease transmission in open wards in the United States.

Another innovation he brought back from his most recent overseas trip was the type of mask and gown he wanted the medical staff to wear when they were on duty. The mask could more accurately be described as a hood, covering the whole of the head and with a slit provided for the eyes. Those who knew about these things said it most resembled the first type of gas masks used by the British Army, with the bottom of the mask hanging loosely around the lower part of the face and neck. The design meant that there was air space between the breathing orifices — nose and mouth — and the material of the mask, something Fetherston believed reduced the risk of infection. It also reduced the gag effect induced by some masks. Finally, a medical gown somewhat similar to a laboratory coat was put on, with the lower part of the mask tucked into it. [15]

As the rooms were being fitted out and masks and gowns for medical staff sourced, additional baths and toilets were being plumbed in and additional electric lights installed. Finally, Ben Matthews called another meeting of all the doctors resident in the city of Prahran. The meeting was very well attended and once more Richard Fetherston spoke to his fellow doctors. He explained what Prahran had already put in place for its citizens and those present — at his request — all agreed to assist at the Armadale emergency hospital. Fetherston thanked them all and informed the meeting that a roster would be drawn up and the doctors would be asked to take charge of the hospital for a two-week period. As well, a resident medical officer would be installed at the hospital while every effort would be made to adequately staff and supply the hospital. [16]

While the hospital remained an outstanding centrepiece of Prahran's response to pneumonic influenza, in truth it was the centrepiece of a very large mosaic. Some of the pieces around it may have seemed a little odd at times, though. At the beginning of the outbreak, all libraries in Prahran had been closed, *"it being well-known to librarians that books from a public lending library are fruitful as disease carriers."*[17] Another large piece was the inoculation program undertaken at the town hall depot. Assisted by other doctors, medical students and Red Cross volunteers, Fetherston's inoculation program would eventually see some 14,000 Prahran residents being given the full Coryza vaccine treatment. That figure represented a third of Prahran's residents, a figure well above the national average. [18]

Richard Fetherston seemed to be at the heart of everything that happened. On 19 May, he gave a free public lecture on pneumonic influenza, a lecture that included practical demonstrations by Matron Burrowes and other staff from the Armadale emergency hospital.

Later, when the epidemic had passed and there was time to undertake some kind of accounting of what had happened, the figures for the City of Prahran told an interesting story. In just two days short of exactly six months, the Armadale State School emergency hospital admitted

716 patients. Of that number, 43 died, a figure that represented 6% of the admissions, and is a figure in line with other areas around Australia. However, the Prahran Council's Annual Report for 1919 states without equivocation that those 43 deaths were the only fatalities in the city that were directly attributable to pneumonic influenza. In a city of 49,433, the figure represents 0.08% of the total population, well below the rate recorded in any other municipality anywhere in inner city Melbourne or Sydney, the areas with the highest death rates of all. [19]

Even if the figures are not completely accurate — another 32 deaths were attributed to "infectious diseases" — they reveal the outstanding success in disease control in Prahran during the dark months of 1919. Richard Fetherston, Ernest Willis and Ben Matthews could be justifiably proud of what they achieved, and the residents of Prahran could be justifiably thankful for their presence. Not every Victorian municipality was a Prahran, though, and not every municipality had that kind of leadership either.

———◇◇◇◇◇———

They weren't to know it, of course, but the outbreak of late January-early February was just a first wave, as frightening as it was. To give some idea of the impact, and the numbers, two weeks after Victoria was declared an infected state, on 11 February, 2,766 cases of pneumonic influenza had been reported to authorities and 219 of those patients had died. On 16 February, which would turn out to be the busiest day for hospital admissions, the main metropolitan hospitals reported that they were treating 1531 influenza patients. They also reported 967 vacant beds, but that was a function of staff rather than patient shortages.

A week later, the situation was easing. One Melbourne newspaper led with a front-page story saying that, *"viewed generally, the influenza position today shows a slight improvement on yesterday, though there were eight deaths. Reports from the hospitals continue satisfactory, admissions showing a large decrease."*

Those reports from the hospitals broke down the overall impression that had been given. The eight deaths had occurred at five hospitals, two each at Melbourne, St Vincent's and Exhibition Hospitals and one each at the Brunswick and Footscray Hospitals. There had been 40 admissions that day, compared to 73 the previous day, but still six more than two days prior to that.

To that date, 354 pneumonic influenza patients had died in metropolitan hospitals while another 66 had passed away in country hospitals or private homes. A number of doctors who were asked, while wanting to avoid any specific predictions, believed it was now a time of optimism, especially when the present death rate was compared to that from just a few days earlier. The overall figures were good, too, with 32 metropolitan hospitals treating 1374 patients of whom 40 had been admitted that day. [20]

The Medical Advisory Committee had been monitoring all these statistics as closely as any of the newspapers and at its meeting on 2 March decided it was time to loosen some of the restrictions the State government had imposed. It recommended that, from the following day, hotels be allowed to reopen and that, in five days' time, theatres, picture houses and other places of public amusement also be permitted to open. A proclamation to that effect had been gazetted by the government the previous evening, when it also chose to release the text of the report Health Minister John Bowser had received from the Committee:

*"The epidemic of influenza appears to be somewhat less severe. Cases are still occurring in great numbers. On 2 March there were still 1291 cases in the metropolitan hospitals. Cases already pneumonic are still being admitted. Seven deaths occurred on 1 March and eight on 2 March.*

*The Committee suggests that a public meeting warning should be given as the risks from influenza are still considerable, and that all reasonable precautions should be continued by families and individuals. The prohibition should continue against convalescents or contacts travelling into clean districts...The Committee should again emphasise the necessity for medical attendance at the earliest possible stage. Crowds should still be avoided. Residents in the suburbs who have business in the city should travel, if possible, at hours when crowds will not be encountered."*[21]

As well as easing the social restrictions, the State government announced that the emergency hospitals it had established would gradually be dismantled from mid-March and their patients concentrated at the Exhibition Hospital. As well, no more influenza patients would be admitted to either the Melbourne or St Vincent's Hospitals. Perhaps sensing that the epidemic was about to end, the Chief Health Officer also spoke to the press giving the statistics to the last week of March. Dr. Robertson said that there had been 12,672 cases of pneumonic influenza notified to Victorian health authorities and, of that number, 803 had died. 714 of those deaths had occurred in the Melbourne metropolitan area and 89 in the country. By 28 March, the total number of influenza patients had been reduced to 693.[22] The figure was up to close of business on a Friday night. That weekend, the second wave struck.

—⸺◦◦◦◦◦⸺—

This was the bad one. The earlier restrictions that had been in place were reintroduced and the schools that had opened on 18 March were closed once more.[3] The death toll of around 1000 from the first wave would double and then treble before the wave wore itself out at the end of

August. More deaths meant more sadness and more dislocation. Outside Melbourne, the Farmers Cricket Club said they would not be competing in the next season of the Ballarat Cricket League after the deaths of five of its senior players. And, once again, the public health system came close to collapse.

There was still enough blame to go around. The Melbourne *Age* gave a hint of what was happening behind the scenes on 21 April when it asked, *"Is it a sign that the game is played out when the Influenza Advisory Committee starts to try to clear itself of responsibility at the expense of the Government and the Health Department? The Committee has presented the Minister of Health with a report that is remarkable in its innocence. It points out that more accommodation for influenza patients is required. This fact has not altogether been hidden from other observers. During the last few weeks, a daily average of 100 sufferers from influenza had to be denied hospital accommodation because there were no beds or nurses available."*[24]

The extract was from a very long article, an essay detailing how committees, boards and departments were blaming each other for first failing to make adequate preparations and take adequate precautions before the epidemic hit and then being caught short by many of the restrictions and preventative measures that were introduced, some of which were recommendations championed by those very committees, boards and departments. The Advisory Committee that launched the attack on unpreparedness for a possible second wave was the same Advisory Committee that had recommended scaling back all the restrictions.

As in New South Wales and elsewhere, the second wave was less virulent but more contagious than the first, and it was this factor that threatened to overwhelm the public health system. Health Minister Bowser approached the Commonwealth about the possibility of taking over the Army Base Hospital in St Kilda Road; the approach was rebuffed. The Health Department then looked to increase the capacity of the

Exhibition Hospital while it also tried to recommission isolation wards that had been decommissioned just a few weeks earlier.

All through this, the Melbourne newspapers continued to chart the epidemic on a daily basis:

> *"Yesterday, forty-three deaths were registered; thirty-six in the metropolitan area, two at Ballarat and one at Geelong, Ballarat East, Cape Nelson, Edenhope and Warragul. There were 114 admissions to and 108 discharges from the metropolitan hospitals yesterday, leaving 1344 patients in hospital last evening. The deaths in the hospital numbered twenty-three, which will be included in the subsequent notifications of registrars."* [25]

There was no upside to the impact of the second wave. The closure of isolation wards and emergency hospitals meant that sufferers admitted to hospitals would now be nursed by professionals from the time of their admission. There was even a downside to that, however, as it meant that hospitals were now turning away patients they would have previously admitted. The newspaper article quoted above concluded by noting that the previous evening, 100 patients had been turned away from metropolitan hospitals.

The total number of deaths attributable to pneumonic influenza will never be known. In Victoria, as elsewhere in Australia, numbers of deaths ascribed to other ailments were actually caused by pneumonic influenza while some of those who died outside hospital, and who were simply noted as dying of old age, general debilitation, fever and the like, were also probably killed by pneumonic influenza. A general estimate for Victoria would put the figure around 4,000 or so, or perhaps a bit higher. Probably three-quarters of the figure were the result of the second wave of infection when the shortcomings and shortfalls in Victoria's public health preparations and responses were cruelly exposed in their inadequacy and for all to see. In terms of pandemic tolls overseas, the numbers were not spectacularly high, in part because the second wave in Victoria may not have been as virulent in Victoria as it was elsewhere. One Victorian newspaper editor summed it up well when he wrote, as the second wave rolled through: *"Victoria has a mild epidemic of influenza and a severe epidemic of panic."* [26]

While the number of deaths could undoubtedly have been worse, it also could undoubtedly have been better, and many of those deaths could and should have been prevented. As the bureaucrats and medical committees bickered over responsibilities and roles, the system was teetering and people were dying. Instead of arguing with each other they should have looked around for a better model than the one that was failing so many Victorians. To New South Wales, perhaps, or if that was too far, to the city of Prahran.

*Nursing Staff & Children Outside the Exhibition Building,*
*Melbourne, 1919*

Museum of Victoria Collection

# CHAPTER 9

# South Australia:
# A Big Picnic and a Little Mutiny

South Australia had always prided itself on being a little bit different to the rest of Australia, as a society founded on modern, progressive theories that, whether colony or state, would lead the world in the passage of progressive social legislation. It must have been something of a shock, then, in late January 1919 when both Victoria and New South Wales were declared infected and closed their borders with South Australia. That shock could explain why the South Australian government seems to have forgotten that the quarantine camps that sprang up at Serviceton on the Victorian border and Cockburn on the New South Wales border were their responsibility. They may be cut a little slack over Serviceton, the place where railway gauges changed over, because the town itself was in Victoria, but Cockburn was clearly in South Australia and may have become a disaster area had not the residents of the nearest town, Broken Hill, come to the assistance of the travellers trapped there. Otherwise, South Australia appeared fairly well placed to face the threat of pneumonic influenza.

South Australia had prepared for a possible outbreak well in advance and as an embarkation/disembarkation point also had considerable experience in matters of quarantine. The peak public health body in South Australia was the Central Board of Health and its chairman, Dr. Ramsay Smith, had been very proactive in his preparations. For some weeks, Smith had been in regular contact with both the Prime Minister's and Defence Departments discussing what he considered to be a very promising set of circumstances. Acting Prime Minister William Watt had authorised local defence officials to work closely with the South Australian government and, as a result of this, the Central Board of Health was now authorised to call upon military medical men and nurses, plus other ranks, and to utilise military hospital equipment and medical supplies should the need to do so arise. Smith himself had completed the negotiations with the senior military and AAMC officers in South Australia.

As a result of the discussions led by Ramsay Smith, the Mitcham Army Camp, located seven kilometres south of central Adelaide and the largest military facility in South Australia, had been reserved for use by the state if pneumonic influenza struck. [1] Arrangements were also made regarding the secondment of ambulances, medical officers and nurses, military tents for distribution among public hospitals, and for the services of non-commissioned officers and army orderlies.

Smith's Central Board of Health also laid down a set of procedures for dealing with suspected cases of pneumonic influenza. As soon as a possible case was reported to health authorities, police would isolate the suspect's premises and the person would be removed to an isolation hospital. The reporting doctor and a health official from the local Health Board would discuss the case and, if necessary, approach the Central Board of Health for an expert consultant or a bacteriological investigation, to be organised through Adelaide Hospital. If the case was indeed one of pneumonic influenza, the state's Chief Medical Officer would report it to Federal quarantine authorities. The notification of that one case could see the entire state declared infected.

The Central Board had also drawn up a list of precautionary measures for the general public to follow. The measures had already been published in newspapers, but the Board was also planning to have them printed in placard form for posting in shops, workplaces and the like. Finally, as soon as Victoria and New South Wales were gazetted as infected states, and thus the risk of South Australia becoming infected rose dramatically, an order suspending all annual leave for South Australia police was issued by the South Australian government. If pneumonic influenza was to come, they would be prepared for it. [2]

---

It was already there. Late in the afternoon of 28 January, a patient was admitted to Adelaide Hospital suffering from influenza-like symptoms. That patient's condition deteriorated overnight and, now confined within the hospital's isolation ward, he was put on the hospital's list of "seriously ill" patients. By the end of that day, he had been joined by 16 other patients, all displaying similar symptoms. Twelve of those 16 were staff or patients who had contracted the influenza while in hospital; the remaining four were members of the general public, one of whom had just arrived in Adelaide from Melbourne. Some of the cases appeared to be quite mild while there were doubts whether two of the cases were actually influenza at all.

By 30 January, a new case had appeared in another ward at the hospital and several more had been admitted from outside. Because of this, the hospital was closed to visitors, except in special circumstances. The Medical Superintendent at the hospital, Dr. West, believed that the contagiousness of the cases they were seeing was such that it would be necessary to open a dedicated isolation hospital, and speculated that it might be at the Mitcham Army Camp.

That same day, the bacteriological tests came back confirming that several of the early patients, including some hospital staff, were indeed suffering from pneumonic influenza. The news triggered a number of responses. It also led to a rush for inoculations across Adelaide. Most of those involved in the rush were individuals seeking inoculation from their own general practitioners, but the entire staffs of several banks and large city firms were vaccinated en masse. At the same time, the Central Board of Health issued nearly 500 doses of Coryza vaccine for the inoculation of officers from local boards of health and hospital employees who may have come into contact with infected patients. General free inoculation was not yet considered necessary, but arrangements for it had been put in place. Possible sites for inoculation depots had been identified by local health boards with doctors assigned to each. South Australia was ready.[3]

The state had earlier been given the opportunity to test her maritime quarantine defences against the disease. On 27 December, the troopship *Boonah* arrived from Western Australia. She was carrying around 430 troops, half her usual complement, and Adelaide newspapers were quick to point out that all the troops who had developed pneumonic influenza, as well as those expected to develop it, had been left behind at the Woodman's Point Quarantine Station. While the public might have been reassured by such observations, health and quarantine authorities were still not prepared to take any chances with the disease and all returning troops would be placed in quarantine at the Torrens Island Quarantine Station. There, newspapers assured readers, *"extensive preparations are being made for their reception and entertainment."*[4]

The length of time the returning soldiers would spend on Torrens Island would depend on whether or not any fresh cases of pneumonic influenza were detected; if not, the soldiers could expect to spend seven days there before being allowed to continue their journeys home. Again, the local newspapers told readers that the facility had been completely upgraded in recent years and was now capable of housing 230 persons, patients and contacts, in some comfort. The *Boonah*, though, was carrying eight officers, 26 non-commissioned officers and 400 other ranks, so some modifications needed to be made at the facility. The permanent accommodation was supplemented by tents and marquees, with the Red Cross providing extra comforts for the men.

It went well. There were no new cases detected, the men undertook their daily inhalations and played endless games of cricket except when the weather was simply too hot. At the end of seven days, they were given a final medical check and were sent on their way. Almost exactly one month later, another troopship arrived off Adelaide; the outcome would be very different this time.

<hr />

When Dr. Ramsay Smith finished talking to the press on 29 January, having detailed the Central Board of Health's preparations to deal with any outbreak of pneumonic influenza, he handed over the briefing to the commander of all Australian Army resources in the state, Brigadier General John M. Antill, for an update from the military perspective.[5] Antill told the reporters that there was just one troopship off Adelaide and it was being held in quarantine purely as a precautionary measure. It had not yet been decided whether or not the men who were on it, bound for Adelaide and the eastern states, would be held aboard the ship or disembarked and sent onwards by train. And that was part of the problem.[6]

The troopship that Antill was referring to was the *Somali*, one of the smaller P&O liners that before the war had never carried more than 160 paying passengers on a cruise. This time, however, she had sailed from Devonport, near Plymouth in south-eastern England, carrying around 1000 Australian soldiers returning to their homeland. They were not ordinary soldiers, either; all were registered as B Class, meaning they were unfit for further active service. Nor had their journey to Adelaide been straightforward. Leaving England, the *Somali* had sailed through the Mediterranean to Port Said, at the western end of the Suez Canal. The men thought they may have been given shore leave there but fear of Spanish flu prevented that. It was the same story at Port Suez at the other end of the canal and at Colombo. When *Somali* anchored off Semaphore beach on the coast directly opposite the city of Adelaide, those aboard had been at sea for the best part of two months.

Nor had it been a pleasant trip by any reckoning. To add to the frustrations of being cooped up on a ship that was far too small for purpose, from Colombo onwards the only fresh water available was for drinking only and the ship had also run out of soap. Despite the fact that many of the troops had health issues, there was only one doctor aboard and he was soon run off his feet. *Somali* anchored off Fremantle on 19 January and the 104 returning Western Australian soldiers were allowed to disembark; no-one else would be allowed ashore. At Fremantle, those aboard were also told that Australia was now under strict quarantine, and that they would be required to have formalin steam baths and inhalation treatments each day, and — if there were no outbreaks of influenza aboard — native South Australians would be disembarked at Adelaide.

*Somali* took on extra water at Albany, which relieved some of the stress for those aboard, but again no-one was allowed ashore. The ship finally anchored offshore from the Semaphore pier early in the morning of Tuesday 28 January. Shortly afterwards, two medical officers came aboard to check the men but left without saying anything to ship's captain Warner or to Major Harry Arnell, the officer in charge of the remaining soldiers aboard the vessel. Shortly after 9 a.m., Captain Warner informed Arnell that he had received a signal from authorities ashore saying that, although no signs of influenza had been found aboard the *Somali*, quarantine officials had decided that it should remain in quarantine for another seven days.

It took Major Arnell another four hours to pass this information on to the soldiers and what he actually passed on to them was not precisely what Captain Warner had told him. Rather, the message Arnell passed on was that the South Australians would not be disembarking that day as there were concerns that the ship might be "contaminated." Arnell gave the men no indication of when the South Australians among them might be allowed to disembark.

All the men aboard were disappointed with the outcome; the South Australians were not just disappointed, they were furious. It had not been a pleasant voyage for anyone, but if there had been a positive about it, that positive was that the *Somali* had been a clean ship with not a sign aboard of anything resembling a case of pneumonic influenza. So clean, in fact, that the Western Australians aboard had been allowed to disembark soon after the ship had arrived at Fremantle. There had been nothing noted on the ship since, making the decision to delay their landing, for however long that delay might be, simply incomprehensible. Angry enough to want to do something about it, the South Australians sought out the one man they thought might know what best to do, "Gunner" Yates.

George Edwin Yates had been born in Staffordshire, England, in 1871 and after moving to South Australia with his family, found far more opportunities in Adelaide than he might reasonably have expected in the county of his birth. By 1916, he was 45 years of age and was also the member for Adelaide in the Australian House of Representatives. Despite his age and position, in October of that year, George signed up for service in the Australian Army. To do so, he fibbed a little bit, knocking five years off his actual age and giving his occupation as "labourer." Drafted into a field artillery unit — hence the nickname "Gunner" — he arrived in France in time to take part in the great battles of 1918 at Villers-Brettoneux, Morlancourt and Hamel. He also fell ill and was evacuated back to Australia shortly before the Armistice was signed.

"Gunner" Yates possibly had more reason than most for wanting to get ashore. Waiting for him there would be his wife, his sister, his daughter and a grandchild he had never seen.

---

When approached by several soldiers for his advice, Yates intuited that it was not yet the time for confrontation. Instead, he suggested they organise a petition outlining their disappointment that, at this very late stage, their ship was being placed in some form of quarantine while their homes and their loved ones were almost within eyesight. After so long, for the South Australians, this had become an intolerable situation. When the other soldiers on the ship, those from the eastern states and Tasmania, learned of what the South Australians were doing, a number said that they would also like to offer their support. Private George Friend, a New South Welshman who had served in the 38th Battalion, volunteered to organise a second petition.

Yates tried to present the completed petitions to Major Arnell, but the officer refused to accept them. In the conversation which followed, Arnell said that he could not and would not support the men, something that would be implicit if he accepted the petitions. Yates' response was to detail why the petitions were drawn up in the first place, outlining the depth of anger among the South Australians. He concluded by telling

Arnell that, should the soldiers' requests not be met, he believed almost anything could happen. After Yates left, Arnell was so concerned by what he had heard that he contacted shore authorities himself to see if the South Australians could be disembarked; he did not receive a reply.

The day grew increasingly hot and the men gradually split into small groups, seeking shade and discussing what to do next. The standoff continued the next day as well, with shipboard life just a repeat of the many days that had gone before. It was the same again the following day although there were now rumours, confirmed in men's minds by their very telling, that the South Australians were about to be disembarked. These rumours seemed to be confirmed when, on the morning of Friday 31 January, the men were ordered to parade in full uniform and hand in their kitbags and hammocks in preparation for disembarkation. After assembling at 9.30 a.m., the men were told that a tugboat would be arriving at 10.30 a.m. to ferry them to shore. They were still there at 1.30 p.m. when Arnell dismissed them, saying that he had just learned that there was no room for them on Torrens Island.

Understandably disgusted by what they had just been through, some of the men took out their frustrations on their kit bags, throwing them into walls and onto the deck, kicking them and the like. To the men, it was working their way through their anger and frustration; to Major Arnell, it was wilful damage to government property.

The men had now been on the *Somali* for 54 days, and that afternoon a number of impromptu meetings were held all over the ship. George Yates attended several of these and at one of them at least, the suggestion was made that the men should simply lower the ships' boats and make their own way to shore. At 4 p.m., concerned about what he was hearing and extremely concerned that the pent-up anger was about to explode, Yates sought an urgent meeting with Warner and Arnell. He told both that the South Australian soldiers were stretched to breaking point and that unless they received a satisfactory answer from shore authorities in the next two hours they would take matters into their own hands.

Ship's captain Wagner told Yates that he was aware of the plan to take the ships' boats and row to shore and appealed to Yates, as a current member of the Federal Parliament and as someone with influence over the men, to stop any such thing from happening. As for himself, Wagner told Yates that he would take whatever steps he thought appropriate to stop the boats from being lowered.

After the meeting with Yates, Wagner and Arnell instructed their officers to remove all equipment from the boats. Arnell also sent a cable to the Senior Medical Officer at Port Adelaide, a Dr. Hone, informing him of what had happened and reiterating that he considered the situation aboard the *Somali* to be serious. At 5.30 p.m., a reply was received from authorities ashore suggesting that, if the soldiers aboard obeyed all instructions, *Somali* would be released from quarantine at 7.30 a.m. the next day. Just to be on the safe side, while these communications were being exchanged, Wagner had taken his ship some distance out to sea, making it practically impossible for any of the boats to be rowed to shore, especially as all their oars had been removed.

Soon afterwards, the ship was informed that it would be at least another two days before they could disembark, and the mood aboard *Somali* began to turn very ugly. Just on dusk, Dr. Hone himself came out to the *Somali* in a launch to explain to the officers, and to the men as well, the vital importance of the quarantine system. By now, that system was becoming increasingly irrelevant to the men. And so it was that when Hones attempted to return to the launch for the trip back to Port Adelaide, a group of soldiers prevented him from doing so. Hone was told that he would not be released until the *Somali* returned to Adelaide and the soldiers aboard were allowed ashore. Hone had little choice other than to agree to the conditions.

*Somali* returned to her anchorage off Semaphore early the next morning and soon afterwards a tugboat arrived to transfer the South Australians to the Torrens Island Quarantine Station. As they stepped ashore there, George Yates and George Friend were both arrested by military police who informed them that they would both be charged with mutiny.

---

Like several other states, there was no massive explosion of cases to mark the outbreak of pneumonic influenza in South Australia but rather a steady drip of cases that slowly built up the numbers. Nor did the disease seem to be particularly virulent, in this first wave at least. It soon became obvious that there would be too many hospital admissions for a single isolation ward at the Adelaide Hospital but too few to justify the significant outlay that reconfiguring the Mitcham Army Camp would entail, so another venue was sought and, as in Victoria, the answer was found in the state's Exhibition Building.

Almost a decade younger than Melbourne's Exhibition Building, Adelaide's had been built in part to celebrate the 50th Jubilee of Queen Victoria's ascension to the British throne with the added fillip of also celebrating the 50th anniversary of the founding of the colony of South Australia. Located at the eastern end of North Terrace, its location was very good and its conversion into an isolation hospital relatively easy. The temporary hospital was opened at midnight on Saturday 8 February when 45 cases from Adelaide Hospital were transferred there. Its Resident Medical Officer was Dr. Ethel Ambrose, one of the first female doctors to graduate from Adelaide University and its Matron was Miss Lucy Tremlett, an experienced military nurse.

While a hospital was being fitted out and put into operation at the

Jubilee Exhibition Building at one end of North Terrace, discussions about the Jubilee Oval at the other end of North Terrace were also beginning. The declaration of Victoria as an infected state and the closure of its border with South Australia had trapped a number of holidaying South Australians in their neighbouring state. It was a problem that authorities struggled with for several weeks although, to be fair, they did have other issues to attend to. Eventually the Central Board of Health decided that, once transportation had been arranged, the temporary emigres could be returned to Adelaide, to a facility to be put together at the Jubilee Oval, in a prime location near the main railway station and down the road from the Exhibition Hospital. Work on the new facility commenced on 19 February.[7]

Two special trains were organised to bring the South Australians home to Adelaide. At the Melbourne end, the organisation was undertaken at the direction of the Honourable Edward Anstey, Member of the South Australian House of Assembly, Commissioner for Crown Lands and, most appropriately, Minister for Repatriation. Anstey's departmental deputy was responsible for the second train. Two South Australian nurses who had also been in Melbourne were also involved in a nursing/policing capacity. Part of all their roles was to ensure that none of the returning passengers attempted to evade the quarantine restrictions. All the passengers were required to sign a declaration before a Justice of the Peace, stating that they had not been exposed to infection prior to leaving Melbourne and that they had taken every precaution to ensure they were not carrying the disease. Breaching the declaration would result in a hefty fine of £100.

The two trains, with dining cars attached, travelled in tandem to Murray Bridge where the second, carrying more passengers and with the Mount Lofty Ranges ahead, was split into two with a new locomotive towing the second half. The three trains arrived at Adelaide's main railway station at 30-minute intervals, starting at 10 a.m., during the morning of Wednesday 26 February. At that station, passengers were transferred to a smaller shuttle train for the short trip to Jubilee Oval, thereby avoiding contact with the general public.

Before the train departed Melbourne, Ramsay Smith had sent a telegram to Edward Anstey suggesting that, when they arrived at the Jubilee Oval, he and one of the other passengers, Justice Alexander Buchanan of the South Australian Supreme Court, take charge and form committees to oversee the day to day activities within the camp. Smith also thought they would all be satisfied with what they found at Jubilee Oval. The day before the trains were due to arrive, bedding and stores of various kinds arrived at the site in a continuous stream. One hundred square military tents were deposited there and then erected on the turf of the oval. Smith thought that two people per tent would suffice, unless they were children.

Allocation of quarters would be left to the repatriates and the committees they formed. Central Board of Health officials, overseeing the fit-out, believed that if the weather was hot, many of the single men would probably prefer to sleep in the grandstand, in the open, rather than under cover. Either way, as well as the tents, there was ample accommodation for up to 500 people in the showground annexes; that number would probably fit in the Mechanics Hall alone. There were enough iron bedsteads for much more than that number, the Board believed the lavatory arrangements were adequate and additional showers and plunge baths had been installed. The camp was also given its own telephone and post office.

All meals would be served in two sittings in the pavilions beneath the stands, and a catering staff would be provided for as long as the camp was open; that staff would have their own camp next door. Dr. Alexander Kradowski had been appointed medical officer in charge and had agreed to live in the camp while carrying out his duties. The two nurses travelling aboard the train, Sisters Cook and Oldham, had also agreed to remain in the camp with their fellow-travellers. Any of those travellers who showed the slightest signs of influenza would immediately be placed in an isolation tent. Otherwise, things would very much be left in the hands of the camp committees. Those who stayed there did not later refer to their time in a quarantine camp; rather they would speak about "The Big Picnic."[8]

—⸺◦◦◦◦◦⸺—

Upon arrival, the passengers set about making themselves at home. Despite expectations, the single men voted to take over the Mechanics Hall as their main dormitory, promptly renaming it the *South Australia Hotel*. Unattached women, hopefully with tongues tucked firmly in cheeks, opted for the Livestock Show Hall. Married couples, elderly singles and families with children were set up in the tents on the oval. Those on the outside of the camp considered its occupants detainees and sent them food parcels — tinned fruit, soup and a very large consignment of fresh grapes — as well as small comforts like tables and kerosene lamps. Those on the inside simply set about making themselves as comfortable and entertained as possible.

Soon after their arrival, Anstey and Buchanan went to work and by day's end there were committees covering health, housing, sanitation, entertainments and presentations. A daily check-up of all would be conducted by Dr. Kradowski — soon famous for his infectious smile — assisted by nurses Cook and Oldham. Apart from that compulsory check, the day's activities revolved around a range of games, sports, concerts and poetry recitals. One of the residents would later recall that, *"The daily routine was soon well-established: bath, breakfast, thermometer drill* for women, committee meetings for the few, spraying of tents and removal of dustbins, dinner at 12.30 or 1.30, cricket, thermometer drill for men, afternoon tea parties, tea at 6 or 7, and the concert or less public entertainment in the evening."[9]

Their final night at the Jubilee Oval featured a concert and a presentation ceremony at which speeches of appreciation were made to Minister Anstey and Justice Buchanan, Dr. Kradowski was cheered to the echo, prizes were awarded to the more competent poets and votes of thanks were expressed for the work of the nurses, Misses Cook and Oldham, and to Mr. Griffith and Mr. Heaton. All repatriates were released on 4 March, some expressing sadness that the Big Picnic was over. There was a small epilogue; after their release, a group of former residents put together a booklet entitled, *Normal: Souvenir of the Quarantine Camp, Jubilee Oval, Adelaide, Feb. 26 — March 5, 1919*. One of the more unusual products of the pneumonic influenza, the little booklet featured short essays of reminiscences and some of the better poems written and recited there.

---

The disease never did seem to take off in Adelaide or anywhere else in South Australia, for a while at least. On the afternoon of 13 March, the state was declared to be free from pneumonic influenza, just six weeks after it was declared infected. South Australia became the first state to achieve that feat and although the state's status would once more be changed to 'infected' a month later, that reflected the situation in the country rather than in Adelaide. By the end of March, there were just seven patients in the Exhibition Hospital.

The Big Picnic would not have an encore. The Exhibition Hospital would remain open and operational for most of 1919. In June, its administration and control were transferred from the Central Board of Health to the Adelaide Hospital. In September, part of the emergency hospital was converted into a permanent isolation ward with a 100-bed capacity. Patients elsewhere in the hospital were transferred to the new ward while the remainder of the complex was fumigated and returned to its original use as an exhibition space.

---

As cases of pneumonic influenza declined and declined in Adelaide, hotspots erupted elsewhere. In late March, an outbreak at Wallaroo on the coast in the mid-north of the state saw the local Rechabite Hall hurriedly pressed into service as an emergency hospital. Further north again, the disease struck hard at Port Pirie. There, on 26 March, 146 cases had been reported with two deaths recorded there the previous day. As soon as it became obvious that Port Pirie was a pneumonic influenza hotspot, the Central Board of Health ordered the closure of all local schools, churches and places of entertainment. Two open-air picture shows had to be cancelled and a saleyard marketplace where meat, vegetables, fruit and dairy products were sold direct to the public was ordered to shut down.

At war's end in 1918, an army hut in excess to demand at one of the camps around Adelaide had been shunted by rail up to Port Pirie where it was gifted to the local YMCA. With the outbreak of pneumonic influenza in the town, it was taken over by the Board of Health's Hospitals Department for use as a temporary hospital. It was soon filled to capacity. On 3 April, for instance, the number of new cases in South Australia included 25 at Pakenham, just two at Adelaide but a staggering 46 at Port Pirie. [10] During the Easter period there, police were stationed on all roads leading to the town, turning back those who wanted to enter, or to leave. With 883 cases reported in the town and district, Port Pirie would have more cases than any other rural locality in South Australia.[11] Further to the north the exact figures would never be known.

After South Australia was officially declared infected, those travelling north from Adelaide were quarantined in a makeshift camp at Oodnadatta, the head of the railway line in South Australia. Pneumonic influenza did not appear in the area until around the middle of the year, but all those in the far north of the state were aware of it. In particular, rumours about the disease had reached the Aboriginal communities based on or near the stations adjacent to the overland telegraph line running through Central Australia from Adelaide to Darwin. Many of the Aboriginals immediately went bush, returning to a more traditional way of life, but quite a few remained working on the stations and visiting the small settlements that existed in the semi-wilderness.

The arrival of the disease in the north of the state coincided with the mid-year reorganisation of the medical response in Adelaide, most notably the restructuring of the Exhibition Hospital. A number of the nursing staff there were now available for redeployment, and several took the opportunity to move where communities were calling out for assistance and relief. One of those who left was Matron Lucy Tremlett, bound for western New South Wales. Another was one of her senior nurses, Mary Kelly. Apart from three weeks at the Mount Barker emergency hospital, Kelly had been in charge of the women's ward at the Exhibition Hospital since its opening.

Learning that nurses were needed at Oodnadatta, Kelly volunteered for service there and was soon on a train heading north. At Quorn, then a major railway hub near Port Augusta, the stationmaster boarded the train with a telegram for Nurse Kelly. From that she learned that a serious case of pneumonic influenza had been found on an outback station, and her assistance with it was requested. Kelly left Quorn soon afterwards, travelling on a cattle train this time, and was on that train the following day and into the night. They stopped at a railway siding that seemed to be in the middle of nowhere but waiting for her there was a boy with a small cart and a pair of horses.

During the rest of the night the little party travelled to the station's homestead, a distance of around 40 miles (65 kilometres), arriving there at 8 a.m. with both horses badly knocked up. At the homestead, Mary Kelly found the boy's bed-ridden father suffering from double pneumonia but not pneumonic influenza. He was in a very bad way, though, and had received no form of medical treatment whatsoever. With Kelly's ministrations, plus the few medications she had brought with her, the pastoralist's health returned quite quickly. Mary Kelly was taken back to the railway siding and was soon en route to Oodnadatta once more.[12]

At Oodnadatta, Kelly found that the area's Europeans and Afghans were coping well with what seemed to be a milder form of pneumonic influenza than she had encountered elsewhere. She learned, however, that the local Aboriginals were suffering badly, with reports of numbers dying in outlying camps without receiving any form of medical attention. She also learned that a local missionary who had a team of donkeys and a covered wagon was visiting those camps, collecting sufferers who were capable of travelling and bringing them back to a camp he had established for them a kilometre outside Oodnadatta.

Mary Kelly was the only nurse in town and soon realised that her expertise was most needed at the special camp set up for Aboriginals. There, she found her new patients in what she described as *"an incredibly filthy condition,"* and with the assistance of other local Aboriginals firstly washed and cleaned her patients and then set about helping them to recover. While there had been several deaths at the camp before Kelly arrived, there were only two after she took charge. A few weeks later, the last of her patients had returned to their families and it was September. The epidemic in Oodnadatta was over and Mary Kelly was able to go home. With the end of the outbreak in Oodnadatta also came the end of the epidemic in South Australia. [13]

---—◦◦◦◦◦—---

At the time of the outbreak, South Australia was the fourth most populous Australian state, with a population of 495,160 of whom just over 50% resided in metropolitan Adelaide. 540 of the state's residents succumbed to pneumonic influenza, with the state recording Australia's second lowest death rate, after Tasmania. There were nodes of infection in Adelaide, with Port Adelaide and Adelaide city recording the highest number of infections. There were also nodes of infection in the rural and regional parts of the state, although the number of cases reported in Port Pirie, 883, was more than three times higher than the next hotspot, Mount Gambier. [14]

The real figures were higher than that. The statistics collected from outside established settlements are either non-existent or extremely doubtful. The major statistical study undertaken on the epidemic in South Australia suggests a total figure of between 44 and 191 for those areas. The Central Board of Health did not record Indigenous status and may not have included any Indigenous South Australians in any of its accounting. It does not appear to have identified any Aboriginal deaths at all, yet we know that numbers did die, some in a tent camp outside Oodnadatta and probably many, many more in small camps scattered across the South Australian outback.

The Angel of Death's wings fluttered lightly over South Australia. There were just six deaths among patients at the Torrens Island Quarantine Station and perhaps 300 more across Adelaide and its suburbs, and those spread over a six-month period. The pattern, in Adelaide in particular, was that preparation time before the disease's arrival was put to good use, on Torrens Island and at the Exhibition Hospital and Jubilee Oval. The low rates of virulence and infection allowed Ramsay Smith and his Central Board of Health to apply resources when and where they were needed. Preparation worked, and more preparation worked better, for most of the state at least.

# CHAPTER 10

# Queensland:
# A Little Late, a Little Light

Pneumonic influenza came late to Queensland giving public health, quarantine and government authorities there several months to watch the progress of the disease in the southern states and plan their own responses accordingly — or not. Things had started promisingly enough. In late November 1918, following the Melbourne conference, trained and volunteer nurses in the Brisbane metropolitan area were invited to register with the office of the senior health official in the state, the Commissioner of Public Health. For those outside Brisbane, local municipal authorities were also asked to register nurses in their respective areas. And that was about it until the new year of 1919.

After the confirmed outbreaks in New South Wales and Victoria, on 29 January 1919 Queensland declared pneumonic influenza an infectious disease, within the meaning of the state's Health Act, and introduced a number of regulations to address the threat posed by the disease. From that day forward, all local authorities had to notify the Queensland government of any cases of pneumonic influenza which occurred in their areas, with the proviso that the cases had been diagnosed by a qualified and authorised medical practitioner. Those doctors were given quite extraordinary powers to deal with the kinds of situations that might arise if the disease struck. They could, for instance, direct a patient to remain in isolation at home or in a hospital. They were also given the authority to have people detained if they were believed to have been at risk of contracting pneumonic influenza. That individual could also be compelled to undertake 10-minute sessions in an inhalatorium on three successive days and to also be inoculated with an anti-influenza vaccine.[1]

Queensland's first line of defence, though, would be a strict border quarantine. The main quarantine station in southern Queensland was the Lytton Quarantine Station, a federal facility on the outskirts of Brisbane, on the south side of the Brisbane River where it enters Moreton Bay. Queensland authorities, including politicians and health officials, worried that escapees from the quarantine station would not have far to travel to bring the disease into metropolitan Brisbane, and had called for a new quarantine station to be established on one of the many islands in Moreton Bay; they were calls studiously ignored by the Commonwealth.

On 4 February, 260 returning soldiers were landed and placed in quarantine at the Lytton facility. That evening, four of the soldiers broke out of the station and made their way to Brisbane, where they caught up with friends before being tracked down and detained by military police in the early hours of the following day. It was a clear warning of what could happen and, in the aftermath, a reinforced guard of 16 officers and 340 other ranks was placed at Lytton. The Queensland government also tried to prevent a repeat of the outbreak by approaching the High Court of Australia seeking an injunction to prevent the Commonwealth from landing any more returning soldiers at sites where it would be difficult for state authorities to keep the men in isolation restriction.

Justice Gavan Duffy declined to grant the Queensland government an interim injunction on 10 February and adjourned proceedings to a date to be fixed. Rallies and demonstrations were held in Brisbane protesting the decision and the continued use of the Lytton Quarantine Station, but they made no difference in the end. [2]

———∞∞∞———

As well as the quarantine camp established at Wallangarra (see above), a second camp was established at Coolangatta, just across the Tweed River from the New South Wales town of Tweed Heads, on 5 February. The two towns lived in a somewhat symbiotic relationship (as they still do) and there were several days of confusion as the residents sorted out themselves and their services. There is no denying the success of the three main quarantine camps in southern Queensland, though. Of the 5,321 people who passed through those camps and into Queensland, not one person was diagnosed with pneumonic influenza. [3]

———∞∞∞———

Initially at least, authorities had a bit less success in their efforts at prophylaxis. The Health Department planned to build a number of inhalatoria to support the frontline of quarantine, and construction of them was well underway before someone discovered that Queensland had absolutely no supplies of zinc sulphate, the key component in the whole process. Fortunately, they were able to source supplies from interstate and were thus able to operate the inhalatoria at the quarantine camps they had established. At Coolangatta, the steam used in the process came from a conventional stationary vertical boiler, while at Wallangarra the inhalatorium was constructed at the railway station where the steam would be provided by a locomotive. Other inhalatoria were constructed in Brisbane and aboard a punt, to be used by passengers whose ships had been allowed to enter the Brisbane River.

Then nothing happened, for a while at least. February came and went, March came and went, and April was almost gone when, on the 30$^{th}$ of the month, the Commissioner of Public Health declared the state to be pneumonic influenza free. Two days later, he had to backtrack a bit and admit that there were cases of the disease being treated in Brisbane Hospital. It was, in fact, considerably more serious than that. The first official death from the disease in Queensland had occurred on the day the Commissioner declared the state to be free of the disease. The death had occurred at the Lytton Quarantine Station and the victim was a passenger from an interstate steamship. There would be more deaths at Lytton, where 62 cases of quite severe infection were being squeezed into a facility designed to hold 40. Three days later, Brisbane newspapers reported, *"Influenza Outbreak in Brisbane,"* a fact confirmed by acting Premier Edward Theodore who, on 2 May, officially disclosed that a number of pneumonic influenza cases were being treated in an isolation ward at the Brisbane General Hospital.

The spread of the outbreak in Brisbane was quite rapid, and by 15 May the Health Department had been notified of 1100 cases, plus another 452 patients who had already been admitted to hospital. That number had quadrupled two weeks later when official notifications of infections in the Brisbane metropolitan area alone totalled 4,452. By then, a range of restrictions were in place, gazetted by the Theodore government on 9 May. The regulations, which would remain in place until 19 July, mandated the closure of churches and Sunday Schools, other schools and colleges plus, *"places of public amusement or resort, theatre, hall, dancing room, gymnasium or other places where persons regularly or occasionally congregate or assemble for worship, education, meeting, amusement, entertainment, dancing, physical culture or athletics."*

Shortly after the new regulations were released, the Brisbane Boxing Stadium announced that it would be removing its roof, thereby qualifying as an open-air venue and thereby, too, — notionally at least — being able to continue to operate. It quickly learned that this would not be the case.

———⟶◦◦◦◦◦◦⟶———

The Queensland government, unlike those of most of the southern states, did not appoint or activate an overarching advisory committee to oversee and coordinate all efforts to deal with the outbreak. Instead it created Joint Health Boards covering two or more local government areas, each charged with checking and then preventing the spread of pneumonic influenza in their designated zones. The enthusiasm of those local boards may have been tempered somewhat on 16 May when the State Government also announced that it would only cover two thirds of the costs incurred in fighting the influenza epidemic and that payments would only be made when the disease had been eradicated.

The State Government established its major emergency isolation hospital at the Brisbane Exhibition Grounds and chose to use existing channels to send out the messages it wanted the general public to hear and heed. It was especially cognisant of the effectiveness of newspapers, especially the larger Brisbane dailies like the *Courier*, and in addition to providing information and updates through newspapers, the Commissioner of Public Health would regularly release information via pamphlets, circulars and public notices, forwarded to local health boards and hospitals for display and distribution.

The Health Department offered the local boards more concrete assistance as well. It was the department who printed the "S.O.S./FOOD" cards and sent them out to suburban and regional health boards for distribution. In the inner Brisbane suburb of Toowong, for example, the cards were distributed throughout the area by the senior male students from the Toowong State School, a process they completed in two days.

189

In areas like Toowong, when a member of a household became infected, the house was isolated and quarantine rules were applied. Only the most serious cases from that household would be sent to hospital because there, like elsewhere in Brisbane and across the state, the public health system started to be overwhelmed.

A recent academic study of the Queensland response to the pneumonic influenza epidemic in Queensland in 1919 observed that, at that time, *"personal health remained firmly within the private domain provided for by a tripartite system of self-help, charity and minimal government support."*[4] The State government devolved as much of the responsibility, and the cost, of the response to the disease as it could. Where the wearing of face masks was compulsory for all persons for periods of time in New South Wales, in Queensland they were made compulsory only for those nominated to wear them by health officials in the various jurisdictions.

The vacuum left by the State government had to be filled by local and volunteer groups; they became the primary carers, feeding and nursing friends and neighbours because nothing else was available. The ambulance services simply could not cope and a large proportion of those taken to hospital travelled there in private vehicles. The Red Cross Women's Emergency Corps, which had provided sterling service during the war, once again swung into action. Their volunteers provided nourishment — beef tea, barley water and more substantial foodstuffs — for households and individuals suffering from influenza. With many men still to return from war service, the burdens in Queensland, as elsewhere, fell primarily on the state's women. And, with numbers falling ill, those burdens increased when services such as gas and transport were rationed.

Some of the newly established local health boards utilised state schools as emergency isolation hospitals, provided the school was empty and the state government approved the proposal. Part of the formal agreement allowing this to happen specified that the school buildings had to be fumigated and cleaned and all furniture returned to its proper place before the facility was handed back to the Education Department. A further complication was that, even with several months to prepare for an outbreak, many parts of Queensland ran short of all medicines almost as soon as the epidemic hit. These factors ensured that, more often than not, Queenslanders who contracted pneumonic influenza would be treated in their own homes rather than in institutions. Ironically, it would later emerge that this was by far the cheapest way to treat patients.

The outcomes could have been a lot worse, given the state government's relative lack of input. That it wasn't was due to the work of many family members and many volunteers. The Red Cross has already been mentioned, but there were two other Brisbane-based organisations that did amazing work. On the north side of the Brisbane River was the Women's Emergency Corps and on the south side the Women's Help Committee. At the height of the epidemic, the activities of both organisations were reported upon daily by the Brisbane *Courier,* and those reports make fascinating reading.

The Women's Emergency Corps, originally formed in 1914 and based on an English organisation of the same name, was run under the auspices of the Anglican Church and drew volunteers from a much wider cross-section of service and support clubs. Branches would be formed all over Brisbane and their primary responsibilities would become patrolling the streets, usually twice a day and on bicycles, visiting homes and, where necessary, arranging for medical assistance, helping with any household work and assisting in the distribution of food. At its peak, the Women's Emergency Corps boasted 1000 volunteers. It was far larger than the Women's Help Committee, but the south side of the river also saw the formation of neighbourhood Vigilance Committees which performed the same role. [5]

After the initial confirmation of its presence, pneumonic influenza spread rapidly through Queensland. The number of patients isolated at the Brisbane General Hospital and the Exhibition grounds continued to grow, peaking at 320 on 20 May. The number would remain above 300 until the end of May and would not drop back to single figures until August. Within a few days of the outbreak in Brisbane, the disease had reached Ipswich and, two weeks later, the first cases were recorded in Toowoomba. Tracing the progress of the disease into rural and regional Queensland shows how it travelled along arterial roads and railway lines, and how spikes in infection often followed agricultural shows and bush race meetings.

The disease went north, too, initially by sea to the major ports scattered between Brisbane and Cape York, and then inland along road and rail lines. Within a week of the outbreak in Brisbane, the first case was reported in the central Queensland town of Rockhampton. There, within a month 40 people had succumbed to the disease and almost 250 others were in hospital. New cases would continue to appear in Rockhampton until August, the longest duration of continuous infection for any town in Queensland. The spread of the disease, and the difficulties of dealing with it and its victims brought a harsh truth home to Queenslanders.

The rail network was designed to service Brisbane and its hinterland, and to facilitate the carriage of people and goods from there to other parts of Australia, primarily to the south and primarily through Wallangarra. The closure of the border, and the bottleneck it created at Wallangarra, should have been a warning to state authorities. There were also feeder lines going inland from port towns like Rockhampton, Mackay, Townsville and Cairns but, like Brisbane, they were primarily east-west lines rather than radial networks. There was no rail connection to the far north of the state and the roads to there were not designed for a lot of heavy-duty traffic. Coastal shipping was the preferred method of transportation on the eastern seaboard of Queensland.

In good times, there were few issues with Queensland's transportation system. By no stretch of the imagination could 1919 be considered good times and the maritime strike which started that year, on top of the epidemic, reduced much of central and north Queensland to the edge of subsistence. At different periods, it looked as though slow starvation was a real possibility for significant numbers of Queenslanders. The Commonwealth chose not to intervene, and a quite desperate situation was only narrowly avoided when the Queensland government was forced to charter shipping to carry the supplies necessary to keep its own citizens alive.

Queensland would survive the pneumonic influenza epidemic, but a minimum 1111 of her citizens would not.[6] The real figure may well have been significantly higher, but problems with attributing cause of death and the fact that many deaths in remote and Indigenous communities may not have been reported at all have contributed to what is undoubtedly a conservative figure. It is difficult to know whether more people would have survived had the Queensland State Government adopted a more interventionist approach, like the government in New South Wales. Because it didn't, numbers of community groups stepped into the vacuum and they certainly prevented a lot of deaths, and a lot of misery, from occurring. And perhaps, after all, these things cancel each other out.

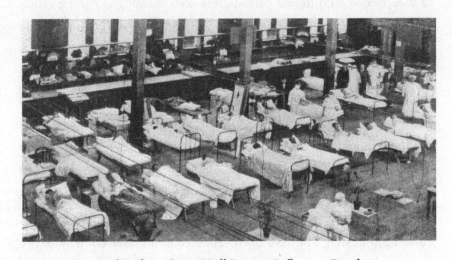

*Hospital Beds in Great Hall During Influenza Pandemic,*
*Exhibition Building, Melbourne, February 1919*

State Library of Victoria

# CHAPTER 11

# Western Australia: Friction at the Edges

Western Australia is vast: it could swallow Western Europe and still have a bit left over. In 1919, it was also sparsely populated, with the greatest concentration of people in its south-western corner. Most of them lived in the Perth-Fremantle conurbation, but there were significantly-sized towns on the coast below, Bunbury prominent among them, in an arc that stretched all the way around Cape Leeuwin to Albany and Esperance, the old whaling ports on the edge of the Australian Bight and the Southern Ocean. There was also a sprinkling of towns on the western and north-western coastline, Geraldton, Cossack, Broome and Derby among them. Inland was a vast emptiness, largely unexplored by Europeans who held the interior of the state to be of little value. The one exception to this was the area concentrated on Kalgoorlie, Boulder and Coolgardie, home to some of the richest goldmines in the world and the land gateway to travellers from the east. The basic facts of geography dictated the course of pneumonic influenza and, in many places, also dictated the response to the disease.

Western Australia had a sometimes-fractious relationship with the Commonwealth during the first two decades of Federation, and events in early 1919 almost guaranteed that the relationship would continue to be bumpy. With both New South Wales and Victoria proclaimed infected states and with both, notionally at least, completely closed, it came as something of a surprise when Dr. Everitt Atkinson, Western Australia's Public Health Commissioner, announced on 30 January that the trans-Australia Express, the rail link between the eastern and western halves of the continent, would be stopped at the railyards at Parkestown on the southern outskirts of Kalgoorlie. All passengers would then be inspected and held in quarantine for four days.

Dr. Atkinson went on to say that arrangements had been made with the Commonwealth, who ran the trans-Australia service, to accommodate the passengers. Separate tents and marquees would be erected to house any suspicious cases while police authorities in Kalgoorlie had sworn in a number of special constables, with a permanent officer in charge; that group would oversee the security of the quarantine.

On the actual quarantine side, health authorities at Boulder and Kalgoorlie had been deputed to administer the quarantine regulations and would be assisted in this by three local health inspectors with an additional two inspectors from the Western Australian Health Department. An inhalation chamber was to be erected onsite, and all passengers would be required to pass through it before they were released. The train had both sleeping and buffet carriages, and passengers and crew would remain aboard during the quarantine period. Any one of those passengers or crew displaying symptoms of influenza would immediately be removed from the train and treated and housed in the canvas accommodation until they recovered.

It went pretty much the way Atkinson suggested it would. The trans-Australia Express, carrying its normal dozen or so crew and 116 passengers, arrived on time and was shunted onto a siding at Parkestown. Shortly after its arrival there, all aboard were examined by the local health officials; all were found to be free of influenza. Afterwards, they settled back into their carriages to wait for four days of doing nothing to pass. [1]

---

The response from Canberra was not long in coming. The next day, Western Australia's acting Premier, Hal Colebatch, received a long communication from acting Prime Minister William Watt. Watt expressed disappointment that the trans-Australia Express had been placed in quarantine and was further disappointed that the train's crew were apparently expected to now take full responsibility for the passengers. Watt also showed annoyance that at least one train in each direction would now have to be cancelled before the period of quarantine ended. Watt concluded with the observation that there was no reason for Western Australia to have done what they did, and it was clearly a breach of the November agreements.

Colebatch had no option but to reply to the prime minister. In that reply, he stated quite categorically that what Western Australian authorities had done in stopping the train was done in strict accordance with normal quarantine procedures. Furthermore, the arrangements at Parkestown had been worked out between local representatives of the Western Australian Public Health Department and the Commonwealth Railways. Colebatch believed that the cancellation of two trains was a small price to pay to keep his state free of infection. He concluded by saying that no further action was planned until the next trans-Australia Express arrived at Kalgoorlie. [2]

On 1 February, the Public Health Commissioner announced that the next trans-Australia Express, due into Kalgoorlie the next day, would also be placed in quarantine. During the afternoon of 3 February, the 116 passengers from the first train were released from quarantine, with most catching that evening's express train to Perth. The train itself was moved to the Kalgoorlie railyards during the morning of 4 February; it had to be moved because of space concerns at Parkestown. By the end of 4 February, there were two more trans-Australia Express trains in quarantine there.

William Watt was furious with the actions of the Western Australian authorities, especially when he learned that two more trains had been placed in quarantine. South Australia, where the trains originated, was still officially a clean state and to Watt, the actions in Kalgoorlie seemed to have been driven as much by local health officials as they had been by the Western Australian government and its Chief Health Officer. Watt said, and said in no uncertain terms, that the Commonwealth intended holding the Western Australian government directly responsible for all costs associated with holding the trains in quarantine and for making good any damage which may occur.

Then came the sting in the tail. Watt informed acting Premier Colebatch that unless the Commonwealth received an assurance that no further trains were to be detained, and that those already held would be released, the trans-Australia Express service between Port Augusta and Kalgoorlie would be stopped. He also gave a deadline of 5 p.m. on Wednesday 5 February. [3] Colebatch and Premier Henry Lefroy, when he returned to work, remained firm in their resolve which was only strengthened when South Australia was declared infected on 8 February. Both sides stuck to their guns and it would be three months before regular transcontinental services resumed. At least the land border was well and truly shut.

In Perth, the combination of the city's relative isolation and the effective land and maritime quarantine restrictions put in place kept pneumonic influenza at bay until the middle of the year, with the first confirmed case outside Woodman's Point not being reported until June 1919. It was not an especially virulent form either, and contagion only spread following the ignoring of restrictions the government put in place, most notably after the Peace Day celebrations in King's Park on 19 July. Once more, though, many of the battles would be fought in regional centres, and Bunbury makes for a well-documented example.

———◦◦◦◦◦———

Simon Crownson Joel was born into a prominent Melbourne Jewish family in December 1873 and was determined to become a doctor from an early age. Graduating in medicine from Melbourne University, young Simon — he usually referred to himself as Crownson Joel — travelled to London for postgraduate studies there. While undertaking those, he met and fell in love with a young woman named Kate Davies; it was a feeling she reciprocated. With the agreement of her family, Kate followed Simon back to Melbourne, where the couple married. It was and would remain a happy marriage, one that produced two sons, Bernard and Neville, and a daughter they named Maxine.

In 1898, the young couple moved to the other side of Australia, to Bunbury in Western Australia. At that time home to 4,000 people, the bustling little seaport town welcomed the Joels when they arrived, he to take up a position as a junior doctor in an established practice, she to raise a young family. The Joels seem to have fallen in love with everything about Bunbury. Within a few short years, as well as his private practice, Simon had become Bunbury's Health Officer and Deputy Quarantine Officer. A decade after moving to Bunbury, the Joels took an extensive holiday, Simon and Kate taking their young family to London, travelling via Melbourne so the children could meet all their relatives in both cities.

The Joels had not been long back in Bunbury before Simon, already a Justice of the Peace, became the Medical Officer for the Bunbury branch of the Royal Surf Life Saving Association when it was formed in 1910. It was an honorary position, and sat alongside other honorary positions he held, including one that was a bit out of the ordinary. Simon Joel was always on-call for the Goldfields Fresh Air League when they sent up to 300 children of all ages to the large holiday facility they had built just behind Bunbury's main beach. [4]

The Joels, and their commitment to Bunbury, did not miss a beat when the First World War broke out. Simon immediately volunteered and joined the Australian Army Medical Corps as a captain. Just as quickly, he was appointed Area Medical Officer for Bunbury. Kate Joel worked in support, organising a range of community functions to support the frontline troops. In October 1917, for instance, she was busy organising a "Plain and Fancy Dress Ball" to coincide with the opening of the Bunbury Show on 7 November. Proceeds would go towards the purchase of Tommy Cookers for the troops. It was no surprise that the Joels, Simon in particular, would be at the forefront when the threat of pneumonic influenza came to Bunbury.

As the public interest, and public reporting about the *Boonah*, Woodman's Point and pneumonic influenza was reaching a peak in early December, Simon was invited to address a special meeting of the Bunbury Health Board, called to discuss ways of preventing a pneumonic influenza outbreak in the district. He spoke well, arguing that there was a need for a committee to oversee the various preparations that would be needed and of the need, too, for prophylactic measures, especially as Bunbury was a port town.

Expanding on that point, the doctor suggested that a small committee could look at such issues as investigating what arrangements might be most appropriate for the transportation of patients to hospital and the delivery of food to the homes of the victims. Such a committee or working group could consider as well the compilation of a list of paid and volunteer labour that might be required, reviewing motor transport options and availability, and the registration of persons who were willing to assist in running the inoculation depots that would be set up. Joel said that he believed that individual communities would very much have to look after themselves if the disease struck, and a good starting point would be identifying where those who contracted the disease would be housed and treated.

Turning to the steps that had already been taken, Joel said that he had requested a supply of vaccine from health authorities in Perth, and that he expected it to arrive in the next few days. While the vaccine would not prevent the disease, it would certainly mitigate its consequences. At that point, the Bunbury Local Health Board voted to form itself into an Influenza Advisory Committee to commence putting into place a program based on what Simon Joel had just outlined.[5] The newly-formed committee then agreed to meet once again three nights later, and Simon Joel was invited to attend that meeting as well.

A number of actions came out of that first meeting of the new Influenza Committee. It decided that an advertisement would be placed in local newspapers calling for volunteers, male and female, with some knowledge of first aid. Those volunteers could assume neighbourhood control positions if an outbreak of pneumonic influenza occurred in Bunbury. The city's Medical Board, assisted by Simon Joel, would at that stage assume full control of the town's response.

With the general lines of responsibility agreed, Joel informed the others that the influenza vaccine had arrived and that public inoculations would be held at the council offices at 3 p.m. on Wednesdays and Saturdays, while private inoculations could also be arranged through general practitioners. Continuing, he suggested that a new committee or sub-committee be formed and given the specific task of preventing and/or controlling potential outbreaks. It could place advertisements and articles in newspapers detailing the symptoms of pneumonic influenza and outlining the benefits of early inoculation. The bottom line should be that if anyone exhibited any of these symptoms, they should immediately go to bed and seek medical assistance.

The committee also needed to ensure that quarantine measures were enforced, and that adequate medical and nursing resources were available. Food and household necessities would need to be stockpiled and, if the outbreak was large enough, a suitably furnished building to be used as an emergency hospital would be required. Finance would also be needed to pay the domestic and nursing staff at that hospital while food and transport would also need to be provided. To contain any outbreak, schools, churches and places of entertainment would also have to be closed.[6]

The meeting closed with a resolution to take over the Bunbury State School should an outbreak occur and to use the school's excellent cooking facilities to provide sustenance for the patients. It was a decision in line with an announcement made a few days later by the Western Australian Commissioner of Public Health, who had been given special powers to requisition the use of buildings, premises and items needed in connection with the treatment of influenza patients. The Commissioner offered assurances that a reasonable sum would be paid for the purchase or hire of those items. Finally, in the run-up to Christmas, the Bunbury Board of Health issued a circular to all residents giving exhaustive instructions in regard to the prevention and treatment of pneumonic influenza. All, then, sat back to see what 1919 might bring.[7]

———◇◇◇———

They were given a preview shortly into the New Year. In early February, a minor scare quickly escalated when a former soldier who had returned to Australia aboard the *Boonah* was reported to have contracted pneumonic influenza while living on his property at Brunswick, near Bunbury. The man had actually gone duck hunting and returned home cold and wet. A few sniffles developed into a cold and Simon Joel was summoned from Bunbury to treat him. Joel correctly diagnosed a common cold but because of the man's background aboard the *Boonah,* recommended to the family that they self-isolate for a few days and also notified health authorities in Perth of the case. That was probably where the rumours of pneumonic influenza — and a small media storm — originated.

It was a false report, but it did kick-start the preparations for a possible outbreak in Bunbury after little had been done there since the start of the year. A week after the soldier fell ill at Brunswick, on 8 February a public meeting was held in the Bunbury Council Chambers to discuss a general response to the threat. Although the meeting had been widely advertised in local newspapers, only between 15 and 20 residents attended. The Mayor, William Thomas, opened the meeting by saying his council believed that the key to overcoming the disease was organisation and that he believed as well that it was very prudent to act before the disease actually appeared. He added that it was particularly important to have a number of ladies who would be prepared to offer their services to assist qualified nurses should the need arise. Thomas then handed over to the Council's Health Officer, Dr. Simon Joel.

Joel took the mayor's closing point as his opening observation. Victoria, which he knew well, had been required to ask New Zealand for 100 nurses and they had already run out of hospital beds. To him, as to the mayor, the secret was preparation and organisation, and he proceeded to outline just what the council proposed.

As Simon Joel explained it to the small audience, the first phase of preparation was to bring together a body of volunteers to support the trained nurses in their vital work. Those volunteers would be required to work as cooks, to clean up and to generally maintain the emergency hospital that the council would set up. The second phase of the preparations would be protection and treatment. The making of face masks would need to be started as soon as possible as masks had a preventative value. Inoculation, while also valuable, primarily acted to moderate the effects of the disease. For the moment, though, a working bee to start making the gauze masks would be a good start. The third phase would be the care of the sick in their own homes. If the disease did come to Bunbury, every house would need to be checked to ascertain whether or not there were sufferers inside.

At the conclusion of Dr. Joel's address, all those present formed themselves into an action committee and agreed that, if they had not already been, they would be inoculated. They also agreed that further measures and meetings would flow from that night's presentations.[8]

---

By not arriving too soon, pneumonic influenza gave Bunbury time to prepare. After the initial burst of activity in February, things went quiet until June when, on the back of reported cases elsewhere in the state, the Bunbury City Council again chose to act pre-emptively. It decided that if an outbreak did occur in the town, the Council's Health Committee would formally take over the Fresh Air League's premises for use as an emergency hospital. The facility had been designed to accommodate between 200 and 300 children and could provide accommodation for that number of adults. The committee believed it would be adequate for the numbers they expected to be affected.[9]

---

The council was advised that the Fresh Air League facility could be made fit for purpose for a sum of £75 and that the state's central health authorities had agreed to provide that amount. All the materials they needed to do the job had been purchased and all that was now needed was legal authority to take possession of the site. As can sometimes be the case, the Goldfields Fresh Air League had been blissfully unaware of Bunbury Council's plan for their holiday camp and responded vigorously when they learned of it. They would not hand the buildings over voluntarily and appealed to the council, *"to give the kiddies a chance for their yearly holiday."*

In fact, the Fresh Air League said, they would only give up their Bunbury site if they were compelled to do so by the Commissioner of Public Health; several telegrams later, that is precisely what happened. Shortly afterwards, a comprehensive inventory of everything at the facility was undertaken by representatives from the Bunbury Health Committee and the matron in charge of the facility, a Miss McCallum. After some relatively minor repairs to the roof of the main building, the Fresh Air League premises were ready to become an emergency hospital by the end of June. [10]

There were a few more loose ends to be sorted out before all concerned could be certain that everything that could be done had been done. At Simon Joel's suggestion, Bunbury was divided into wards, each of which would be given a patrol. Each patrol would be made up of volunteers under the direction of the Railways Ambulance Corps, trained first aid responders. By the middle of the month, though, only five ladies had volunteered to be trained as nursing aides. Mayor Thomas and Simon Joel learned that more would have volunteered if they had been assured that their jobs would be held for them should they be called away to assist in nursing. The two men took up the challenge to do just that and by month's end, 22 people had volunteered to become nursing aides and medical orderlies. A local nurse, Sister Eaton, had also volunteered to tutor them all.[11]

An ambulance had already been secured from the State Railways, but the Health Committee believed another might be necessary and authorised an approach, which was ultimately successful, to the Bunbury Harbour Board. The local Red Cross also stepped up their preparations. Mrs. St. Barbe-More told the committee that she would ask all her lady members to step forward if they were required. In the meantime, she would begin to organise all the catering requirements for the emergency hospital and also undertook to arrange for the kitchen to be staffed. Finally, Kate Joel had earlier suggested establishing a convalescent home for those recovering from the disease and had identified Bunbury State School, again because of its extensive kitchens, as the ideal venue for this. Now, at the end of June, she confirmed that she would organise the facility.

The situation had progressed to the point at which Mayor Thomas could say that, in his opinion, Bunbury was now as well-prepared as anywhere in Western Australia to confront the influenza epidemic. Unfortunately, the mayor then became something of a victim of his own success.

———◇◇◇◇◇———

It all started with innocent enough discussions about two things: nurses and outsiders. While the numbers of both trained and volunteer nurses were gradually building up, neither Simon Joel nor the Influenza Committee believed the numbers were yet sufficient to deal with a major outbreak in Bunbury. They would continue to advertise and continue to work closely with the local Red Cross branch and, on 15 June, Joel met with the Bunbury Railway Ambulance Corps branch to see if there was a possibility of them being available en masse if an epidemic struck the town. Who they and the other volunteers would be nursing then became something of a matter for debate.

William Thomas, in his capacity as mayor of Bunbury and in his various other roles on health and influenza committees, was not comfortable with the thought that all the hard work that he and the others had put in might ultimately benefit people for whom it was not intended. For its hinterland, Bunbury had become the service centre for dozens of smaller settlements, some just small villages of a few cottages, others more substantial centres of up to 400 residents. At a meeting of the Health Board in mid-June, Thomas spoke of the likelihood of people from those outlying areas flooding into Bunbury, seeking assistance, should an outbreak of pneumonic influenza occur in that part of the south-west. He spoke with passion and conviction and was joined by others, with a general agreement that those outside Bunbury had been given time enough to make their own preparations, and those who represented Bunbury had a responsibility to put the welfare of their constituents ahead of the welfare of those lived outside the town's boundaries.

The only one present to question the need to lock all non-residents out of the medical system they had set up was its architect, Simon Joel, who asked for clarification of a number of points. Despite this, the Board agreed that no infected person should be brought into Bunbury from outlying areas and then quickly moved on to other business. That other business included approving the employment of a trained nurse and a competent cook for the Fresh Air League emergency hospital and listening to a report from the Town Clerk who informed the Board that the inhalatorium at the Electric Light Works had been completed and would be used primarily for those who had been in direct contact with infected persons. [12]

Within a couple of weeks, Simon Joel realised that he was being quoted as supporting the idea that only residents of the municipality of Bunbury should be treated in Bunbury's facilities if they contracted pneumonic influenza. That was an idea that affronted both his professional ethics and his personal preferences and being associated with it was something he was not prepared to let stand. It had never been a position he approved of, either publicly or privately, and so he wrote to all local newspapers to make that very point. After his letters were published, it was all smiles and handshakes and by the end of the month, the Bunbury authorities agreed that all sides' positions had been misunderstood.[13] That was just as well because, after a scare when several Bunbury residents contracted bad cases of seasonal influenza, the pneumonic type arrived in the town in early August.

---

The months of planning and preparation paid off immediately. When Simon Joel confirmed Bunbury's first case of pneumonic influenza on 3 August, everything went according to plan and within four hours an emergency hospital at the Free Air League site was opened, staffed and taking care of its one patient. Two weeks later, there were seven patients at the hospital, five men and two women. Four of them were regarded as being seriously ill, two were classified as just ill and one was convalescent. From that point on, admissions increased during late August and into September but there were never more than 20 or so patients in the hospital while for most of those six to eight weeks, when the epidemic was at its height, the daily average was just 10 patients.

There was no real pattern to the outbreak, with cases coming in from all over the town. Several were also admitted from outlying districts, something which raised absolutely no issues as there was no real pressure on Bunbury's medical facilities. At no time was the emergency hospital at more than one-tenth of capacity while there were rarely more than a dozen or so being treated in their own homes. It was even possible to make some minor upgrades to the hospital during this period when some issues emerged with the plumbing. In mid-September the senior medical orderly at the hospital contracted the disease but there was no disruption to its ongoing operations. The Health Board even paid his wages while he was ill, having received approval to do so from Perth.

The last case in Bunbury was admitted to the emergency hospital in late September and, after a relatively mild attack, was discharged to her home in early October. By 14 October, the decision had been made to return the hospital to the Fresh Air League, and the main building was completely cleaned and disinfected, even those areas that had not been used. An accounting at the end of the month revealed that the hospital had admitted 55 patients in the six weeks it had been in operation; just two of those patients had died. Hospital staff had treated another 400 patients in their own homes. Most of those cases were very mild and a number of them were believed to have actually been seasonal influenza. One of the home patients had also died. Post-mortem examinations of two other people, neither of whom had sought medical assistance, revealed that they had also died of pneumonic influenza. [14]

In his Annual Report, published later that year, Bunbury Mayor William Thomas would say:

*"We can certainly claim to have done all in our power and that with a commendable promptitude to meet the occasion. Our best thanks are due to the ladies of Bunbury who offered their services as nurses and in other capacities and for the timely and judicious assistance rendered by them to combat the outbreak. It is with gratitude that I have to record that the outbreak has apparently reached its limits throughout the state and to thank the general public for its effort to support the Council to maintain the health of the town."*

Mayor Thomas had a lot to be thankful for. With a death rate of less than one-tenth of a per cent, the Bunbury district had one of the lowest death rates of any Australian municipality. The infection rate there was also incredibly low while the inoculation rate, which would eventually approach 40%, was one of the highest to be found in Australia. The planning, preparation and prophylaxis depended in some part on the good ladies of Bunbury but also, and in large part, to the foresight and determination of one man, Dr. Simon Crownston Joel, and his name was conspicuous by its absence in the mayor's speech.

---

The pneumonic influenza epidemic did not have as great an impact on Western Australia as a whole as some had predicted, although that impact could be extremely severe in particular communities and neighbourhoods. The rate of infection was comparable with that of Queensland, but the number of deaths in Western Australia was 540, half of Queensland's total and the same as that of South Australia, which also had a considerably lower rate of infection.[15] At the height of the epidemic in mid to late September, the Perth metropolitan area was averaging around 15 to 20 new cases a day, with two deaths also being the daily average. Figures from around the state would have almost doubled those numbers.

As elsewhere, the death toll may have been considerably higher than the official figures suggested. In early 1920, a two line story appeared in a number of Australian newspapers: *"Reports that eighty-three Aboriginals have died of influenza at Beagle Bay in the north-west of Western Australia have been received."*[16] Whether or not the report was accurate in all respects is partly irrelevant as it is what lies behind such stories that is important. There were many deaths that went unrecorded in Western Australia because they occurred among the fringe-dwellers. Half a dozen here, 83 there. In Western Australia, possibly more than anywhere else in Australia, the battle against pneumonic influenza was fought on the fringes, at Kalgoorlie, at Bunbury and at Beagle Bay.

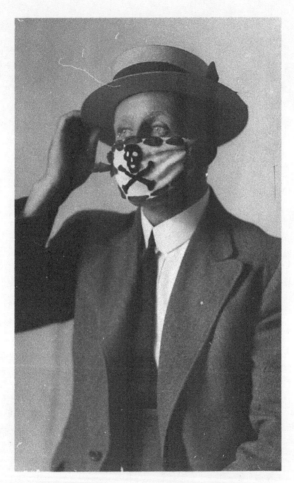

*Wearing the compulsory mask, brought in to combat the epidemic of flu in 1919.*

State Library of NSW

# CHAPTER 12

# Tasmania and T.I.: The Outliers

Tasmanians put great faith in the fact that they lived on an island, one whose surrounding seas provided an ideal quarantine barrier against many threats, with the main threat in early 1919 being the spread of pneumonic influenza from the mainland of Australia. Their faith was strong but in late January 1919, when both New South Wales and Victoria were declared infected states, Tasmanian Premier Walter Lee decided that faith backstopped by practical measures was a lot better than faith alone.

On 29 January, Premier Lee urgently requested an additional 20,000 units of both Coryza A and B vaccines from Melbourne. More actions followed in quick succession. A quarantine station for returning soldiers was established at Barnes Bay on Bruny Island, with an additional overflow facility put in place at the old Claremont Hospital. Troops were required to remain in quarantine for seven days in conditions that could best be described as "challenging." [1] It was months later, on 15 August, that pneumonic influenza claimed its first Tasmanian victim, a young woman who was the niece of a councillor from New Norfolk and who died in the Hobart suburb of Sandy Bay.

The government response to this was immediate. State Cabinet met during the morning of Saturday 16 August and, acting on advice from the

Tasmanian Medical Advisory Board, issued a proclamation introducing a range of restrictions to be imposed to deal with the threat of an epidemic. All schools, churches, libraries and places of indoor or outdoor entertainment where numbers of people were likely to congregate were ordered to close throughout the state. The same prohibition applied to all military parades, football matches and agricultural shows. Only three persons could occupy bar areas in hotels, and then only for five minutes each. Face masks had to be worn in public conveyances carrying more than three persons and were strongly recommended for all people moving in public spaces. The Blind Institute in New Town was to become the main emergency isolation hospital while the Claremont Hospital would become a convalescent home. Cabinet also said that the restrictions would be reviewed "in a short time."[2]

The arrival of the disease prompted some limited signs of panic in Hobart, most notably among newspaper journalists rather than the public at large. The *Mercury,* the city's main newspaper, announced the outbreak of pneumonic influenza under a banner headline, and then went on to report that:

> "Now that the people have been convinced that pneumonic influenza is here, and that they are not going to help themselves otherwise than by courageously facing the situation, they are calmer than they were over the weekend. Yesterday the chemists continued to do business among people in search of preventatives, but the majority of their time was occupied in making up medical prescriptions.[3] The disease is spreading more rapidly each day, and the number of serious cases yesterday showed a marked increase over previous days. The health authorities have been kept exceedingly busy replying to a host of enquiries and demands for requirements, and the officers of the Municipal Relief Depot made

*over a hundred visits yesterday, distributing drugs and comforts and
assisting distressed families."*[4]

---

Fighting outbreaks of disease, like politics, is best treated as a local exercise, and in this Tasmania was no different to the rest of Australia. Six
days after the first death occurred, Tasmanian authorities declared the
outbreak of an epidemic and across the state communities large and small
swung into action. In the largest of those communities, Hobart, the main
hospital immediately appealed for old bottles so that medicines could be
dispensed to those requesting them, a number that increased by 50% in
the days following the outbreak. There was also a realisation that there
were not enough doctors and nurses in Hobart, so efforts to bring in more
also commenced with the declaration of the outbreak.

Most of those extra doctors and nurses came across from the
mainland, and to make it a bit sweeter for some, the Tasmanian Branch
of the Nurses Association negotiated for those nursing patients with
pneumonic influenza to be paid a third more than their usual salary.
One of the doctors brought in by the State's Chief Health Officer was
placed in the Public Health Office to assist in departmental work but
the others were posted to where they were most needed. Requests for
replacement doctors had already come in from several quarters. At the
Mental Diseases Hospital in New Norfolk, both doctors were already ill,
as was the only doctor in the east coast town of Swansea. All three were
temporarily replaced by doctors currently working in Hobart.[5]

Across the river from Hobart was Bellerive, essentially a dormitory
community for the state capital. When the number of cases there
suddenly doubled and then trebled in late August, town authorities also
undertook decisive action. Bellerive State School was taken over and

quickly converted into an isolation hospital. Two wards, one for men and one for women, were completely equipped with furniture, spare clothing, cutlery and other necessities, all donated or loaned by local residents. The entire process of creating a new emergency hospital took just a few hours and the former state school was then ready to receive patients. Within just a few more hours, six of them had been admitted.

The disease caused considerable distress among the suburbanites of Bellerive, owing to the fact that many families were impacted at the same time. To help alleviate some of the problems, the Bellerive Council divided the suburb into sections and supported the setting up of a vigilance committee in each section. The main role of those committees was to make regular calls to every house in the section. Where appropriate, reports on what was found and what was required were forwarded to Bellerive's Central Depot, which was responsible for despatching the type of assistance needed by the particular household. The depot also received donations of money, clothes and food. Bellerive also looked towards establishing its own isolation facilities and had taken possession of a fully equipped ambulance, capable of carrying four patients.[6]

At the end of August, an assessment was made of the impact of pneumonic influenza on Tasmania. In two weeks and two days, the disease had killed 47 people and perhaps a dozen more; some deaths that had been attributed to seasonal influenza were more likely to have been pneumonic. Of that total, 34 had occurred in Hobart with another six each in Launceston and Queenstown. There did not seem to be a discernible pattern to those being struck down, with victims ranging from small children to the elderly. However, 19 of those who perished were between the ages of 20 and 34, seemingly in the prime of life. It was also spread out across the island. There had been 35 fatal cases in the south, eight in the north and one in the north-west. By then, though, it also seemed to be abating.[7]

It wasn't, and little outbreaks, fortunately limited in both size and virulence, continued across the state. At Queenstown, in the west of the island, both of the town's doctors were among the first residents to fall ill with the disease. In one way, the town was then lucky because it was a key part of the operations of the nearby Mount Lyell Company, a mining giant with an almost paternalistic attitude to its workers. As soon as the doctors contracted the disease, the company arranged for a doctor, six nurses and a pharmacist to be brought across from Melbourne. The group arrived in Queenstown, having travelled via Burnie, on 31 August. Three of the nurses remained in Queenstown while the others proceeded a little further to the small town of Gormanston where the company had established its own temporary hospital.

Queenstown Council also arranged for the services of a locum, a Dr. Tymms, who arrived at just the right time. After a pause of two weeks in early September, pneumonic influenza returned with a vengeance, and it was estimated that close to 80% of the town's population, then estimated at 5,000, including the neighbouring settlement of Gormanston, contracted the disease. Most displayed mild symptoms, and could be treated in isolation in their own homes, but the numbers were too great for the town's hospital, so the Imperial Hotel (now the Galley Museum) was fitted out as an auxiliary hospital, capable of holding up to 50 patients. At the same time, the local State School was taken over for use as a convalescent home. [8]

———◦◦◦◦◦———

The monthly update for September showed that 103 Tasmanians died as a result of pneumonic influenza that month. The trend line was definitely heading down again, though, with just a few cases and no deaths during the final days of September, a trend that continued into October. [9]

The state's Medical Advisory Committee met in Hobart on Friday

26 September to consider the question of whether or not to ease the restrictions, given that the epidemic seemed to be over. It was decided to suspend the regulations pertaining to all outdoor gatherings from the next day and publish a notice to that effect in all major newspapers on the following Monday. The restrictions relating to indoor entertainments, picture shows and theatres would be relaxed from 6 October, with the situation being closely monitored during that time.[10]

It seemed to go well, and on 8 October the Tasmanian Government removed all restrictions on people congregating. To many in the state, including newspaper editors, this action suggested that authorities believed that the epidemic was over, although some of the wiser among them expressed a degree of caution. The *Huon Times,* for example, said that there was always the possibility of a second wave, and that if one arrived it could be much worse than the first. Unfortunately for some, the lifting of the restrictions came too late. Most of the various football competitions, at the heart of many communities, were not continued with premierships being awarded to the clubs that were on top of their ladders when the competition was suspended.

There would be a second wave, and its effects would be felt especially hard in the north and north-west of the island.

———◦◦◦◦◦———

Circular Head was a municipality in the far north-western corner of Tasmania, encompassing towns like Stanley and Smithton. During the second wave of the outbreak, the Circular Head Council set up temporary hospitals, carefully recording that the cost of doing so was £362. One of the hospitals was established in the urban centre of Stanley and the other at Black River, a remote camp for workers then pushing railway lines into the remote areas of the state. The latter was considered vital because the disease had already reached the camp and would claim at least two victims there. As well as carefully costing those hospitals, the council staff spent quite a bit of time preparing a detailed claim for reimbursement from the State government. [11]

In the north-west, though, Devonport would become the epicentre of the outbreak. At the beginning of the first wave, the Devonport High School was closed for seven weeks from 18 August until 7 October when Devonport returned to normal in the belief that the disease had passed. It hadn't and in mid-October a number of influenza cases that included at least one fatality convinced a senior nurse who lived and worked in the town that pneumonic influenza had returned. As soon as that fact became obvious, the Health Department reimposed the restrictions it had originally introduced on 3 September. The police approached all local groups and organisations to inform them of this reimposition while the local branch of the Red Cross once more stepped into the breach, some of its volunteers reportedly working day and night. [12]

In West Devonport, too, arrangements had been put in place to address the first wave of influenza. To begin with the local council decided to set up the West Devonport State School as an emergency hospital, and several nurses were engaged to work there. When no epidemic eventuated, the nurses were let go and the school reverted to its original use. Within days of that, the second wave hit. This one had a major impact on both Devonport and West Devonport. On 23 October, for instance, 300 new cases of influenza were reported in the district, bringing the total since the original outbreak to 1000. Fortunately, it seemed that a significant proportion of these were seasonal rather than pneumonic influenza.

For a time, every business in the area was either closed or understaffed. Of a total staff of 17 at the Devonport Post Office, for several days there were just three employees on duty, each working 15 hours a day. Assistance was sought from Launceston while the Devonport Council was roundly criticised for its epidemic response of simply hiring a single nurse and seeming to hand over its responsibilities to the Red Cross. They were responsibilities the Red Cross itself struggled to meet, for although it had two nurses on its books, it had to issue urgent calls for volunteers to help in the distribution of food, clothing and other comforts from their depot. They also needed assistance with transportation, saying even a horse and buggy would be helpful. [13]

The situation was grave enough for one of the specialists employed by the Public Health Department, Dr. J. G. Hislop, to be despatched to the north-west to report and advise on what was happening there. One of Hislop's first actions on arriving in Devonport was to call for three additional nurses from Hobart; they arrived the following night. The day after his arrival, the doctor made a flying visit to the town of Sheffield, 20 kilometres inland from Devonport, and that evening met the local influenza advisory committee. He was informed that there had been 17 deaths in the district in the past 10 days, and the committee thought that some of them may have been caused by pneumonic influenza. Hislop was able to confirm that several of the patients he was shown were certainly suffering from that disease.

After checking that all the restrictions had been reintroduced in Devonport and Ulverstone, the two major towns in that part of Tasmania, Hislop returned to Hobart to write his report for the government, confident that he and they had done everything that could reasonably be expected of them. [14]

—•◦◦◦•—

Twenty kilometres up the Derwent Valley from Hobart is the town of New Norfolk, established in the first decade of the 19th Century by farmers relocated there from Norfolk Island. Among a number of claims to historical fame, New Norfolk was where Governor Arthur directed the construction of an "Invalid Depot" in 1827, an institution in which people with substantial mental problems could be housed and treated. Almost a century later, in 1919, the facility was known as the Mental Diseases Hospital and was run by the Mental Diseases Hospital Department. At that time, it was used primarily as a treatment facility for children with intellectual disabilities and, as such, was an unlikely candidate to become a centre for research into pneumonic influenza, but that was what it became.

Because it had the capacity to spare and was already set up and equipped as a hospital, the Mental Diseases Hospital was early identified as a centre for the treatment of persons suffering pneumonic influenza. During the outbreak, it would handle 175 patients, of whom 44 were positively identified as infected with pneumonic influenza; 11 of which died. It would also see some pioneering work into pneumonic influenza undertaken by two outstanding clinicians based there, Dr. Peter Lalor and George Haddow. Lalor was the namesake and grandson of the miners' leader at the Eureka Stockade and Haddow was the Mental Diseases Hospital's Laboratory Officer.

Lalor and Haddow started their investigations with one of the most obvious by-products of the disease, the sufferers' sputum. The laboratory examinations they undertook revealed the presence of a number of organisms — pneumococci, streptococci, influenza bacillus, gram-positive diplococci, staphylococci and gram-negative diplococci. These appeared in most victims, sometimes all of them together and sometimes just a couple, but their examinations revealed the presence in all sufferers of one of these organisms, gram-negative diplococci. Lalor and Haddow hypothesised that the presence of that particular form of diplococci was a marker of the difference between normal, seasonal influenza and that of the pneumonic variety.

The two men then cultured gram-negative diplococci from blood samples of two of their most severely impacted patients, something that had not been achieved anywhere else in Australia and possibly in the world. Post-mortems were conducted on all those killed by the disease, and they revealed the presence of the diplococci in every case. While not wanting to overstate the case, Lalor said that what he and Haddow found might be the first step in developing a vaccine to actually protect against the disease, rather than just mitigate effects. As well, the two men found that recovered patients continued to carry gram-negative diplococci in their sputum, suggesting a possible method of disease transmission.

In the end, it may not have mattered all that much in attempts to thwart the disease but, nevertheless, it was a fantastic achievement for a small hospital at the end of the world. [15]

---

Tasmania's second city, Launceston, proceeded along the same path as the rest of Tasmania, with two waves of the disease involving numerous infections and a lower than average death rate. Its response to the disease was impacted, however, by the same shortage of nurses that was being felt elsewhere in the state. When the first wave hit in August, the Launceston City Council was quickly made aware of the impending shortage and equally quickly contacted Whitelaw's Nursing Bureau in Melbourne to arrange for 30 registered nurses to be sent to Launceston by the first available boat. It also took the first steps towards establishing its own nurse's bureau.

The council and the headmasters of the various state schools in Launceston were also involved in setting up a city-wide organisation to cope with the epidemic, something along the lines of the neighbourhood watch or vigilance committee structures that had been established elsewhere in Tasmania and on the mainland. City officials also worked closely with volunteer organisations like the Red Cross. Council and the local branch of that society soon came up with a rather novel way to address the shortage of nurses. Many qualified nurses in the community — some retired and others having switched careers — were uncomfortable about volunteering to nurse patients suffering from pneumonic influenza, especially if they had families of their own. What was now proposed was that the Red Cross nurses would assist patients with pneumonic influenza, and the volunteer nurses would take over the rest of the patients. Aligned with that was a request that persons requiring assistance because of illness to first contact the Red Cross who would then assign them a nurse. It was a simple and elegant solution, and it worked.

---

In his later Annual Report, the Chief Health Officer of Tasmania, Dr. Emanuel Morris, surveyed the health outcomes for the state for 1919-20.[16] During that year, there had been 898 reported cases of pneumonic influenza resulting in 171 deaths. Hobart, with 293 cases and 65 deaths, was followed by Launceston with 144 and 28, Zeehan with 149 and two, New Norfolk, 70 and 12, and Devonport with 33 and 10.[17] The first case was reported on 15 August 1919 and the last on 13 October. The epidemic lasted roughly eight weeks and, unlike on the mainland, it appeared almost simultaneously all over the state. Because of this it was not possible to say just how or when it appeared.[18]

The raw figures tell only part of the story. Tasmania did not suffer either the absolute numbers or the infection rates of the mainland states but had faced its own particular challenges. The greatest of these was the suddenness of the outbreak in August; it was like the disease sprang to life spontaneously in all corners of the state. This created a number of immediate problems, most notably the shortage of nurses and other health professionals. The various cities and towns did find ways to address this and, in the end, the arrangements they made enabled them to make it through.

Common sense was also well to the fore. In Hobart, churches divided the city into 13 wards and made sure that ministers and/or priests were available to individuals and families within those wards, irrespective of their denomination. Soldiers in quarantine on Bruny Island would claim later that they would not have survived the experience without the tobacco and sweets provided by the Red Cross and the YMCA. In both Hobart and Launceston, and perhaps elsewhere, the doyens of society hosted face mask parties, and competed among themselves to create the most colourful and fashionable face mask.

There was also something that was, by and large, missing in Tasmania. Individuals and groups throughout the island state did not seem to be looking for someone to blame for the situations pneumonic influenza brought about. If there was a shortage of medical specialists, bring them in from interstate or coax them out of retirement. If there is no vaccine for the disease, see if we can develop one. The Commonwealth was unpopular in Tasmania because of the shipping crisis, but rather than play the blame game, Tasmanians played the community game and it seems to have worked.

——◦◦◦◦◦——

The last outbreak of pneumonic influenza in Australia occurred on a group of islands to the north of Tasmania, a long, long way to the north in the Torres Strait; it was centred on Thursday Island, T.I. to the locals. Thursday Island, and a cluster of islands nearby, had a population of just over 2000 in 1920. Predominantly Torres Strait Islanders, there were also significant numbers of those with Papuan, Japanese and European heritage, most of whom were Australian. It was an important little outpost for trade in the Torres Strait and between New Guinea, the Straits islands and northern Australia. It also had strategic importance and there were both Australian Army and RAN facilities and personnel on the island as well as quarantine facilities.

On Thursday Island, there was a local council, headed by an elected mayor, and there was a public hospital whose staff was led by Dr. Norman Markwell and Nurse Herring. Markwell, a New South Welshman, had been on the island since 1915. Then 28, he had been accompanied by his wife, Emma, and their first child, a son; they would subsequently have another two sons. Volunteering for an army role as well as his other medical duties on the island, including supporting the quarantine doctor, Markwell was made a captain in the AAMC, and chose to remain on the island at war's end. He was there when the first cases of pneumonic influenza appeared at the beginning of February 1920.

Locals would always blame the Japanese for the outbreak, saying a boatload of sick fishermen or pearl divers arrived in the last days of January. The truth of the allegation was never ascertained but by the 5 February it had spread across the island. It first presented in a mild form but soon turned virulent. Within a week, 200 cases had been reported, among them Dr. Markwell who first displayed the symptoms on 4 February. By 10 February the number of cases had jumped to 400 and there had been nine deaths, including George Byers, a long-time resident and Government Carpenter and Chief Petty Officer Green from the local RAN detachment. Local estimates were that 60% of the island's population had been directly affected.

The hospital quickly became overcrowded, a situation not helped when Nurse Herring also contracted the disease a week after the outbreak commenced. Conditions at the main hospital were eased somewhat when the military established an emergency hospital (for military personnel). The mayor, assisted by his aldermen and members of the hospital committee, stepped into the breach and took over a lot of the service delivery at both the public and the emergency hospital. They also supported the island's second doctor, Dr. Murray, whose normal workload consisted of checking and enforcing quarantine requirements.

To go with staff shortages at the hospitals, there were also shortages of food and medicines. On 10 February, military authorities sent an urgent request for doctors, nurses, medicines and milk to be sent aboard a RAN destroyer, knowing it would take at least a week for that destroyer to arrive. A second major issue they all faced was a dwindling supply of nourishing food for both patients and convalescents. All stocks of meat extract were exhausted early in the outbreak, and by 12 February the only meat available on the island was what was held in the cool rooms of the military bases. On that day, the mayor arranged for a share of that to be made available to health authorities for the production of beef tea for the seriously ill.

That afternoon, the steamship *Victoria* arrived carrying around 15 tons of foodstuffs and other supplies. That provided some relief, but the supplies would, at best, last for only a few days. There were no wharf labourers available either, so the ship had to be unloaded by its own crew. Later that day, Emma Markwell sent an urgent telegram to the new Queensland Home Secretary, William McCormack:

> "Dr. Markwell is in eighth day in influenza and pneumonia. Dr. Murray is carrying on here alone. He says that there are 400 cases up to yesterday on Thursday Island, fifty per cent being pneumonic. The Torres Strait Islands, Badu Moa and Manboie are stricken with disease. There have been only two deaths among the whites but the coloured people are dying daily. Help is badly required." [19]

McCormack revealed that the Queensland government had attempted to send relief supplies to Thursday Island via the steamship *Civoria* which made regular runs to the island. Unfortunately, the ship had sailed from Cairns before the nurses and medical supplies could be boarded. Queensland then approached the Commonwealth and asked whether it would be possible to send the needed supplies aboard a fast naval vessel. They were informed in return that relief supplies were already on their way aboard a civilian vessel.

That vessel was the steamship *Roggeveen*, now expected to arrive at Thursday Island around the 18-19 February. Scheduled to sail from Sydney to Thursday Island, en route from Auckland to the Netherland East Indies, medical and food supplies had been hurriedly loaded aboard before she departed Sydney. The Queensland government also joined in, sending six nurses by train to Gladstone on 13 February. They would join the *Roggeveen* when she called in there. It looked to be touch and go, though, as the islanders waited for relief to arrive. By 16 February, the death toll had reached 27 with a third European, a member of the island's military garrison, among the latest victims. Equally worrying was the lack of nourishing food which was still obviously hampering the recovery of some of the victims.

By 19 February, the *Roggeveen* had arrived, and its nurses were fully engaged while the supplies it carried had been distributed among those who needed them most. By then, the disease had spread to other Torres Strait islands and across to the tip of Cape York, where it cut a swathe through isolated Indigenous communities. Unconfirmed reports put the death toll at the Small River settlement on the mainland at 20, although like all other details about Indigenous deaths during the epidemic, there are many questions about the accuracy of the stories.[20] Those stories were truly disturbing. There were tales of babies being found alive trying to suckle their dead mother and of one family member gradually losing and burying all his family members until he was the only one left alive.

The outbreak was over on Thursday Island by the end of February, although it probably continued a little longer on other islands in the Torres Strait and in remote Indigenous communities at the tip of the Cape York Peninsula. The death tolls from those islands and those communities will never be known but there is some certainty about the figures for Thursday Island itself. There, 42 people died and between 800 and 1000 others were infected. While it could have been worse, it could also have been better, as it seems little had been done to prepare for the possibility of an outbreak. A century on, the course of pneumonic influenza on Thursday Island and across the surrounding islands and mainland settlements can be seen for what it really was, a vicious little battle at the end of a long and draining war.[21]

# CHAPTER 13

# Post-mortem

## I.

By the middle of 1920, health authorities around the world began to assess exactly what their countries and the wider international community had just lived through, trying to chart the course of the pandemic while identifying where it had originated and why it had assumed the particular form it did. The early findings were quite frightening; the later ones would be worse. The first publicly available assessments were put together by British medical authorities and made their way to Australia through the medium of American newspaper reports.

The early British estimate was that the pandemic had caused six million deaths around the world in just 12 months, with half that number occurring in India. By way of comparison, the authors of the British report suggested that the number of those killed or who died from wounds in the armies of France, Russia, Great Britain, Italy, Germany and Austria totalled six and a half million. When the number of casualties sustained by the "minor belligerents" was added, the total — including those still missing — would increase to just over seven million in over four years of war. Using these figures as a basis, the

British were able to conclude that the pandemic had proven to be 10 times as deadly as the war.

The report concluded with some specific examples; the deaths in the American armed forces during the 12 months they were involved in the fighting on the Western Front were 36,154. The deaths in the United States during the months of October, November and December 1918 directly attributable to Spanish flu were about 350,000, nearly10 times as many, making the disease 40 times deadlier for Americans than the war. In the United Kingdom, the threat of air raids by German aircraft, particularly Zeppelin airships, had terrorised large segments of the population. Yet the total number of casualties from those German air raids, both Zeppelins and conventional bombers, was 554. More than 10,000 civilians were killed by disease in the last year of the war.[1] As horrifying as the facts and figures were, they would prove to be serious underestimates.

———— ◦◦◦◦◦ ————

Gathering accurate information grew easier as the century progressed. The first of the "modern" epidemics was the Russian flu pandemic which swept across Europe in 1889-90, reaching Australia a year later. It was also the first epidemic to be widely reported and dissected in contemporary newspapers, enabling readers to both gain an understanding of the disease and track its movements across countries and across continents. The reporting of the Spanish flu pandemic was even better, especially when wartime censorship restrictions were removed, and when combined with the release of official figures, allowed researchers and reporters to put together a more accurate and comprehensive picture of what characteristics were unique to the disease and the true extent of the damage it wrought.

Using more sophisticated research methodologies, the initial

1919 figure of six million had grown to 20 million by 1927, and then continued to grow. A figure of 30 million was posited in 1991, and in 2007, a tentative figure of between 50 and 100 million was offered as a final estimate. At the time that all these figures were published, those putting them forward were at pains to stress that they were probably on the conservative side of the actual death toll. The final figures were also calculated by determining that the actual mortality rate from the disease was somewhere between one and two per cent of the affected population, hence the final figure of 50 to 100 million. [2]

It would be clearly established that the Spanish flu pandemic killed more people than the total number of combatants and non-combatants who perished during the First World War. Epidemiologists would determine it was second only to the Black Death plague pandemic, six centuries earlier, in terms of rates of mortality and numbers killed. Those epidemiologists also found an unusual characteristic of the 1918-20 pandemic. Most similar outbreaks claimed victims who were overwhelmingly at either end of the age spectrum, the very young and the elderly, giving the mortality profile a distinctive "U" shape. Spanish flu/pneumonic influenza had a third cohort who seemed especially vulnerable, young adults between the ages of 20 and 40. This gave the disease's mortality profile a distinct and unique "W" shape.

Other interesting facts were also uncovered. The mortality rate could vary quite widely; in 24 of the American states impacted it was 0.3 %, and even lower rates were recorded in Australia. At the other end of the scale, Bombay (Mumbai) recorded a mortality rate of 6.2%. [3] World-wide, Spanish flu killed around 20% of those who contracted it, compared to a rate of around 1% of those who caught normal, seasonal influenza. As well as the human cost, there were attempts to put some kind of economic cost on the pandemic. In the United Kingdom, for instance, actuaries calculated that insurance companies paid out twice as much in influenza claims in 1918-19 as they did in almost five years of war claims. The one thing there was never total agreement about, however, was where the disease originated.

———◦◦◦◦◦———

The first possible explanation for how the pneumonic influenza/Spanish flu pandemic arose was published in early 1920 while the disease was still active in several parts of the world, including Australia. A report originating in the United Kingdom, prepared by the Local Government Board there and first published in the United States, suggested that influenza had reached epidemic levels in China and Japan in March 1918 but was not reported in Spain until May that year. The authors of the report went on to suggest that the disease had in fact originated in China and had travelled to Europe via North America while conceding the possibility that the disease may have actually originated in North America. In the United Kingdom, the Royal Navy's Grand Fleet and elements of the British Army suffered the first casualties while the first civilian victims were found in Glasgow in May 1918.

In what was termed the "Autumn Epidemic," the principal seaports of Liverpool, Southampton and Portsmouth were next affected, but the virulence of the disease was relatively low. As the disease moved to the inland centres, its virulence seemed to increase. Systematic studies undertaken at Manchester during the summer outbreak showed that those most affected by the disease were aged between 15 and 45 years. However, this profile changed during the second wave later in the year. Then, for males, the greatest impact was on those aged from two to 15 years and, for females, between one and 45 years. The study concluded with the important observation that some of these variations could be explained by the development of different strains of the disease.[4]

The general view for a long time was that the pandemic started at an army base in Kansas in the United States, where an influenza-like illness was first reported in January 1918, one which may have been a mutation of the Avian flu virus transmitted from nearby poultry farms. The disease was then spread by infected soldiers as they travelled along the land and sea transportation routes that took them to embarkation ports on the east coast of America, often stopping at other army bases on the way. It travelled across the Atlantic with the American Expeditionary Force (AEF) and landed with them in Europe; Brest, the AEF's main disembarkation point reported an outbreak, possibly the first in Europe, in April. From the army camps behind the Western Front, the disease spread out into the civilian population. By June 1918, it had crossed the lines to Germany with the rest of western and eastern Europe following soon afterwards.

That view of the outbreak was also subsequently challenged. Another fruitful research trail tied the spread of the pneumonic influenza virus, now classed as a strain of the H1N1 virus, halfway around the world and linked that passage to the movement of Chinese labourers recruited to work behind the British and French lines on the Western Front. Researchers began with the observation that China appeared to have suffered a lower mortality rate than most other nations, suggesting that there was a degree of immunity in the population because of an earlier exposure to the virus. Plus, a respiratory illness that struck northern China in November 1917 was identified a year later by Chinese health officials as identical to the Spanish flu.

In the wake of the bloody battles of attrition on the Western Front in 1917, the Allies needed to free up as many troops for the frontlines as they could. One way to do so was to release rear-echelon soldiers for the front and this led to the formation, under joint British/French control, of the Chinese Labour Corps, a body that would eventually bring 94,000 labourers from northern China to southern England and France. Shipping those labourers around the southern tip of Africa was considered too time-consuming and would tie up too much shipping, so British officials decided to ship the labourers to Vancouver where they would be put on trains for the trip across North America to Halifax for embarkation on the ships that would carry them to Europe.

Because of anti-Chinese feelings then widespread throughout western Canada, the trains carrying the labourers were sealed. They were also guarded by special Railway Service staff who acted as security, too, when the Chinese rested in rail side camps surrounded by barbed wire. No reporting on the passage of the Chinese across the country was allowed, censors stopping the stories before they made it into print.

There is ample evidence that significant numbers of those labourers were carrying illnesses with them. The first mass movement, in late 1917, saw 25,000 Chinese labourers transported halfway around the world. Of that number, 3,000 would end up in medical quarantine with flu-like symptoms as they traversed Canada. In their isolated camps along the railway lines, their Canadian doctors treated their sore throats with castor oil before sending them back to the trains. Some of those doctors blamed the various symptoms on the "innate laziness" of the Chinese. But they were needed to support the summer battles planned for 1918 and so, on 2 March, a ship loaded with 1899 labourers left the Chinese port of Wehaiwai despite the fact that locals could not be hired because some form of plague was rampant in the port.

The first Chinese labourers arrived in southern England in January 1918 and were soon shipped across the Channel to France. There, so many of them fell ill that a designated Chinese hospital was established for them at Noyelle-sur-mer, where hundreds of them died. While not suggesting the Chinese labourers were the only source of infection, researchers believe the strain they were carrying may have mutated in spring 1918 and suddenly become much more virulent and much more contagious than before. [5]

More recently, an argument has been put forward that the appearance of pneumonic influenza almost simultaneously in places as far apart as Britain, South Africa, India and Australia during a relatively short period in the second half of 1918 indicates that there may have been a period of "seeding" when the infection arrived but remained dormant until triggered. Evidence to support the argument comes from a study of influenza spikes across nations in previous years, particularly in the United States in 1915-16. [6] Perhaps it was all of these factors; perhaps it was none and the scientists and epidemiologists have missed something.

---

The conventional wisdom for the impact of pneumonic influenza on Australia's population is that around 40% of that population of just over five million people contracted the disease and around 15,000 of those who did so perished. By way of comparison, a century on, common or seasonal influenza is estimated to be responsible for around 3,500 deaths a year. In the United States, the pandemic killed far more people than the number the country lost in the First World War. This was not true for Australia, which lost 62,000 young lives in that war.

In terms of mortality rates, Australia fared much better than the rest of the world, with a rate generally calculated as being less than 3 per thousand. By way of comparison, the rate was 4.3 in England and 5 for Europeans in New Zealand. Around the world, the mortality rate was much higher among Indigenous peoples, a trend repeated in Australia. Because of accounting methods, sometimes tinged by racism, the true number of Indigenous deaths in Australia will never be known. However, if we look at the stories from places like Thursday Island and Oodnadatta, and listen to the rumours from places like Beagle Bay and the Cape York Peninsula, we must accept that the number of Indigenous deaths was far higher than the official figures suggest.

A number of possibilities have been put forward for the lower mortality rates in Australia. Here, as in Europe, those who had caught and survived the Russian flu pandemic in the early 1890s had developed a form of immunity which helped them survive Spanish flu as well. This was also offered as a partial explanation for the "W" shaped mortality curve. Another theory is that, in Europe in particular, the disease attacked populations already weakened by the privations caused by four years of bitter warfare. Perhaps, but that does not explain why Australia's overall rate was significantly lower than that of the United States and New Zealand, two countries which — like Australia — had only been touched lightly and indirectly by the war.

There was a general belief at the time that the disease was less virulent by the time it reached Australia, but that explanation doesn't hold up when pockets of high infection and mortality rates still occurred around the country. The characteristics of the disease were the same here as elsewhere, too, with the same "W" shape and the same attack on those normally considered least likely to succumb; 99% of the deaths in Australia occurred in those aged under 65 years.[7] The lower Australian rates must be due to other factors, a significant one probably being the time Australia had to prepare for the disease which, in turn, allowed Commonwealth, state and municipal authorities to prepare for the onset, something many did well and others not so well. Maritime quarantine was in large part responsible for giving the country that extra time.[8]

There were some lessons learned in Australia, to be filed away until the next pandemic arrived. The first was that the outbreak was finite and followed a particular course. In Australian towns and cities, the period from the first case until the end of the wave was usually from six to eight weeks. In army camps and quarantine stations, and aboard troopships where people were crowded together, the cycle was sometimes reduced to three to four weeks.[9] Australians also learned that aspirin was something of a miracle drug. It did not cure pneumonic influenza but proved extremely effective in alleviating the symptoms, lowering a patient's temperature and easing the aches and pains that accompanied the disease. Production and sales of aspirin around the world more than doubled between 1918 and 1920.[10]

Inoculation was also a success story of sorts. Doctors and public health officials all eschewed claims that the Coryza vaccine produced by CSL, and its variants produced in New South Wales and elsewhere, would prevent those inoculated from contracting the disease. They did, however, claim that it could help to reduce the severity of the symptoms and despite rumours of deaths attributed to bad batches of the vaccine, it had an overall take-up of close to 20%, with a total of 819,000 Australians being given the A and B strengths of the vaccine.[11] In some localities that proportion rose to 40% and above, generally where vaccination was presented as part of a larger suite of anti-infection measures. Research in Australia and overseas later suggested that inoculation did, in fact, have something of a preventative effect. Somewhat ironically, over-congestion at some inoculation depots may actually have contributed to the spread of the disease.

Two other elements of the Australian response were of more dubious value. One was the use of face masks, compulsory at some places and at some times, voluntary at others and widely ignored in many areas. Post-epidemic research would suggest that cloth masks, such as those widely used throughout the epidemic, might actually have increased the risk of infection for the wearer.[12] But, if they did nothing else, they were a visible reminder of an invisible pathogen and highlighted the need for caution. Similarly, there was no real evidence that inhalatoria actually achieved anything beyond public awareness and a host of good stories about their construction and operation. They, too, were not without their critics. Crowding people together and then exposing them to the elements in clothes damp from a steam spray was considered especially problematic. New South Wales discontinued their use in April 1919.

----◦◦◦◦----

Not only was New South Wales the best-prepared state when pneumonic influenza finally arrived, it was the state which undertook the most comprehensive review when it was gone. To begin with, in April 1919, the state government appointed a Committee of Claims, *"to deal with the various claims made for compensation on account of loss sustained by reason of the closing down of business places, etc., consequent upon the influenza epidemic..."* [13] The claims were actually against restrictions imposed by the government to combat the epidemic, and were facilitated by the passage of the Influenza Epidemic Relief Act 1919, given Royal assent on 23 December 1919.

The Act allowed claims for business-related rent, rates and taxes, interest, insurance premiums, wages, living expenses and lighting charges. It stimulated an avalanche of claims, the majority of which were not covered by the terms of the act. The most common claimants were private schools, wine and billiard saloons, hotels, picture theatres and live performance theatres. Out of claims totalling in excess of £200,000, the New South Wales government would pay out just over £30,000.

New South Wales was also able to compile the most detailed and complete picture of what happened during the outbreak. Between January and September 1919, pneumonic influenza killed at least 6,387 people in the state, infecting as many as 290,000 people in Sydney alone. Densely populated areas suffered the highest mortality rates, with metropolitan Sydney recording some 3,902 deaths, a figure that represented just over 60% of the state's fatalities. Within that death count, males represented 60% and of that number nearly 40% were industrial, blue collar workers. That was the single largest occupational group and was equal to the combined number of deaths in the commercial, primary production and transport and communication sectors. In comparison, just 208 deaths came from the professional class of male workers.

Even with all the hard work, staff shortages meant that there were never more than 2,000 hospital beds available in Sydney between January and September. During that same period, there were 25,000 hospital admissions of people suffering from pneumonic influenza. Little wonder, then, that some 814 medical and nursing staff themselves contracted the disease that year. That was from a total primary nursing and medical staff of 1488, and while the figure was in excess of 50% of that staff, only 12 of those who contracted the disease died, a figure in line with the general mortality rate in the wider population. Where there was a significantly higher death rate among health workers, such as at the Woodman's Point Quarantine Station, it was attributed to the staff having no prior exposure to the disease. [14]

The other reason New South Wales' efforts to moderate the impact of pneumonic influenza were as successful as they were could be found in the uniform, state-wide approach adopted there. Using predominantly volunteer medical practitioners, 1260 inoculation depots were established across the state. In them, more than 404,000 people were inoculated with 819,636 doses of vaccine being administered in a six-month period. This represented about a quarter of the population of the state, while in Sydney the proportion was much higher, up to 40% in parts.

New South Wales was also home to one of the sadder little stories to come out of the larger tragedy of the pandemic. At the outbreak of the war, hundreds of Germans and Austrians living in Australia were rounded up as enemy aliens and placed in internment camps. The largest of these camps in New South Wales was at Liverpool, and there were still hundreds of internees held there when pneumonic influenza struck in early 1919. Dozens of internees had died in the camp during the war, some from communicable diseases, and now numbers of others died at a time when they should have been home with their families, whether that home was in Australia or overseas.

Some 190 internees were buried in the Liverpool Cemetery and in the years after the war the Australian government was approached by the German War Graves Commission which asked that they be allowed to place headstones on the graves of the German nationals. It was a request supported by the Imperial War Graves Commission, which believed the Germans had been exemplary in the care and maintenance they had provided for Australian war graves in their territory. Before they proceeded with that project, however, the German Commission spent a considerable amount of money creating a distinctive memorial in Sydney's Rookwood Cemetery. On it were inscribed the names of German nationals who died while interned in Australia.[15]

---

At the other end of the organisational scale was Queensland, who just seemed to muck through. Officially, at the end of the epidemic, the state's death toll was less than one thousand, a figure that may actually have been around half of the actual total because of glaring omissions and shoddy record-keeping. The epidemic also highlighted the fragility of the state's infrastructure, especially in the area of transportation. Recent research[16] has illustrated how the disease left south-eastern Queensland, carried aboard coastal shipping to central and northern Queensland seaports. There, the railway lines built to move people and produce between the hinterland and the coast now carried pneumonic influenza as well.

When that coastal shipping was significantly reduced, due to a combination of industrial action and Commonwealth intervention, large parts of rural and regional Queensland came perilously close to losing people to starvation as well as disease. That they didn't was due in large part to the actions of individuals within government rather than to the government itself. In that at least, Queensland exemplified how Australia survived the pandemic as well as it did.

## II.

John Cumpston was as responsible as any individual for Australia's success in keeping the death toll as low as it was. In some respects, his actions once the outbreak occurred are puzzling; when a valid state response clashed with Commonwealth policy, he would blindly back the Commonwealth even when it was demonstrably wrong. However, it was what he did before the outbreak that was so effective in the end. Cumpston championed the November 1918 medical conference in Melbourne and there pushed for unanimity on a number of measures. Quarantine was to be the first line of defence and, behind that, layers of preparation and prophylaxis at the state and municipal levels. The agreements reached there quickly fell apart but the principles behind them didn't, and that was John Cumpston's greatest contribution.

In 1921, Cumpston was made Director-General of the new Commonwealth Health Department while also retaining his position as Director of Quarantine. A number of awards came his way during the next decade, including a Companion to the Order of St. Michael and St. George (CMG) from the King. In 1927, the League of Nations Health Committee recommended to the League's General Assembly that Dr. John Cumpston be appointed an Assessor, a specialist advisor to the League and its peak award in public health. It was an appointment Cumpston said was one of the highest honours a public health official could be paid. [17] John Cumpston died in his adopted home town of Canberra in 1954.

Jeanie O'Kane, the redoubtable mother of Rosa, was determined that her daughter's death at Woodman's Point while nursing ill soldiers, would not pass without notice. At home in Charters Towers, she organised a fundraising campaign to generate enough money to erect a suitable memorial over Rosa's grave. As that was being organised, the Defence Department notified Jeanie of their intention to remove the remains of all the service personnel who had been buried at Woodman's Point to a new war cemetery in Perth. Jeanie stood her ground, saying that she wanted her daughter's remains to stay where they had been buried with such simple grace in December 1918. Nurse Hilda Williams' family took the same stand and today the young nurses still lie side by side at Woodman's Point, Rosa's grave marked by an impressive granite obelisk and Hilda's by a simple wooden cross. In the century since the nurses' deaths, much of the old Quarantine Station has reverted to bushland but the graves are maintained by the Friends of the Woodman's Point Recreation Camp. [18]

Jeanie O'Kane also applied for a war pension in the months after Rosa's death. Originally rejected, Jeanie wrote to the Governor of Queensland, Hamilton Goold-Adams, seeking his support for her application. She described how Rosa *"made the supreme sacrifice when she volunteered to nurse the pneumonic influenza patients of the plague-stricken transport* Boonah." Jeanie said that her daughter died of the very disease she and the other nurses were battling, and went on to describe her daughter as, *"a fine type of Australian girl, of marked ability, and a girl of great possibilities had God spared her life."* [19]

Jeanie O'Kane reapplied for a pension, this time documenting her dependence on Rosa during the last 12 months of her daughter's life. Her claim was re-assessed and she was granted a pension of two pounds a fortnight. Jeanie would eventually return to teaching, and in coming years worked at Liontown, near Rockhampton, and Gympie before returning to Charters Towers where she taught until her retirement in 1924. Jeanie Elizabeth O'Kane passed away on 6 July 1936 at the age of 77, survived by her two sons and their families. Until the day she died, Jeanie said that losing Rosa was the greatest tragedy in her life.

———◆◆◆———

At their courts martial in Melbourne, both George "Gunner" Yates and George Friend pleaded not guilty to all charges, and even the prosecuting officer conceded that there had been no mutiny aboard the *Somali* and that none of the returning soldiers had broken quarantine. This seemed to have had only passing impact on the court and both men were sentenced to terms of detention, Yates to 60 days and Friend to 30. With regard to both men, though, the court did recommend mercy on the grounds that discipline aboard the *Somali* was, *"to a certain extent, relaxed."* The court also pointed out that quarantine authorities had not informed Major Arnell of their intentions within a reasonable period. Military reviewing authorities chose not to exercise mercy and ordered that the men be held at Victoria Barracks in St Kilda Road until they could be transferred to their own districts.[20]

George Yates' period of detention did not work out as he had been led to believe it would. He had expected to serve his sentence in Adelaide but was taken from Victoria Barracks to the Broadmeadows Army Camp. From there he was taken to Sydney where he believed he was to be placed on a ship bound back to Adelaide. He wasn't, instead being lodged in the old Darlinghurst Gaol where he spent most of his time locked in a cell. When his father became ill, Yates was taken back to Adelaide, arriving there on 12 April; his father died two days later. Yates was then placed in a compound at Fort Largs where he spent his days doing menial labouring and cleaning tasks. His only consolation was that his wife could visit him each day until he was released on 3 May.[21]

After his release, George Friend returned to a life of anonymity in Sydney while George Yates went in another direction. Yates did not lose his parliamentary seat of Adelaide because of his conviction, but he did lose it at the next general election in 1920. However, he won it back in 1922 and held it until Labour suffered a landslide defeat in 1931. From then until he turned 78, George "Gunner" Yates continued to run for parliament, sometimes as a Labour candidate and sometimes as an independent, sometimes for state parliament and sometimes in a federal election; all of these candidacies were unsuccessful. George Yates died in Adelaide in 1954, aged 88 years.

———◇◇◇◇◇———

Every crisis throws up heroes, and the pneumonic influenza pandemic in Australia between 1918 and 1920 was no different to other crises in that regard. Some of those heroes were public servants like John Cumpston, some were elected officials at Commonwealth, state and municipal levels, and many were anonymous volunteers doing bicycle patrols through suburban streets, babysitting in homes visited by the disease or preparing meals for those who were unable to prepare their own. Then there were the frontline medical professionals, several of whom have been detailed in earlier pages, who knowingly put their own health on the line day after day in those dangerous times.

Richard Fetherston, who did such magnificent work in the City of Prahran, continued in his various medical roles well into the 1930s. He died at his home in St Kilda in June 1943, predeceased by his wife and survived by two sons and a daughter. His life and work are commemorated through the delivery of the triennial Richard Fetherston

Memorial Lecture, held in Melbourne and expounding on a subject related to maternal welfare.

When the outbreak was over, Nurse Mary Kelly returned to Adelaide from Oodnadatta, resigned from nursing and opened a hairdressing salon for ladies in Pirie Street, Adelaide, almost equidistant from the Exhibition Hospital and the Jubilee Oval.

Simon and Kate Joel and their young family remained in the family home in Stirling Street, Bunbury, after the epidemic passed. Simon established his own medical practice in 1922 and also developed an interest in dairy farming, buying and developing several properties in the district. In late 1934, Simon took his family to Melbourne to spend time with relatives there before sailing to England to catch up with Kate's family. A few days before they were due to depart, on 18 December 1934, Simon was involved in a terrible road accident when he pulled out to pass a tram on the wrong side in Wellington Parade, Melbourne, and crashed head-on into an oncoming tram. Simon died of his injuries on 19 February 1935.

Dr. Peter Lalor and George Haddow pushed hard to develop an effective vaccine for pneumonic influenza while also trying to save as many lives as possible working at Tasmania's Mental Diseases Hospital in New Norfolk. They were not successful in this, but their research provided a fruitful direction for others to follow. Peter Lalor returned to Victoria after the epidemic had subsided to take up the position of Medical Superintendent at the Sunbury Hospital. While there, he passed away suddenly in 1927, aged just 39. George Haddow became a senior bacteriologist in Tasmania's Department of Public Health while also working at the Royal Hobart Hospital. In March 1939, the 59-year-old delivered a lecture at that hospital and afterwards, heading home, suffered a massive heart attack and died in the street outside.

The spectre of pneumonic influenza hung over Australia for a long time. Throughout the 1920s and 1930s, newspapers printed reports of possible outbreaks such as in in Broome and Bega, and on hotspots of seasonal influenza that seemed to be unusually virulent or unusually contagious. Somewhere in those reports, the words "pneumonic influenza" would inevitably appear. The Great Depression of the early 1930s removed some of the focus, as did the rise of totalitarian states. The last vestiges of a focus on influenza pandemics were swept away by the human disaster that was the Second World War.

Despite the threat of a Cold War that might suddenly heat up, and the insidious danger from international terrorism that was increasingly front and centre from the 1970s onwards, the second half of the Twentieth Century was markedly better than the first half, in Western nations at least. But then, as one century segued into another, new threats emerged from the natural world. Avian flu and Ebola, SARS and MERS followed one another in quite rapid succession until, a century after the pneumonic influenza pandemic, a new pandemic — COVID-19 — emerged to once more challenge public health systems.

Dimly remembered lessons and experiences from the Spanish flu of 1918-20 suddenly became apposite, relevant to the threat posed by the new viral disease emerging from Asia. Protecting the borders became paramount. Where once quarantine had been the main weapon, a century on the modes of international travel had changed to the extent that quarantine stations and quarantine inspections were never going to be adequate. Instead, the federal approach — as it was clearly a federal issue — was to close the borders to all but returning Australians and to place those in a form of quarantine, self-imposed isolation, when they did return. A century on, a main threat of contagion emerged at Australia's major seaport; the ocean liner *Ruby Princess* would be the 21st Century equivalent to the *Niagara* and the *Boonah*.

Dr. Brendan Murphy became something of a natural successor to Dr. John Cumpston, while the states' Chief Medical Officers stood in the footprints of Richard Fetherston and Simon Joel. The arguments between states over border closures and restrictions on gatherings and movements were refreshingly familiar, as were the debates over the use of facemasks and medicines. Perhaps the only major item missing from the Spanish flu pandemic was the use of inhalatoria. Otherwise, Covid-19 called forth a lot of memories as well as a major concern. In an era of climate change, where extreme weather events that statistically occurred once a century now occur on an almost annual basis, epidemics are also becoming pandemics with increasing frequency. From Swine flu to Avian flu and from SARS to MERS, there has been a worrying increase in pandemic disease this century.

A century ago, Australia survived the first of the modern pandemics, albeit at some cost, and looks to have survived the latest. There are lessons to be learned from both, lessons that just might help us survive the next.

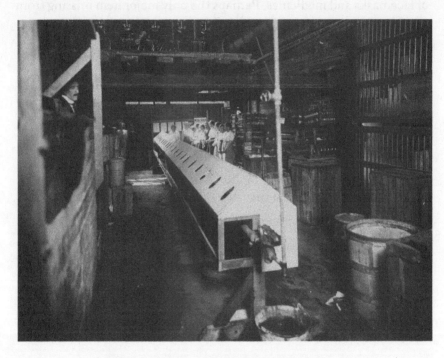

*Workers waiting to use the 'inhalatorium' at the*
*Kodak Australasia Pty Ltd factory in Abbotsford, 1919*
Museums Victoria

# The long voyage of the *Boonah*

For the men aboard the *Boonah,* the days must have seemed interminable and some of them no doubt hoped for a slight cough or a rise in body temperature because that would at least get them back onto dry land. There was not a lot for them to do, the smell of the ship just wouldn't go away and there was always the chance that, rather than a mild dose of pneumonic influenza, they might develop a full-on infection in which case their troubles might be over a lot sooner than they hoped. Quarantine authorities had deemed it necessary for a full week to elapse with no further infections aboard the ship before it could be declared free of the disease, a clean ship, and then allowed to go on its way. With new cases occurring on-board every day, the date of departure just kept getting pushed back.

Their plight did not go unnoticed by the general public of Perth where there was a genuine fear of pneumonic influenza as well as a real desire for the men aboard the ship to be treated with compassion. The public also recognised that there was a tension between those competing priorities, and the letters to the editors of the major Perth newspapers at that time reflect that tension. They reflect anger growing to outrage at the idea of keeping healthy troops penned up on a ship where new infections were reported every day; to many it seemed the logical outcome of that policy would be the inevitable infection of everyone aboard.

Landing them all at Woodman's Point would simply overwhelm the facilities there, and there was still a lot of disquiet about the location of the quarantine station on the mainland anyway. Many letter writers, reflecting wider community concerns, pointed out what was — to them at least — the obvious solution. There were two significant islands just off the coast from Fremantle, Rottnest and Garden Islands. Both had facilities and infrastructure capable of supporting large numbers of people while they passed through quarantine and, being islands, both offered containment and isolation.

The initial response from state health and Commonwealth quarantine authorities was that holding the men aboard *Boonah* was the most appropriate response as it meant they were better able to keep checking the men as they were together in a contained area rather than spread out somewhere else. It appeared to be a hollow claim when those same authorities were urging the general public to keep themselves isolated and not congregate anywhere in any significant numbers. As the wrangling between the various authorities and an unedifying exchange between the State Minister for Health, Sir Hal Colebatch, and key federal figures continued, local opinion solidified and, led by the Returned Soldiers' League, protest meetings were held, culminating in a major demonstration, attended by thousands, on the banks of the Swan River. A semi-ultimatum was delivered by that meeting: do something about the men on the ship or we will.

The build-up of pressure produced a result. After sitting at anchor in Gage Roads for nine days, *Boonah* was declared free of infection and allowed to depart for Port Adelaide at 2 p.m. on the afternoon of Friday 20 December. The folly of the original declaration became apparent when four more cases of influenza aboard the ship were reported within

24 hours of that departure. Rather than return the men to Woodman's Point, they were isolated from the others and put ashore at the quarantine station at the next port of call, Albany.

That stop was necessary because *Boonah* was not carrying enough coal to make the run across to Port Adelaide with what she carried in her bunkers. While anchored in Gage Roads, authorities had not allowed her to be refuelled over concerns that the infection might be brought ashore during the process. They, apparently, did not have the same fears about Albany but the waterside workers there certainly did. Through their union, they expressed grave fears about the dangers they would face when resupplying *Boonah.* The union negotiated with all the relevant authorities, including the *Boonah's* owners, seeking an agreement for compensation for any labourer who became ill, lost time at work or had to be quarantined for influenza after working on the ship.

When it became obvious that there was still a lot of negotiating to do, the simplest of all solutions was found. A coal hulk was loaded and towed out to the *Boonah* where 400 men took 12 hours to load 340 tons of coal into the bunkers. At 8 a.m. on 24 December, Boonah finally departed on the last leg of the journey to Port Adelaide.

After spending Christmas Day at sea, *Boonah* arrived at Port Adelaide at 3 p.m. on 28 December. Fourteen new cases of influenza had occurred as the ship crossed the Bight and those men were immediately taken to the isolation hospital on Torrens Island. The other troops remained on board overnight and at 8 a.m. the following morning they were also transferred by lighters to the Torrens Island Quarantine Station for their compulsory period in isolation. *Boonah* was back where the voyage to the war had started10 weeks' earlier. The men enjoyed a hot bath, followed by a hot meal, and then settled in to enjoy their stay on the island.

They found conditions on Torrens Island a great improvement on everything they had experienced in the preceding two months. They were accommodated in wooden buildings, had adequate ablutions facilities and the food was plentiful and of a high quality. During the summer days there they had plenty of opportunity for sports and other outdoor activities during the daytime although they found there was little to do during the evenings. Those who had avoided contracting the disease, together with those who had recovered from it, were held for three weeks on Torrens Island, and there was not another death among the *Boonah* troops during that time.

At the end of that time, the troops were told they could now go home. The South Australian troops were simply taken back to the mainland and given travel vouchers, but it was a bit more complicated for the others. Some 170 Victorians opted to travel by train to Melbourne, arriving there on 20 January 1919. A number of other Victorians, plus those from the other eastern states and a small contingent of New Zealanders were taken aboard the troopship *Leicestershire,* which also sailed to Melbourne, arriving on 22 January. From Melbourne, troops from New South Wales and Queensland returned home by train while those bound for Tasmania crossed Bass Strait aboard the ferry *Loongana.* By the end of the month, they were all home.

---

By that time, most of those taken from the *Boonah* to Woodman's Point were also being released and heading home. Twenty-seven of them would forever remain at Woodman's Point, buried in the small cemetery there alongside the four nurses who died while doing their duty in nursing gravely ill soldiers.

---

*Boonah,* too, eventually returned home to Germany. In 1925, she was purchased by the North German Line of Bremen who promptly renamed her *Witram.* In 1937, she was renamed once more, becoming the *Buenos Aires,* and at the outbreak of the Second World War she was requisitioned by the German Navy. While serving as a troop transport, *Buenos Aires* was sunk by a British submarine, HMS Narwhal, between Denmark and Sweden in May 1940.

———◦◦◦◦◦———

*Boonah's* companion vessel returning to Australia across the Indian Ocean, and carrying a number of doomed nurses, was the *Wyreema.* After that voyage, *Wyreema* was used to carry the French General Pau and his staff back to their home country, via the Mediterranean after the French had concluded an official visit to the Antipodes. From southern France, the liner sailed to Liverpool where her crew were struck down with pneumonic influenza; out of a total of 140 crew, all but four contracted the disease and 15 of them died. She returned to Australia via Salonica, collecting Australian service personnel en route, and after being reconditioned in Sydney, was returned to her owners in September 1920.

# ENDNOTES

## Introduction

1. *www.rba.gov.au/calculator/annualPreDecimal.html*

## Chapter 1. Incubation

1. *Argus,* Melbourne, 29.5.18, p. 9
2. *Courier,* Brisbane, 26.11.18, p. 6 provided its readers with a potted history of influenza as it was then understood, and that article was reprinted in many other newspapers. However, quite a lot of what contemporary scientists, and astrologers, thought about influenza was wrong. It is caused by a virus and there are three types, A, B and C, with Type A causing the most severe infections. The virus itself is constantly mutating making it impossible for humans to develop permanent immunity.
3. *West Australian,* Perth, 3.6.18, p. 4
4. Ibid, 26.6.18, p. 7. See also *Herald,* Melbourne, 22.6.18, p. 9
5. See, for example, the *Mail,* Adelaide, 22.6.18, p. 1, *Star,* Ballarat, 15.7.18, p. 1, *Journal,* Adelaide, 15.8.18, p. 1 and Beaumont, p. 443
6. The Broadmeadows Army Camp influenza outbreak was widely reported in Victoria and interstate. The most comprehensive reporting was in the *Herald,* Melbourne, 16.8.18, p. 8, 17.8.18, p. 17, the *Age,* Melbourne, 17.8.18, p. 12, 19.8.18, p. 6 and the *Telegraph,* Brisbane, 17.8.18
7. *Age,* Melbourne, 9.10.18, p. 9

8. *Age,* Newcastle, 21.9.18, p. 1

9. *Sun,* Sydney, 26.9.18, p. 1, *Sun,* Newcastle, 28.9.18, p. 5

10. *Herald,* Melbourne, 24.9.18, p. 1

11. *Bathurst Times,* 28.9.18, p. 3

12. *Daily Telegraph,* Launceston, 12.10.18, p. 8, *Advertiser,* Adelaide, 5.10.18, p. 9 and *Herald,* Melbourne, 5.10.18, p. 15

13. *Register,* Adelaide, 7.10.18, p. 9

14. Ibid, 9.10.18, p. 7

15. NAA: A2:1919/452. Watt, a Victorian, was Treasurer in the Billy Hughes Nationalist government of the day. When Hughes went to London in April 1918, Watt became acting Prime Minister, a position he held until Hughes returned from the Versailles Peace Conference in August 1919.

16. Ibid

17. *Age,* Melbourne, 9.10.18, p. 10

18. *Daily Telegraph,* Sydney, 10.10.18, p. 1 and 15.10.18, p. 4

19. *Daily Telegraph,* Sydney, 29.10.18, p. 8

20. *Sun,* Sydney, 26.10.18, p. 5

21. *Daily Telegraph,* Sydney, 16.10.18, p. 8

22. Ibid, 24.10.18, p. 4

## Chapter 2. Prophylaxis

1. NAA: A2:1919/452. Imperial protocols at the time required head of government communications between members of the British Empire i.e. Prime Minister to Prime Minister, to be channelled through the respective heads of state, i.e. Governor-General to Governor-General.

2. Ibid

3. Ibid

4. For good examples of these articles, see *Daily Telegraph,* Sydney,

16.10.18, p. 8, *Herald,* Melbourne, 12.10.18, p. 7 and *Daily News,* Perth, 12.10.18, p. 7

5.   The telegram from the Governor of Ceylon is found in A2: 1919/452 while the reports from around the world are contained in the *Herald,* Melbourne, 22.10.18, p. 7, *Argus,* Melbourne, 28.10.18, p. 4 and 29.10.18, p. 5.

6.   The description and figures are based on a detailed outline of the process that appeared in the *Herald,* Melbourne, 30.11.18, p. 22

7.   NAA: A2:1919/452

8.   In 1934, the Coast Hospital would be renamed Prince Henry's Hospital.

9.   *Courier,* Brisbane, 21.11.18, p. 7

10.   *Herald,* Melbourne, 12.10.18, p. 17

11.   *Telegraph,* Brisbane, 19.10.18, p. 7

12.   This section is based on interviews Dr. Robertson gave as well as extracts from the Victorian Health Department's pamphlet. Additional details, *Herald,* Melbourne, 6.11.18, p. 8, 8.11.18, p. 3 and 18.11.18, p. 8

13.   Ibid, 22.11.18, p. 4

14.   *Argus,* Melbourne, 27.11.18, p. 4

## Chapter 3. An Ounce of Prevention

1.   *Daily Telegraph,* Sydney, 23.11.18, p. 1

2.   *Argus,* Melbourne, 22.11.18, p. 6

3.   The full letter was originally published in the *Herald,* Melbourne, 28.11.18, p. 13

4.   Also known as Western Samoa, the island group had been a German possession until a small New Zealand military force convinced the local German garrison to surrender.

5. HMAS *Encounter* was an elderly light cruiser that had spent most of the First World War patrolling in the Indian and Pacific Oceans.

6. HMAS *Fantome* was a sloop and had also spent most of the recent war on patrol duties, operating firstly out of Singapore and later out of Suva.

7. NAA: A2: 1919/452 provides most of the information for this section.

8. The estimated death toll in Samoa was between eight and nine thousand in a country whose population was less than a hundredth of Australia's. Se Shanks for additional detail on the Samoan outbreak.

9. Ibid

10. Ibid

11. *Herald,* Melbourne, 23.11.18, p. 16

12. Ibid, 30.11.18, p. 22

## Chapter 4. Woodman's Point

1. *Daily Herald,* Adelaide, 24.10.18, p. 3

2. Although now referred to as "Woodman Point", all contemporary accounts refer to the site as "Woodman's Point" and that is the terminology I will use.

3. *Daily News,* Perth, 24.10.18, p. 7

4. Mitchell was also a well-known Perth sportsman who before the war had played senior football for Perth in the Western Australian Football League.

5. *Telegraph,* Brisbane, 19.10.18, p. 7. One of those in isolation, a Chinese crewman, died at Woodman's Point on 4 November but the cause of his death was unclear.

6. Much of the detail about Arthur Thwaites in this section is taken from his Army file, now held in the Australian Archives.

7. One of the infantry reinforcements was Private Oscar Clifford, and he would later write of his experiences for his local newspaper in

New South Wales. It is a fascinating document and can be found in the *Windsor and Richmond Gazette,* 10.1.19, p. 10

8. HMAT A 36 had not always been known as the *Boonah*. Built for the Deutsche-Australis Line, based in Hamburg, she was originally named *Melbourne* and regularly sailed, via Antwerp, to Adelaide, Melbourne and Sydney. Launched in 1911, the ship was seized by Australian authorities in Sydney upon the outbreak of war and subsequently renamed and put into service as a troop transport. Manned by Australian officers and crews, *Boonah* would complete five return journeys between Australia and the United Kingdom, four carrying troops and one carrying just cargo.

9. That would prove to be quite a lengthy process and the men were still in prison when *Boonah* departed for Australia. They would return on a later troopship.

10. *Windsor and Richmond Gazette,* 10.1.19, p. 10

11. At some point after leaving Fremantle but before arriving at Durban, Thwaites had been promoted to the substantive rank of sergeant.

12. NAA: B2455: Thwaites, Arthur Charles

13. Jeanie's maiden name was also O'Kane, making her transition to marriage just that little bit easier.

14. After her children grew up and set out on their own journeys, Jeanie O'Kane sold the newspaper and returned to her first love of teaching, a career she pursued well into her sixties.

15. *Wyreema* was an Australian steamship used primarily on domestic runs with additional cross-Tasman voyages. Requisitioned by the Australian government on 23 September 1918, this was her first voyage as a troopship.

16. Many of the reflections and observations in this section come from a diary written by Susie Cone, one of the volunteer nurses, as they are recorded in Ruth Rae's *Scarlet Poppies*.

17. Rae, p.92

18. *West Australian,* Perth, 25.4.33, p. 4

19. Not all the funerals were as dignified as Rosa O'Kane's. One of the soldiers in quarantine would later write that, *"One of the nurses recently buried had her coffin placed in the grave by the bearers and left there to await the completion of the ceremony by the quarantine minister."* *Windsor and Richmond Gazette,* 10.1.19, p. 10

20. Ibid

21. This section is based on a later letter written to the Perth *Daily News,* and published on page 8 of its edition of 12 August 1937. The author of the letter was Dorothea Foster, a social activist and prolific letter writer. Foster herself served in the AANS during the First World War and clearly knew what she was writing about. The claims she made have not been rebutted.

22. The most comprehensive and accurate accounts of this incident were those written by participants in the events. Three such accounts appeared in newspapers, the *West Australian,* 28.9.29, p. 5, the Perth *Australian,* 24.12.18, p. 1, and the Mount Gambier *Border Watch,* 28.8.30, p. 2. This final account does, however, contain some factual inaccuracies.

23. *Australian,* Perth, 24.12.18, p. 1

## Chapter 5. Hiatus: December 1918-January 1919

1. NAA: A2: 1919/452

2. In 1928, a deeply depressed Wray would commit suicide by crawling into a large drain and cutting his own throat.

3. *West Australian,* Perth, 10.12.18, p. 4

4. The descriptions of the Torrens Island Quarantine Station are taken primarily from an article in the *Advertiser,* Adelaide, 25.12.18, p. 9

5. *Mercury,* Hobart, 4.12.18, p. 4

6.  Ibid, 9.12.18, p. 4
7.  Ibid, 27.12.18, p. 5
8.  *Herald,* Melbourne, 7.12.18, p. 20
9.  Ibid, 14.12.18, p. 14
10. Hodgson, p. 65
11. *Herald,* Melbourne, 2.1.19, p. 1
12. Ibid, 23.1.19, p. 14
13. Ibid. The Melbourne *Herald* provided the most comprehensive and detailed reports on the outbreak of pneumonic influenza. This quote was from one of several reports on the same page on 23 January. Updates were possible as the *Herald* was published in several editions each day.
14. Ibid, 24.1.19, p. 9
15. Ibid, 25.1.19, p. 3
16. *Daily Telegraph,* Sydney, 28.1.19, p. 5
17. *Herald,* Melbourne, 27.1.18, p. 5
18. Ibid, 28.1.19, p. 1

**Chapter 6. Public Policy, Private Pain**
1.  A2: 1919/452, 24.3.19
2.  Ibid
3.  McQueen
4.  Saint, p. 77
5.  Hodgson, p. 49
6.  Michael Adams
7.  Hodgson, p. 49
8.  McQueen
9.  A2: 1919/452
10. A1: 1919/2364

## Chapter 7. The Heart of the Matter: New South Wales

1. That civilian was never identified and never traced.
2. Quoted in Saint, p. 68
3. Most thought the camp would only be needed until the end of February but it would remain in place until 17 May 1919 and, during the three months of its existence, at least 3715 people would pass through it.
4. According to the Queensland government, the fees they charged covered only three quarters of the costs they incurred. The same regime was used at the second quarantine camp Queensland established at Coolangatta. See Hodgson, p. 114
5. The full story is given in considerable detail in the New South Wales Health Department's post-epidemic report, p. 152
6. Saint, p. 67
7. NSW Health Department, p. 159
8. Ibid, p. 150
9. Ibid, p. 160

## Chapter 8. A State of (Some) Denial: Victoria

1. Melbourne *Herald*, 28.1.19, p. 1
2. Melbourne *Herald*, 29.1.19, p. 1
3. Ibid
4. Melbourne *Herald*, 4.2.19, p. 8
5. Melbourne *Herald*, 4.2.19, p. 9
6. Beaumont, p. 524
7. *Age*, Melbourne, 4.3.19, p. 4
8. *Herald*, Melbourne, 17.2.19, p. 8
9. *Age*, Melbourne, 3.3.19, p. 5
10. *Herald*, Melbourne, 17.2.19, p. 8
11. *Telegraph*, Prahran, 1.2.19, p. 4 and *Herald*, Melbourne, 28.1.19, p. 9

12. *Age,* Melbourne, 1.2.19, p. 1

13. *Standard,* Malvern, 8.2.19, p. 2 and *Telegraph,* Prahran, 8.2.19, p. 5

14. *Standard,* Malvern, 15.2.19, p. 3

15. *Herald,* Melbourne, 15.2.19, p. 10

16. *Age,* Melbourne, 7.2.19, p. 8

17. *Telegraph,* Prahran, 1.2.19, p. 4

18. City of Prahran, *Annual Report — 1919*

19. Ibid

20. *Herald,* Melbourne, 22.2.19, p. 1

21. *Age,* Melbourne, 4.3.19, p. 4

22. *Weekly Times,* Melbourne, 12.4.19, p. 32

23. Armadale was one of the schools that hadn't reopened, its students taught in a number of local Sunday School classrooms.

24. *Age,* Melbourne, 21.4.19, p. 4

25. *Age,* Melbourne, 30.4.19, p. 10

26. Ibid, 1.5.19, p. 6

## Chapter 9. South Australia: A Big Picnic and a Little Mutiny

1. Mitcham Army Camp was located where the suburb of Colonel Light Gradens now stands.

2. *Register,* Adelaide, 30.1.19, p. 7 and *Daily Herald,* Adelaide, 30.1.19, p. 3

3. *Register,* Adelaide, 30.1.19, p. 7

4. *Advertiser,* Adelaide, 25.12.18, p. 7

5. Regarded as one of the strictest disciplinarians in the Australian Army, and a stickler for rules and regulations, Antill had served at Gallipoli, Palestine and on the Western Front. Found unfit for active service because of ill-health, Antill had returned to Australia in 1917.

6. *Register,* Adelaide, 30.1.19, p. 7

7. Created as a sports ground in 1895, Jubilee Oval also hosted segments of the annual Royal Adelaide Show.
8. *Advertiser,* Adelaide, 26.2.19, p. 7
9. Marie Larsen
10. *Age,* Melbourne, 3.4.19, p. 8
11. Kako, et al, p. 51
12. *News,* Adelaide, 12.1.31, p. 4
13. Ibid, 10.12.26, p. 13
14. Kako, et al

**Chapter 10. Queensland: A Little Late, a Little Light**

1. Helen Smith
2. Hodgson, p. 118
3. Ibid
4. Ibid, p. 54
5. See Wood, Buch and Smith for further details.
6. Kako, et. al

**Chapter 11. Western Australia: Friction at the Edges**

1. *Kalgoorlie Miner,* 30.1.19, p. 3
2. Ibid, 31.1.19, p. 6
3. Ibid, 6.2.19, p. 3
4. Based on the health and well-being theories of an Irish nobleman, the various international branches of the Fresh Air League established facilities, generally campsites, for children in particular, places where they could spend most of their time in the clean, fresh air.
5. *South West Times,* Bunbury, 9.12.18, p. 3
6. Ibid, 14.12.18, p. 5
7. *Herald,* Bunbury, 18.12.18, p. 2
8. *South West Times,* Bunbury, 11.2.19, p. 1

9.  Ibid, 10.6.19, p. 3

10. *Herald,* Bunbury, 28.6.19, p. 5

11. *South West Times,* Bunbury, 28.6.19, p. 5

12. Ibid, 14.6.19, p. 5

13. Ibid, 17.7. 19, p. 3

14. *Herald,* Bunbury, 3.12.19, p. 1, and *South West Times,* Bunbury, 19.12.19, p. 8

15. Kako, et al, p. 49

16. *Advocate,* Burnie, 13.2.20, p. 4

## Chapter 12. Tasmania and T.I. : The Outliers

1.  NAA: A2: 1919/967

2.  *Mercury,* Hobart, 18.8.19, p. 5

3.  There was soon a booming market in oranges as many people believed they would stave off the illness.

4.  *Mercury,* Hobart, 19.8.19, p. 5

5.  Ibid, 28.8.19, p. 5

6.  Ibid, 27.8.19, p. 5

7.  *Examiner,* Launceston, 17.9.19, p. 4

8.  *Mercury,* Hobart, 14.6.54, p. 4, and *Advocate,* Burnie, 22.4.32, p. 8

9.  *World,* Hobart, 13.10.19, p. 3

10. *Zeehan and Dundas Herald,* 27.9.19, p. 2

11. *Advocate,* Burnie, 13.4.20, p. 4

12. *Mercury,* Hobart, 27.10.19, p. 5

13. *Advocate,* Burnie, 24.10.19, p. 2

14. *World,* Hobart, 6.11.19, p. 4

15. For a more complete outline of the men work, see *Advocate,* Burnie, 7.11.19, p. 2.

16. Morris, a previous Medical Superintendent at the Mental Diseases

Hospital at New Norfolk, had only been in the job since May 1919, prior to which he had served with the AIF in the Middle East.

17. Subsequent accounting would revise the total number of deaths up to 240 but at a rate that was the lowest in Australia. See Kako, et al.

18. *World,* Hobart, 21.10.19 and *Mercury,* Hobart, 27.11.20, p. 13

19. *Express & Telegraph,* Adelaide, 13.2.20, p.2

20. *West Australian,* Perth, 21.2.20, p. 7. Try as I might, I was unable to identify the location of this settlement.

21. Unless specifically cited, this section is based on a number of reports that appeared in the *Express & Telegraph,* Adelaide, 13.2.22, p. 2, *West Australian,* Perth, 21.2.20, p. 5, *Courier,* Brisbane, 11.2.20, p. 7 and *The Week,* Brisbane, 20.2.20, p. 22

## Chapter 13. Post-mortem

1. *Times,* Victor Harbour, 7.5.20, p. 4

2. Saint, p. 84

3. Ibid, p. 71

4. *Mercury,* Hobart, 17.1.20, p. 7

5. Dan Vergana

6. Saint, p. 70

7. Helen Smith; another writer attributes this phenomenon to something known as "cytokine storm," where the immune systems in young people react so well to an infection that the reaction overloads the system and actually kills the young person. See Davies.

8. Between October 1918 and April 1919, across all Australian ports, 228 vessels and a total of 73,844 persons were subject to quarantine. Saint, p. 65

9. Hodgson, p. 52

10. Ibid, p. 269

11. Beaumont, p. 523

12. Saint, p. 86

13. New South Wales State Archives

14. Saint, pp. 81-2

15. *Advocate,* Burnie, 20.1.30, p. 2

16. Hodgson, p. 2

17. *Recorder,* Port Pirie, 11.3.27, p. 4

18. In 1920, Nurse Ada Thompson's remains were exhumed and reinterred at Fremantle Cemetery. Most other service personnel buried at Woodman's Point were reinterred at the Perth War Cemetery in 1958.

19. Queensland State Archives

20. *Age,* Melbourne, 10.3.19, p. 11

21. *Express and Telegraph,* Adelaide, 5.5.19, p. 2

## A note on sources

This is the first book I have written in a quite specific way, most of the earlier works just developing content as I moved further into their research. For *Pandemic,* I wanted as much as possible to go back to the original people wearing those masks on those quiet streets. In the National Library of Australia's Trove database we have one of the most valuable resources anyone who writes could ever wish to access. Using a variety of search terms, I was taken back to those days of 1918-20, reading in big city and small suburban and country newspaper stories of Spanish flu as it swept across the world and then the less universal and more human stories of what happened when the disease reached our shores. I suspect that I may have read well in excess of a thousand newspaper articles from across the years, finding detail in personal reminiscences and obituaries written decades after the events I describe in this book. The secondary sources came much later, adding some structure and some polish to those earlier first-hand accounts. It is an approach that I found enriching as much as I found great sadness in many of the stories I read. It is also an approach I would recommend to anyone who wants to write social history. All you need is already there, buried away in the recesses of newspapers and journals that are sometimes long-dead but are really just waiting for someone for someone to type a few words into a box and hit "Return." Thank you, National Library.

# REFERENCES

**Official Records**

National Archives of Australia

A1: 1919/2364   *Pneumonic Influenza: Notifiable Disease*

A2: 1919/452   *Spanish Influenza*

A2: 1919/967   *Pneumonic Influenza: Serum*

B2455:   *Thwaites, Arthur Charles*


**Books**

Beaumont, Joan, *Broken Nation: Australians in the Great War,* Allen & Unwin, Crow's Nest, 2013

Jose, A. W., *The Royal Australian Navy,* University of Queensland Press, St. Lucia, 1987

Rae, Ruth, *Scarlet Poppies,* Australian College of Nursing, Canberra, 2015

Roe, Jill, (Ed.), *Social Policy in Australia: Some Perspectives, 1901-75,* Cassell, Stanmore, 1976


**Articles and Monographs**

Adams, Michael, *How one woman's death from Spanish flu caused outrage in Australia,* news.com.au, accessed 19.2.20

Buch, Neville, *The 1918-19 Global Pandemic in the local history of Brisbane,* Value of Local History Blog Post Series

Davies, Glenn, *Sister Rosa O'Kane: A forgotten hero,* Independent Australia, 25.4.19

Derkenne, Jamie, *The Somali Revolt: Diggers and discipline,* Quadrant Online, 25.4.17, accessed 9.4.20

Hodgson, Patrick, *Flu, society and the state: the political, social and economic implications of the 1918-20 influenza pandemic in Queensland,* Ph. D. Thesis, James Cook University, 2017

Kako, M., Steenkamp, M., Rokkas, P. J., Anikeeva, O. and Arbon, P. A., *Spanish Influenza of 1918-19: The extent and spread in South Australia,* Australian Epidemiologist, Vol. 22 No.1, August 2015

Larsen, Marie, *The Great Picnic: 100 years since the Spanish flu in Adelaide,* blogs.adelaide.edu.au

McLane, John Ryan, *Paradise Locked: The 1918 Influenza pandemic in American Samoa,* Sites: New Series, Vol. 10, No. 2, 2013

McQueen, Humphrey, *The Spanish Influenza Pandemic in Australia, 1918-19,* in Roe, Jill, (Ed.)

NSW Department of Health, *Report on the Influenza Epidemic in New South Wales,* Department of Health, Sydney, 1919

NSW State Archives, Engagement and Access Services, *Pneumonic Influenza(Spanish flu), 1919,* www.nsw.gov.au

Saint, Caroline, *A day (nearly) like any other: Healthcare work in an influenza pandemic,* Ph. D. Thesis, University of Sydney, 2017

Shanks, Dennis, *The Influenza Vaccine used during the Samoan Pandemic of 1918,* Tropical Medicine and Infectious Diseases, 2018

Smith, Helen, *The Spanish flu in Queensland,* Genealogical Society of Queensland website.

Vergano, Dan, *1918 Flu pandemic that killed 50 million originated in China, Historians say,* www.nationalgeographic.com, accessed 24.1.14

Wood, Anne, *The evolution and growth of women's organisations in Queensland, 1859-1958,* www.espace.library.uq.edu.au, accessed 7.5.20

## Websites

nma.gov.au/defining moments/resources/influenza-pandemic

# ALSO AVAILABLE FROM WOODSLANE PRESS

Outback
The discovery of
Australia's interior
$24.99
ISBN: 9781921203923

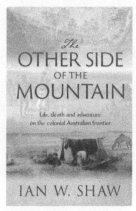

The Other Side of the
Mountain
How a tycoon, a pas-
toralist and a convict
helped shape the
exploration of colonial
Australia
$29.99
ISBN: 9781925868210

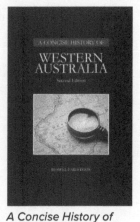

A Concise History of
Western Australia
$29.99
ISBN: 9781921874253

A Concise History
of New South Wales
$24.99
ISBN: 9781925868395

Arthur Phillip
Australia's first
Governor
$29.99
ISBN: 9781921683480

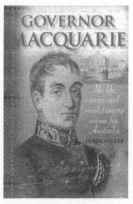

Governor Macquarie
His life, times and
revolutionary vision for
Australia
$29.99

ISBN: 9781921606915

**To order please call 02 8445 2300
or go to www.woodslane.com.au**